Italy

modern architectures in history

This international series examines the forms and consequences of modern architecture. Modernist visions and revisions are explored in their national context against a backdrop of aesthetic currents, economic developments, political trends and social movements. Written by experts in the architectures of the respective countries, the series provides a fresh, critical reassessment of Modernism's positive and negative effects, as well as the place of architectural design in twentieth-century history and culture.

Series editor: Vivian Constantinopoulos

Already published:

Brazil
Richard J. Williams

Britain
Alan Powers

Finland
Roger Connah

Greece
Alexander Tzonis and Alkistis Rodi

Turkey
Sibel Bozdoğan and Esra Akcan

USA
Gwendolyn Wright

Italy

modern architectures in history

Diane Ghirardo

REAKTION BOOKS

*This book is dedicated to my grandchildren, Natasha and Dominic,
and to the grandchildren of others near and dear to me, Alessandra
and Regan Balke, Adele Caberletti, and Braedyn Decker, in the hopes
that they and their generation will leave a cleaner and safer environment
to their grandchildren than ours has to them. It is also dedicated to the
memory of Aldo Rossi, a self-defined pilgrim who really did believe in
making a better world built upon the lessons of the past.*

Published by Reaktion Books Ltd
33 Great Sutton Street
London EC1V 0DX, UK

www.reaktionbooks.co.uk

First published 2013
Copyright © Diane Ghirardo 2013

Printed and bound in Great Britain by Bell & Bain, Glasgow

British Library Cataloguing in Publication Data
Ghirardo, Diane.
    Italy. – (Modern architectures in history)
    1. Architecture – Italy – History – 20th century.
    2. Architecture and society – Italy – History – 20th century.
    3. Architecture – Environmental aspects – Italy – History – 20th century.
    I. Title II. Series
    720.9´45´0904-DC23

    ISBN 9 781 86189 864 7

Contents

Introduction

In Francesco Rosi's cinematic masterwork *Cristo si è fermato a Eboli* ('Christ Stopped at Eboli', 1978), set in Italy during the Fascist period, the painter Carlo Levi, banished to internal exile for his opposition to the regime, departs from the modern Milanese metropolis to travel to a distant corner of Italy's most remote, underdeveloped region, Basilicata. In the film's opening scenes the journey proceeds first by rail, on sleek, modern trains and then on increasingly primitive ones, finally arriving at places not even the rail network reaches, traversing a landscape ever more remote and thinly populated, if nonetheless still intact. In 1992, Gianni Amelio's film *Il ladro di bambini* ('The Stolen Children') led the viewer on a parallel journey, from the vast apartment blocks in the dense and gritty peripheries of Milan to the squalid, speculative and self-built houses and apartments of southern Italy and Sicily. The transformation chronicled by comparison in Amelio's film was appalling: on the outskirts of Italy's second city, the degradation was of a piece with a largely abandoned and ageing industrial landscape only a few decades old, shocking in its vulgar indifference to the grim lives of its inhabitants. In the south, formerly pristine beaches and rugged landscapes sported the fresh scars of poorly constructed, half-finished apartment blocks, empty asphalt playgrounds and parking lots, streets going nowhere. The journeys in these two films are in a very real sense indicative of the transformations Italy's country-side and urban centres underwent over the 150 years since unification in 1871.

This book engages Italian culture and architecture from unification to the present day by considering the production of buildings in dynamic relation to cultural, social and political developments. Post-unification architectural production coincided with a sustained drive to transform into a modern industrial state a country still primarily rural, parts of which had for centuries been under foreign control or in the hands of a papacy averse to modernization. At the same time, Italy holds some of the most prized architecture and art in the world, from antiquity to the baroque to the modern, often packed into the dense historic centres of the peninsula's cities. How to negotiate the claims of the modern city against those of ancient artefacts has vexed planners and politicians since the 1870s, as they struggled to cope with massive migration from the countryside to the cities. Although the debates that raged over these 150 years in the pages of the country's professional and popular press typically concerned matters of architectural style, in this book I argue that such disagreements were largely irrelevant to the building programmes themselves. Far more deeply rooted, intractable and contentious forces help explain the shape and character of Italian architecture and cities today. Successive waves of early industrialization, the heady years of fascist dictatorship sandwiched between two devastating world wars, the corporatization of agriculture, secularization and globalization more generally have all deeply marked the built landscape of Italy. This study examines the modalities of how this transformation took place and the architectural forms it took.

Two types of studies commonly address modern Italian architecture. Book-length studies of particular periods since 1871 generally focus on individual masterworks and major architects, in periods spanning ten to 40 years at a time, with occasional explorations of urban projects in the country's major cities – Rome, Turin, Milan. Broad historical surveys cover the leading architectural accomplishments of the past century and a half, and guidebooks to the modern architecture of a wider range of cities, such as Ferrara, Florence and Bologna, provide accounts of their most prestigious projects and architects. Both types of study constitute important contributions to architectural history, although neither tends to go beyond specific architectural trends or debates among the architectural elite. Here I will focus on more broadly conceived cultural and political issues and make no attempt to offer a standard architectural survey; for those so interested, the bibliography is rich with other readings. Although mostly chronological in sequence, particularly in the first three chapters, in this study thematically arranged chapters overlap chronological periods.

The opening chapters focus on the two most significant early phases of Italian public building programmes: the first spans the period from unification to the outset of the First World War, when attention centred on transforming Rome into the nation's capital. A series of competitions selected designers for new government ministries, military headquarters and monuments in Rome. Giving the national capital a modern appearance and infrastructure, politicians believed, would help forge unity out of the formerly disparate regions. At the same time, politicians believed that participating in international exhibitions and hosting some of its own would present the newly formed country to the rest of the world as an emerging industrial state. Notable examples of the new nation's early buildings include the Palace of Justice, the National Monument to Victor Emmanuel II, the ministries of justice, education and defence, those of the 1911 international exhibition in Turin, and infrastructural works such as major new hospitals. This period of architecture, marked by ornate excess and massive scale, is largely supplanted in the literature by the later Fascist period, when the state began to support Rationalist or modern architecture and to extend building campaigns out of the major cities into regional and provincial centres, as well as to the short-lived colonial empire. These buildings housed organizations linked to the Fascist Party to engage young people, workers, women and the retired in state and para-state groups: Fascist Party headquarters, youth organizations, mother-hood and infancy clinics, after-work and leisure clubs, sports facilities, post offices, and government complexes in North Africa and Ethiopia. The well-known debates among various architectural factions can be under-stood essentially as battles over style and as efforts on the part of all of the groups, especially the Rationalists, to promote a single style as emblem-atic of the Fascist Party. Although differing widely in style and seeking models in different places, the architecture of the two eras nonetheless fulfilled the same goals and can be understood as part of the same, nation-alizing process.

Population movement, industrialization and deindustrialization constitute the leitmotif of Italy over the last 150 years, issues that never disappear, never recede into the background. As a result of the massive effort to industrialize the country, cities swelled with immigrants from towns, villages and rural backwaters. This book considers the infrastruc-tural transformations and additions (including cinemas, cultural facilities and administrative offices) undertaken in the peninsula's major popula-tion magnets; the master plans devised for the burgeoning metropolises; and the speculative and planned housing developments of Milan, Turin, Naples and Rome. It also explores the shanty towns that popped up on urban peripheries; the financing of low-cost, cooperative and state em-ployee housing; and the establishment of new towns near Rome, in Sardinia, in Sicily and elsewhere. Examples include built and proposed projects for suburbs such as Testaccio and E.42 (Rome) and others in Naples, Turin and Milan; public housing in these and smaller cities; garden suburbs; and the transformation of historic city centres such as Brescia and Bergamo. I also consider the modifications to historic urban centres in the struggle to accommodate (however poorly) the demands of cars, buses and trains. The discussion of public housing and suburbs sets up a contrast with singular design projects, from individual houses such as the Casa Malaparte, Capri, to multi-family residences such as the Novo-comum in Como.

In the four decades following the end of the Second World War, renewed housing pressure in the country's metropolises led to government-planned subdivisions consisting of apartment blocks on the outskirts of Italy's major cities. Architects struggled with political concerns relating to architectural form – they wanted to distance their new buildings from those of the dictatorship. Movements in other artistic fields, such as neo-realism in cinema, seeped into architectural debates, but only to a limited degree. Architects found themselves building new quarters far from city centres and beyond the reaches of public transportation systems to take residents to their jobs (conditions immortalized in the books and films of Pier Paolo Pasolini, such as *A Violent Life*). While architects attempted to work out an appropriate architectural language, speculators, cooperatives and public and semi-public entities raced to erect apartment buildings without regard to master plans, infrastructure or even, unfortunately, building codes.

This book cuts across the chronological framework to consider three significant topics: restoration and preservation; competitions; and architectural criticism and post-Second World War debates. Debates over the principles of preservation and restoration are destined to remain unsettled, and not only in Italy, precisely because the array of conflicting interests that invariably attach to them are often irreconcilable. From virtually any perspective, Italian preservationists have much to celebrate – and much to lament.

In 1980 Venice hosted its first architecture biennale, with its centrepiece, La Strada Novissima, a row of facades designed by internationally known architects erected in the historic Arsenale. This exhibition confirmed the growing role of architecture as spectacle, and as a sleek screen for crass development projects that have despoiled the landscape from the Alps to Sicily and the fraudulent skimming of public finances by corrupt politicians. Architects have participated in enterprises riven with fraud, in particular for the football World Cup of 1990, with stadiums rapidly erected in Turin, Milan, Bari and Rome, used two or three times and left to rot once the games concluded. Much the same happened in Turin with the 2006 Winter Olympics, an infelicitous follow-up to the centennial celebration of Italian unification in 1961, which also left abandoned carcasses of flamboyant buildings littered across the city, not to mention staggering deficits that virtually bankrupted the city by 2012.

One chapter also tackles the troubling issues of illegal building and environmental despoliation. As a rule, discussions of housing projects centre on those by prominent architects, but perhaps more important and ultimately greater determinants of the landscape have been the activities of major developers and industrialists. Political control remained in the hands of the centrist Christian Democracy party for nearly half a century (1944–92). In southern Italy in particular, the party gained its electoral strength from its historic ties with organized crime, a pattern briefly interrupted during the late 1990s but quickly restored with the rise of Silvio Berlusconi's Forza Italia and its most recent incarnation, Il Popolo della Libertà (The People of Freedom). Money that flowed to the south for construction and other public works through the Cassa del Mezzogiorno project helped sustain the power of organized crime and assisted the despoliation of the built landscape. While individual families erected humble dwellings on the peripheries of most Italian cities, arguably the illegally built buildings and the shoddy, if legal, structures erected by corporations such as those of Berlusconi have wreaked greater havoc on the landscape.

Throughout the twentieth century, architects and theorists attempted to grasp the role of architecture in a capitalist economy and under diverse political systems, from the monarchy of the first seventy years, to the twenty-one years of Fascist control, to the post-Second World War parliamentary republic. At the same time, they have struggled with a political system founded on personal relationships, known as clientalismo, along with the extensive infiltration of organized crime into Italian politics which, and as a consequence, has led to persistent corruption in competitions for university posts, public projects, and consultantships, not to mention elections. Documented extensively for the first part of the twentieth century, this book addresses more recent examples of such corruption, including the tacit support of unpermitted construction.

Overwhelming as the effects of illegal building have been, those of environmental pollution have been equally, if not more, devastating. This book also chronicles some of the country's simmering environmental disasters, while the final section confronts the ironies of urban growth and its impact on rural Italy. The rush to the cities from the late nineteenth century onwards at times tripled and quadrupled their borders, but it also left in its wake empty farmhouses, rural structures, churches, oratories (small free-standing chapels) and, at times, even entire small medieval towns. Tourists from around the globe, enchanted by a romantic landscape of ruins, purchased, revamped and marketed these buildings, turning them into resorts or centres of new industrial production (of wines and speciality foods) and therefore into landscapes fraught with new contradictions.

The final chapter evaluates the recent contributions of some of Italy's most prominent architects both inside the country and around the world, including those of internationally known 'archi-stars', and concludes with a review of recent projects by a younger generation of Italian architects. As has always been the case in Italy, there are some talented architects whose work merits attention, but the reader will note that these are fewer than those who have added enormous, and awful, structures to the land- scape. In this, Italy does not stand alone; such is certainly the case in many other countries.

> *Perché c'ero, e se c'ero, guardavo, e se anche non guardavo*
> *vedevo, come ancora vedo . . .*

> Because I was there, and if I was there, I looked,
> and even if I did not look I saw,
> as I still see today . . .
>
> Luigi Ballerini, Cephalonia

Roma – Monumento a Vittorio Emanuele II

chapter one

Building a New Nation

To the rousing tune of the national anthem, colourful parades and a bracing display of military might, Victor Emmanuel III inaugurated the monument known as Il Vittoriano, dedicated to his grandfather and Italy's deceased king, Victor Emmanuel II (1829–1878), in Rome in 1911. Designed by Giuseppe Sacconi and begun seven years after the monarch's death, erecting the Vittoriano entailed 26 years of demolition and construction, not to mention lavish expenditure on brilliant white marble and a surfeit of statuary. The apex of nineteenth-century eclecticism, the Vittoriano includes elements of Italian art nouveau (known as Stile Liberty) and both Greek and Roman classicism; its size, materials and isolation detach it from the rest of the city and have earned it nicknames from Romans such as 'the typewriter' and 'the wedding cake'. Initially intended for a site near the ancient baths of Diocletian, by 1884 it migrated to a new, more central location which adroitly shouldered out ancient vistas of the church of Santa Maria in Aracoeli and the Capitoline Hill from the via del Corso, historically the city's main north–south axis. The locational shift accompanied a steady increase in the size of the structure, which looms over everything else in its environs except, perhaps, the distant papal enclave at the Vatican. With this massive urban gesture, the new Savoy monarchy asserted its primacy over Church, ancient republic and medieval city, and also affirmed the government of the newly united Italy's devotion to spectacle and the spectacular.

That same year, 1911, saw the completion of two other monumental structures in Rome for the new nation, the Palace of Justice by Guglielmo Calderini, known to Romans as Il Palazzaccio, 'the ugly palace', and the Mattatoio (slaughterhouse) near Monte Testaccio, an artificial hill composed of potsherds dating back to the first centuries of the Roman Empire. Together with the Vittoriano, these structures testify to the priorities of the new government and to the architectural pretensions associated with it. Monuments and public buildings of the monarchy's first years, dressed out in full, even excessive, ornamental garb, claimed prime land in the city centre and dwarfed their surroundings; on the other hand, planners relegated utilitarian structures and low-cost housing, when they

Giuseppe Sacconi, monument to Vittorio Emanuele II (Altare della Patria), Rome, 1886–1911.

deigned to build them, typically unadorned and of humble materials, to the city's perimeter.

At the same time that construction of the Vittoriano was under way, in the former Savoy capital of Turin Alessandro Antonelli was completing the building that would come to be the city's most recognizable symbol as well as a monument to the transition from traditional building practices to modernism, the Mole Antonelliana (built 1862–89). Initially intended to be a synagogue, then a museum dedicated to the Risorgimento (the nineteenth-century movement for the unification of Italy), the 168-metre-high tower, a soaring iron and clinker brick celebration of the architect's skill. Antonelli's Mole embodied an implicit rejection of medieval, Renaissance and classical aesthetic traditions in favour of an architecture focused on blending traditional structure and materials with modern ones, adapting them to untraditional forms. The Mole represents a set of concerns radically different from those visible in the structures being erected in Rome for the new nation, but, together with those flamboyant public buildings, testifies to the often conflicting imperatives that subsequently engaged Italian architects after the turn of the century.

The modern nation of Italy, born in March 1861, followed a dozen years of struggle. Emerging from centuries of domination by foreign powers in the north and south while parts of central Italy remained in the hands of the papacy, Italy before 1870 was a nation in name only. Despite a thin

Guglielmo Calderini, Palazzo di Giustizia, Rome, 1911.

16 ROMA – Palazzo di Giustizia

Slaughterhouse, Testaccio, Rome. Detail at entrance, 1911.

claim on the national monarchy, Victor Emmanuel, the reigning Savoy king, who hailed from the Piedmont region of northwest Italy, determined to press his case in large part through the construction of a new national capital, by following the example of an earlier generation of Savoy princes who had moulded Turin into the headquarters of its duchy.[1] Ambitious plans to develop Turin in 1860 gave way to equally grandiose and even more lamentable schemes to gut medieval and Renaissance Florence when the latter city's more central location earned it the distinction of supplanting Turin as capital in 1864.[2] As the president of the Royal Academy of Arts charged in a letter to *The Times* in 1899, 'at Florence . . . the Florentine municipality has made a clean sweep of some of the most interesting parts of medieval Florence . . . it has preferred vulgar ostentation to the repose and dignity of venerable association.'[3] This city escaped further Savoy depredation when Rome, as antique seat of imperial power and more recent locus of papal power, became the country's capital in 1871. The triple objectives of the fledgling government were to solidify Savoy claims to the monarchy, to assert the power of the nation over that of notoriously independent cities and regions, and to bring the seriously backward country into line with its more modernized European neighbours to the north such as France, Germany and Britain.

Two concerns animated officials' decisions about the role of buildings in the new era. The mere selection of Rome as the capital already helped

Alessandro Antonelli, Mole Antonelliana, Turin, 1862–9.

gain the monarchy symbolic legitimacy, but to fabricate both the national government's legitimacy and the facilities required of a modern nation, the new regime urgently needed more definitive, more visible projects. Structures for everything from ministries to law courts to monuments dedicated to the Savoy monarchs themselves helped instantiate the nascent monarchy's power within a broad web of dialogues – with other nations, with other aristocratic families both inside and outside Italy, and with the wealthy bourgeoisie and emerging industrial capitalists who had been the crucial architects of the country's unification.[4] Second, officials

16

recognized the need to catch up with other countries already far ahead in the race to industrialize and modernize, which they believed could not be impeded by concern for historic sites. They resisted foreign and indigenous pressures to preserve the architecture and environments of the past. "'Are we to go in rags for sake of being picturesque?" said a syndic [mayor] now ruling one of the chief cities of Italy, to a person who complained to him of the destruction of art and beauty now common throughout the peninsula', one American writer reported.[5] Like the imperial government in Russia, Italy's politicians were eager to industrialize, but they were considerably less willing to include the masses into the political processes that typically accompanied modernization elsewhere. 'I think we all agree that we will not have met the world's expectations if Italy has only seen Rome as an ideal administrative centre', wrote statesman and engineer Quintino Sella in 1879.[6] Rome, in his view, should be the country's scientific and artistic research centre, not just a setting for bureaucrats – and definitely not for industry. Prime Minister Francesco Crispi expressed the ambivalence of the upper classes about industrialization when he observed that

> It is at once fortunate and unfortunate that we do not have the great working-class cities such as those of France and England. Unfortunate, because urban industry in Italy is still in its infancy; and fortunate, because we are not tortured by the dangers such as those to public order in working-class cities.[7]

Beyond the reflections of politicians, descriptions of the 'dangerous classes' figured directly in the 1889 law on public safety.[8] Despite the apparent triumph of modern republican policies, Italian leaders and moneyed classes retained profound doubts about democracy, their views finding expression in Pasquale Turiello's explicit call for rule by a dictator in his book *Governo e governati in Italia* (1882), a sentiment that lingered well into the twenty-first century.[9]

Most of the country's population, overwhelmingly poor and rural but with a fledgling urban proletariat, was conspicuously absent from the government's agenda. Its ranks thinned over the next five decades as immigrants fleeing desperate poverty for the promise of survival, property and even wealth decamped to North and South America. The building programmes discussed below did not engage this class except as labourers; instead, they stood primarily as testimonials to the power of the monarchy, the aristocracy and the bourgeoisie over the disenfranchised masses below them.[10] The Fascist regime extended the administrative building programme to the entire country, to which it added building and social programmes designed to include those overlooked by the earlier government, that is, the urban and rural masses, in an effort to incorporate them within the hierarchical state proclaimed as the fascist ideal.

The building campaigns before and after the First World War took shape around issues of central concern to the country's leaders. Just what an 'Italian' identity would be vexed intellectuals, artists and politicians in the years leading up to and beyond unification.[11] Not surprisingly, the creation of the new Italy's image early on fell in large part to artists and architects, whose musical, pictorial, sculptural, literary and architectural accomplishments would give visible definition to the question. During the first 50 years following unification, the dominant questions concerned what a national Italian architecture would look like, how it would stand up in comparison with the architecture of countries far ahead in the modernization enterprise, how it would relate to local traditions and how it would be possible to fabricate an architecture that would patch together a union out of traditions as disparate as those of Sicily, Lombardy and the Veneto. The ambition initially was to erase local differences, or at least supplant them with a recognizably 'national' architecture that would not be burdened by association with only one of the country's cities or regions. The Monument to Victor Emmanuel famously embodied these values in its deployment of statues and inscriptions celebrating Italy's various regions:

> The inscribed invocations to Cives (citizens) and Patria (nation) declare the secular, national goals of Liberal Italy, while the statues personifying the cities and regions of Italy combine to record the Risorgimento project of unifying traditionally independent and disparate politics into a single nation.[12]

In addition, as David Atkinson and Denis Cosgrove noted, many of the new public buildings in Rome, such as the Palace of Justice, were 'designed in a neoclassical, Beaux-Arts style: intended to express the new international standing of the Italian state'.[13] Leading nineteenth-century cultural critic and professor of architecture Camillo Boito, who generally favoured a neo-medieval style for the new Italian state, put it best when he wrote,

> And as far as style goes, who would ever want to introduce, in a city such as Rome, medieval garb or the ingenious novelties of Frenchified modern art? . . . Rome is the only city where classical academic architecture can somehow be developed today . . . today's architects can take all the elements of the various Roman

architects and compose a modern style, creating a new organism and a new aesthetic.[14]

Although such matters most concerned architects, politicians and their bourgeois constituents viewed them in the context of debates about political alliances with other nations, and as they related to pressing concerns about industrialization and modernization. Such questions did not disappear during the Fascist era; instead, more finely nuanced concerns about producing an architecture at once modern and Italian, local and national, and intent on incorporating the urban masses into the project of Italianization, fascistization and modernization, overshadowed them. Architects as well as figures in literature, art and the new motion picture industry all struggled to understand how they could forge ties with but distinguish themselves from their counterparts in other countries. How different groups attempted to address and, where possible, answer such questions with respect to public buildings is the subject of this chapter.

During the decades between unification and the end of the Second World War, Italy's urban landscape underwent massive transformations. The urban monuments erected in the country's cities and towns included statues honouring the military leader Giuseppe Garibaldi and the new Savoy monarchy; after the First World War came public schools; memorials to fallen soldiers; train stations; slaughterhouses; covered public markets; power plants; stock exchanges and department stores. After 1922 the Fascist regime added monuments to fallen fascists; cinemas; football stadiums; post offices; National Insurance Institute (INA) headquarters and Fascist Party headquarters (Case del Fascio); and gasometri, large vats for reserves of gasoline. Architects also designed buildings for all of the new fascist institutions: an institute for the care of mothers and children, the Opera Nazionale Maternità e Infanzia (ONMI); an after-work leisure organization, the Opera Nazionale Dopolavoro (OND); the veterans' organization, Opera Nazionale Combattenti (ONC); and the youth organizations Opera Nazionale Balilla (ONB) and Gioventù Italiano del Littorio (GIL, or Italian Youths of the Lictor). Just as the cathedral and town hall in the Middle Ages dominated the skyline and public life of citizens, so these new buildings claimed primacy in the modernizing Italian city.

Politics proceed according to images of reality – images often instantiated in constructions, from buildings to monuments to temporary exhibits. The Savoy monarchy and the Fascist regime (as we will see in chapter Three) proposed their respective images of reality in public building campaigns, which allow us to penetrate to the heart of their social and political visions of Italy and Italians.

Italy's unification essentially consolidated the power and aspirations of the country's aristocracy and bourgeoisie, a group, in the views of many contemporaries, apparently immune to the beauty of anything but cash.[15]

> It is for the most part the snug and self-complacent bourgeoisie which rules, and which finds a curious delight in the contemplation of everything which can destroy the cities of the Renaissance and the records of classic Latium, to replace them with some gimcrack and brand-new imitation of a third-rate modern French or Belgian town, glaring with plate-glass, gilding, dust, smoke, acres of stucco, and oceans of asphalt.[16]

So an American critic denounced the attitude prevalent among Italy's prosperous classes. The concerns of the majority of impoverished Italians surfaced only as a fear of being ever vulnerable to pressure from the masses below them, a prospect periodically refreshed for politicians by uprisings or other shocking events. Rebellions in Rimini and Imola in 1874; protest marches by the unemployed and assaults on bakeries in 1889; farmers' insurrections in Sicily in 1893; armed revolts in Lunigiana in 1894; strikes and demonstrations in northern cities in 1898: all evidenced an increasing tension between a government deaf to the needs of farmers and workers and steadily expanding popular movements concerned with the anguished day-to-day search for survival of large chunks of the population. In 1894 the government declared a state of siege in Sicily, violently repressing the fledgling Socialist Party and leagues of agricultural workers, and inaugurating a new season of authoritarian control. Prime Minister Francesco Crispi expressed the views of the ruling classes in 1891 when he reminded the lower classes that the advances of the century then drawing to a close were entirely due to the efforts of the bourgeoisie, and that the lower classes should therefore be quiet, grateful that they were even invited to sit at the table along with those who were always meant to continue ruling.[17]

Growing unrest among the ranks of industrial and agricultural labourers triggered severe repression under Victor Emmanuel II's successor, Umberto I. Two assassination attempts on the king, an unsuccessful one in late 1878 and a successful one in July 1900, solidified the fears of the upper classes about an increasingly informed and radicalized working class. Officials responded to threats from below with the time-honoured devices of repression: limiting the freedom of the press, extensive displays of police and military power, and brutal suppression of any anti-government activity at virtually any scale. Crispi distinguished himself for the brutality with which his government suppressed the bread riots, street unrest and the agitations of early *fasci* (in particular of the Fasci Siciliani) of agricultural workers. His actions met with the approval of the ruling classes, who did not welcome the arrival of the masses into public life. Although the Italian parliament finally removed property qualifications to voting in 1876, they promptly replaced them with a literacy requirement – in a country where 70 per cent or more of the population was illiterate. The tactic succeeded; during the 1890s, barely 10 per cent of the population of 30 million people voted. Parliament did not concede universal suffrage until 1912, and even then, 'universal' referred only to men over the age of 30 who had completed military service.

At best, this part of the population surfaced in contemporary literature and culture as backdrops for the actions of the upper classes. The most telling representations of this hidden population appeared decades later in literature and film, such as in Ermanno Olmi's account of the remoteness of the lives of rural peasants from the momentous events of the nineteenth century, *L'albero degli zoccoli* ('The Tree of Wooden Clogs', 1978), a compelling panorama of lives lived in the shadows as major national events swirled around them. Instead, the petty vindictiveness of the upper classes defending their prerogatives most directly affected the peasants' lives. Thatched huts, remote from shops, churches and the urban amenities with which the upper classes proudly adorned their industrializing cities, populated the countryside of the Po Valley, the Pontine Marshes and other marginal areas. The dust of past centuries on the backs of this repressed population fashioned modern Italy, a fact not lost on contemporary observers. Instead of the richly evocative byways of ancient Rome,

Rural house for colonists in land reclamation project, postcard, c. 1935.

there [is] the stench of engines, the dust of shattered bricks, the
scream of steam-whistles, the mounds of rubbish, the poles of
scaffolding, long lines of houses raised in frantic haste on malarious
soil, enormous barracks, representative of the martial law required
to hold in check a liberated people . . .[18]

For their part, the ruling classes enjoyed the operas of Giuseppe Verdi
and Giacomo Puccini, the landscapes painted by the Macchiaioli, and
fought to have their portraits painted by the artist of European aristocrats,
Giovanni Boldini. Born in Ferrara and trained as an artist in Florence,
Boldini traced his influences both to John Singer Sargent and to the Impres-
sionists. He forged his career primarily in Paris and London, where his
success as a society painter dated back to 1874. His canvases depicting
Consuelo Vanderbilt, Duchess of Marlborough, and other noblewomen
endeared him to the upwardly mobile Italian bourgeoisie, who competed
in particular to have him paint their women, in relaxed but elegant poses,
garbed in quintessentially Gay Nineties dress, rendered vibrantly sensuous
by his sweeping brushstrokes and brilliant colours.

In literature and poetry, that other turn-of-the-century bourgeois hero,
poet and libertine Gabriele D'Annunzio, prompted quite different associations. His affairs with women such as the actress Eleonora Duse captivated the public imagination, and his celebrated novels and poetry
captured the sensibilities of an erotic adventurer.[19] Forced to flee to France
in 1910 to escape his debts, D'Annunzio returned with the onset of the
First World War, having discovered how the excitement, modernity and
adventure of war fired his imagination, undimmed even by the loss of an
eye in combat. Bitterly dismayed by Italy's failure to acquire the Dalmatian
city of Fiume, he led a successful expedition to conquer it in 1919, ruling
as an autocrat for eighteen months before being forced to stand down.
The poet, a decadent with a lust for power, wrote Lewis Corey, was 'most
visible not only in his opera-bouffe seizure and occupation of the city of
Fiume . . . but in his anticipation of the distinctive, despotic doctrines
of Fascism'.[20] Mussolini's Fascist government intrigued him and invited
his support, which he imperiously granted from the retreat on Lake Garda
where he spent the last years of his life writing and entertaining.[21]
Where Boldini's paintings promised status and respectability, D'Annunzio's works and life celebrated the masculine image of the sexual and military adventurer freed from the constraints of a rigid, bourgeois code
of behaviour.

If the amorous adventurer D'Annunzio and the society artist Boldini
titillated the bourgeoisie by upending artistic traditions, the operas of
Giuseppe Verdi provided the soundtrack for the Risorgimento and for

the newly formed Italian nation. Concerts traditionally took place in courtly settings as entertainment for aristocratic audiences, in the private homes of the nobility and prosperous industrial and merchant families, or in prestigious ecclesiastical settings as accompaniment to religious rituals. Such performance venues excluded the petite bourgeoisie, the working class and rural farmers and labourers. The years leading up to and following Italian unification saw the world of music undergo enormous transformation, with the 1840s and '50s characterized by full public performances as well as semi-public ones, often in schools or clubs. Periodicals and posters announced such events, but they also presented smaller ones, including public musical group performances of excerpts from larger works and orchestral arrangements in cafés and public squares. 1863 saw the first true *concerto popolare* in Florence as part of the effort to educate the masses in classical music, and extensive semi-public concerts performed by quartets flourished in Rome, Florence, Milan and Turin. Verdi's operas, with their compelling arias and memorable melodies, made opera more available from the 1840s onwards, precisely through such small public recitals. The very performance of these works in non-traditional settings constituted a challenge to elite music practices, while their themes were often coded expressions of Italians' desire to rid the country of foreign rulers, such as the Austro-Hungarian occupation of northern Italy. *The Battle of Legnano* (1849) recounted the successful campaign to drive Frederick Barbarossa out of Italy in 1176, and *Nabucco* (1842) recorded the expulsion of Jews from Jerusalem by the Babylonian king Nebuchadnezzar, but both were also thinly veiled references to contemporary struggles to liberate Italy of foreign overlords. Scrawled on walls throughout the peninsula, Verdi's very name became a symbol of this rebellion: '*Viva* verdi' signified '*Viva Vittorio Emanuele Re D'Italia*' (Long Live Vittorio Emanuele King of Italy). Following unification in 1861, Verdi wrote the stirring celebration of patriotism, *Hymn of the Nations*, for performance at the Great London Exhibition in 1862. Although Verdi accepted the invitation to serve in parliament, in effect acknowledging his status as an icon of Italian nationalism, he withdrew after five years to leave the task to others, averring that his contribution to the new nation was greater as an artist than as a politician.[22]

At the very time the national government ruthlessly stifled all forms of dissent, it pursued a parallel strategy of spectacle, commemorating itself through international expositions such as that in Rome in 1911 for the 50th anniversary of unification, and its satellite, the Turin International Exhibition of Industry and Labour. The intended audience included both the Italian ruling classes and the international community, who were meant to understand that Italy, too, had modernized. Just as later under

Alfredo d'Andrade,
Borgo Medievale,
Turin, 1862–89.

fascism, image trumped reality. In this respect Italy followed the model of France, which despite numerous urban rebellions mounted no fewer than five major international exhibitions between 1855 and 1900, all of which took their cue from the Great Exhibition of 1851 at Hyde Park in London. In Italy the more immediate response to the trend inaugurated by the London exposition was Turin's first major national exhibition in 1884. Aware that the most popular features of such events were displays of ethnic peoples in simulated natural settings, and not to be outdone by the English or the French, a Turinese group headed by Alfredo d'Andrade mounted an entire medieval quarter (the Borgo Medievale) in the Parco del Valentino, populated by costumed locals occupying humble houses fashioned in line with regional traditions of the fifteenth century. Faithful both to Piedmontese architectural traditions and its construction methods, the project evidenced a rigour of architectural language in compiling elements of notable regional buildings into one harmonious and picturesque whole. Most notably, the district's pseudo-vernacular architecture stood in complete opposition to the heavily ornamented public buildings and bourgeois houses then being erected in Turin and other Italian cities.

All the rage in the second half of the nineteenth century, any country with pretensions to global grandeur in the twentieth century needed to have at least one international exhibition, and Italy was no exception. For the 1911 Turin International, newly prosperous industrial and mercantile elites proudly displayed their products, while the pavilions of European nations boasted of their colonial conquests in reconstructions of primitive villages inhabited by colonial subjects. A national competition

Cesare Bazzani,
Palazzo delle Belle
Arti, Rome, 1911.

addressed three topics: one dedicated to ethnography and the regions, another to the fine arts (both in Rome), and the third to industry and labour in Turin. In the first category the exposition erected a group of ten houses and six apartment buildings near Rome's new Ponte Risorgimento. The area of Vigna Cartoni (now called Valle Giulia), set aside for cultural buildings, welcomed Cesare Bazzani's new Palazzo delle Belle Arti (Museum of Fine Arts) first. Various nations also erected exhibition structures there, but of these, the only one intended to be permanent was Sir Edwin Lutyens's elegant design for the British pavilion; today it is the headquarters of the British School at Rome. Lutyens summoned English Palladianism into the heart of ancient Rome with a pedimented entrance based upon the upper order of St Paul's Cathedral. These two buildings, almost facing one another, illustrate the governing class's preference for the orderly elegance of neoclassicism for buildings dedicated to the arts, while over-the-top display remained characteristic of Italian public buildings in the pre-war years. The earlier Palazzo delle Esposizioni (1880–82) by Pio Piacentini triggered controversy because of the absence of openings on the via Nazionale elevation, despite the Corinthian pilasters and the triumphal arched neoclassical entrance. Determined not to make the same mistake, Bazzani devised a grandiose pronaos (a temple front with a free-standing, colonnaded portico and pediment above) with paired columns atop a high staircase flanked by projecting wings with pilasters, the whole embellished with garlands, festoons, statues and an exuberant bas-relief frieze by Giovanni Prini. Although also designed with a temple front of paired columns and pediment, the Lutyens structure by contrast is an essay in restraint, its clean and elegant pilasters framing simple pedimented windows.

If the historical elements of either classical or neo-medieval architecture appealed to many designers and theorists, such as Camillo Boito, as the best tools for devising an Italian and modern architecture, others flatly rejected any taste of historicism in favour of a new style that swept Europe in the last decade of the nineteenth century, Art Nouveau, known in Italy as Stile Liberty.[23] Designers of the 1911 Turin expo, trumpeted as being international in scope, adopted an entirely different approach from that of earlier Italian exhibitions by embracing exuberant neo-baroque motifs for many of the pavilions, and others the newly florid Liberty style promoted by Raimondo D'Aronco, also designer of the First Exposition of Modern Decorative Arts in Turin (1902). So deeply indebted was D'Aronco's work to international examples that he virtually copied Joseph Maria Olbrich's entrance gate for the Darmstadt Artists' Colony exhibition of 1901, to the outrage of Austrian architects. Erected of cardboard and stucco, none of the 1911 Turin buildings survived, but the so-called Liberty style already boasted a solid group of supporters in cities throughout Italy, most compellingly in houses for the upper classes and commercial and retail buildings. Time has dimmed the political charge of Stile Liberty, which with its internationalist and hence presumably left-wing associations, opponents saw as a frontal attack on historically valid national architectural styles. Indeed, many of Liberty's proponents conceived of it as a deliberate challenge to nationalism and a conservative political agenda, precisely because its supporters engaged such burning contemporary

Edwin Lutyens, British pavilion, Rome, 1911.

Pio Piacentini, Palazzo delle Esposizioni, Rome, 1880–82.

Ciro Contini, Villa
Melchiorri, Ferrara,
1904.

issues as what 'progress' meant at the turn of the twentieth century, what
the role of technology in art should be and whether art should, or could,
have a social and political role. '[Art Nouveau] was always controversial.
Centred on the decorative arts and architecture, its supporters self-
consciously claimed that it was the first international modern style, and
allocated it the role of transformer of European consciousness', argues
art historian Paul Greenhalgh.[24]

Although the style varied from region to region and drew on several
different sources from north of the Alps, including the Vienna Secession,
the characteristic floral motifs ornamented the houses and office buildings
of Italy's prosperous commercial and industrial elite in many Italian cities,
even smaller ones. The acknowledged master of Liberty in Ferrara was
Ciro Contini, an engineer responsible for the style's diffusion in this part
of the Po delta.[25] His Villa Melchiorri (1904), with its curved entrance and
windows, the latter framed by lunettes and refined floral decorations, and
a deep, moulded cornice similarly festooned with vegetation, superim-
posed the new style on an entirely traditional plan. In Milan, exuberant cast-
iron balconies signalled the advent of the new style in apartment blocks
in the city's centre, such as Ernesto Pirovano's Casa Ferrario (1903); in
Turin the Casa Priotti by Carlo Ceppi (1900); and in Rome, the more styl-
ized version of a house-as-castle, Villino Vanoni (1902) by Ernesto Basile.

The Liberty style celebrated sinuous and floral forms, but it also prominently displayed fresh interest in industrial materials such as iron and cast iron, which now provided beams, rafters, columns and studs for office buildings such as Raffaele Canevari's Ufficio Geologico in Rome (1873). In department stores such as the Piatti store in Rome (1900) and Luigi Broggi's Grandi Magazzini Contratti in Milan (1903), the cast-iron elements signalled modernity, as did the extensive fenestration on street elevations that allowed merchants to exhibit their wares in seductively organized window displays, in line with international commercial trends and the emergence of department stores. The quintessential nineteenth-century

Ernesto Pirovano,
Casa Ferrario, Milan,
1903.

Luigi Broggi, Grandi
Magazzini Contratti,
Milan, 1903.

retail structure, the arcade, developed when consortiums of property
owners closed off streets to provide glazed passageways lined with shops;
the international fad spared no metropolis, and Italy's cities were no exception. The most prominent and spectacular arcade, the triumphantly nation-
alistic Galleria Vittorio Emanuele II in Milan by Giuseppe Mengoni (1877),
stood adjacent to the Duomo and sported as its facade a massive triumphal arch. Mengoni's Galleria represented the culmination of a nearly
century-long effort to complete the grand Duomo and the area surrounding it. A directive by Napoleon in 1805 led to the completion of the cathedral's sides and facade, while the grand Piazza del Duomo, proposed by
Mengoni, saw massive demolitions to isolate the cathedral on one end of
a grand piazza, flanked by the Galleria – an altogether obvious assertion
of secular identity at the religious heart of the city.[26] Although most have
been destroyed by war or subsequent development, a few arcades remain,
including Rome's small Galleria Sciarra by Giulio De Angelis (1883), with
eclectic Pompeian frescoes, and the monumental, even more eclectic
Galleria Colonna by Dario Carbone (1914–22, now Galleria Alberto
Sordi). In Turin, the Galleria dell'Industria Subalpina in Piazza Castello
by Pietro Carrera (1877), was a contemporaneous celebration of innova-
tions in the decorative use of cast iron and glass. De Angelis also designed
the Bocconi shops (Rome, 1886–9), today's La Rinascente department

store, and another version in Milan in 1889, for decades the commercial heart of the two most important cities in Italy.

Beguiling as the new Stile Liberty was, powering the Italian economic machine towards the desired modernity and affirming the primacy of the nation called for more prosaic public and infrastructural works, such as implementing the nationwide telephone network, finally nationalized in 1903, a rail system, also nationalized in 1905, and hydroelectric plants and other electrical infrastructure. New roads and new factories began to pop up throughout the country, even in Rome, although the government had already decided not to industrialize the capital city so as to avoid the potentially revolutionary presence of a large urban working class. In many respects such a decision did not depart far from the traditions of papal Rome. 'Here there was no industry, no trade, no agriculture', remarked one late nineteenth-century observer; 'Rome lived an artificial life, never a producing city but only a consuming one.'[27] From the papacy the new state inherited the Tobacco Production Facility in Trastevere (by Antonio Sarti), an enormous, pedimented neo-Renaissance structure with a giant order set on a high base. Then located in a lightly populated area adjacent to the women's jail, the facility became part of the state tobacco

Postcard of the Galleria Vittorio Emanuele II.

Giuseppe Mengoni,
Galleria Vittorio
Emanuele II, Milan,
1877.

monopoly and provided a model for light industry that could be developed around the perimeter of the city, in particular by adopting a simplified historical style not at wild variance with its neighbours.

The Birra Peroni brewery (1908–22) long supplied the region with beer, but despite its industrial functions, Gustavo Giovannoni outfitted the reinforced concrete structure in neo-medieval, picturesque fashion, complete with tower, in an effort to achieve a sympathetic response to the surrounding, newly constructed residential quarter. For a second phase, Giovanni adopted the Stile Liberty. Like many other early twentieth-century industrial structures in Italy, this factory became an extraordinarily successful cultural centre in the first decade of the twenty-first century, the MACRO. To be sure, industrial architecture invited a good deal of formal exploration because specific typologies had yet to be developed.

Pietro Frontoni and Antonio Mazza, Ferrarese sugar refinery, Ferrara, 1899.

Yet where architects in Germany, Britain and especially the United States engaged new materials for the new functions, and hence experimented with the forms new technologies made possible, Italian architects remained locked into historicist repetitions, employing iron for decorative purposes and large glazed windows to facilitate shopping. In the long run, these choices turned out not to have been unwise. Locating industrial establishments in urbanized areas exacerbated design problems, as evident in Giovannoni's laboured efforts to blend the factory into the neighbourhood. More straightforward solutions were possible on sites on the urban periphery, such as in the Zuccherificio Agricolo Ferrarese by Pietro Frontoni and Antonio Mazza (sugar refinery, 1899), a three-storey, unadorned masonry structure recently converted into the University of Ferrara's engineering school. As I discuss in the next chapter, the industrial triangle Turin–Milan–Genoa in northern Italy exploded with factory construction and transformed these cities into modern metropolises, with all the attendant problems. Entire towns came to be dominated by one industry, such as Milan's Gallarate and its textile industry.

Peroni brewery,
Rome.

Industrial development brought not only changes in the economic and social fabric of the country, but in its culture more generally. The new machine age, with its internal combustion engines, aeroplanes, electricity, telephones and even bicycles and submarines, inspired a generation of writers and artists to celebrate the acceleration in movement and the materials that such new devices made possible. Youthful enthusiasm for new technologies converged with the constant search for arts and architecture that were quintessentially modern, Italian and therefore emblematic of the spirit of the new nation. The movement known as Futurism, founded by Filippo Tommaso Marinetti in 1909, coalesced around the exaltation of mechanization in verse, prose, theatrical events and eventually, architectural design. In a Paris newspaper, Marinetti published his first Futurist Manifesto on 20 February 1909, followed by others exalting the intoxicating power and authority of the new technologies. Marinetti emphasized the idea that the new inventions created new people, so it was no surprise that he and other Futurists sang the praises of mechanized warfare. 'We want to glorify wars – the only hygiene for the world

– militarism, patriotism, the destructive gesture of libertarians, the beautiful ideas for which one dies, and contempt for women', sang Marinetti in the movement's opening salvo in 1909.[28] The following year, the scope of his contempt for women blossomed forth in his novel *Mafarka il futurista*, in which an African king, purely by exertion of willpower, gives birth to a divine, gigantic son.[29]

Architecture received its first Futurist expression in the designs of Antonio Sant'Elia beginning in 1912, although the Manifesto of Futurist Architecture jointly authored by Sant'Elia and Marinetti only appeared on 14 July 1914. Sant'Elia's 'Dinamismi' works of 1912–13 initiated his explorations into new structures for the modern city; using a few basic forms (pyramidal, cylindrical, sharply canted buttresses) the young architect from Como studied the ways these forms could be melded into increasingly complex architectural compositions. The *Città Nuova* ('New City') drawings Sant'Elia exhibited along with those of Mario Chiattone during the spring of 1914 evidence the rapturous embrace of new technologies to create an architecture of the future: external elevators, elevated roadways for automobiles, electrical power plants conveyed an image of – without actually setting out a plan for – the new city, so powerfully expressed in the buildings.

The manifesto published in the exhibit's catalogue linked the drawings with the Futurist imperative to reject historicizing impulses in all its forms and to embrace new materials, to then be poetically configured. Historic preservation, classicism, decoration, the charming and picturesque architecture of the nineteenth century, along with slums and areas of urban degradation, would disappear in Sant'Elia's sweeping vision of a new world. For the ancient Vitruvian principles of architecture – firmness, commodity and delight – Sant'Elia instead substituted thrift, use and speed of construction, and subsequent destruction, to accommodate new generations. The timelessness of architecture that stood at the core of building traditions in Italy thus came under challenge. Sant'Elia envisioned a world in which houses did not outlast a generation: 'We will outlast our houses. Each generation must build its own cities' his manifesto proclaimed, in an eerily accurate prediction of what has happened in many countries.[30] There is some irony in the fact that the Futurist ambition to destroy historic Italy's buildings and traditions accurately reflected precisely what government officials at all levels and speculators were doing throughout the country in the decades following unification, as one bitter commentator noted in 1886:

> No doubt it could never be foreseen, never be imagined, by those
> who brought about and permitted the consolidation of Italy into one

kingdom, that the people, nominally free, would become the abject slaves of a municipal despotism and of a barbarous civic greed.[31]

The First World War broke out less than a month after Sant'Elia's manifesto appeared, and he and other Futurists entered the military with great enthusiasm for what Marinetti described as a cleansing force for the youth of Europe. Cleanse it did, for Sant'Elia and others did not return from its battlefields. The future of Futurist architecture in the post-war period lay in the hands of Marinetti, Chiattone, Virgilio Marchi and others, but even though most of its adherents embraced fascism, the architectural movement never regained the vigour and poetic power of Sant'Elia's pre-war designs. Nonetheless, his work acquired not followers but iconic status among Rationalist architects during the interwar years, with Giuseppe Terragni designing and building a Fascist monument in Como based upon one of Sant'Elia's designs.

Along with exhibitions, the second priority of the new Italian state was to erect public buildings to house new national agencies such as the ministries of Defence, Finance, Justice, the Interior, Agriculture and Justice, all located in the capital. By comparison with the Palace of Justice (law courts), the Ministry, with its simple brick elevations set atop a high, rusticated base and framed by travertine quoins, was a model of restraint, unburdened by what can only be described as the excessive ornamentation

Pio Piacentini, Ministry of Justice, Rome, 1913–32.

of the Palace. Law courts erected elsewhere in the country followed the more sober model of the Ministry, such as Marcello Piacentini's design for the Palace of Justice in Messina, Sicily, in 1912. After a terrible earthquake levelled it in 1908, Messina was still undergoing major reconstruction, at the same time that officials inserted new public buildings representing the national government into the damaged urban fabric. Piacentini's initial design proposed a neo-Renaissance palace, but the interruption of the First World War and the turbulent years following its conclusion delayed most of the construction until 1923. By that time, Piacentini had rethought the earlier design, reformulating it into what was then a more modern, stripped classicism, which he declared to have been inspired by Berlin's Brandenburg Gate. Raised on a high podium with a wide staircase, a giant order of Doric pilasters topped by a high architrave marks the main elevation. Three entrances are set in elegant travertine frames, and each of the bronze doors sports reliefs designed by Piacentini. Atop the attic is a bronze and aluminium sculpture by Ercole Drei of the goddess Minerva in a four-horse chariot. Piacentini's subsequent commission for the Palace of Justice in Milan presents a leaner, even more stripped classicism, with none of the echoes of Doric classicism so finely articulated here. Newly expanding cities were also encouraged to erect public buildings, a situation complicated in southern Italy by the disastrous aftermath of the earthquake of 1908, which levelled Messina and seriously damaged Reggio Calabria on the mainland. Ernesto Basile completed the grand new town hall for Calabria in 1914, while rebuilding Messina proceeded more

Antonio Zanca,
Palazzo Municipale,
Messina, 1935.

slowly. Antonio Zanca's design for the Palazzo Municipale in Messina (1935), with its large pediment and gigantic order of pilasters like that of Basile, represented eclectic versions of late nineteenth-century Umbertine classicism.

The electrical, chemical, metallurgical and mechanical industries fuelled economic development in the decades prior to the First World War, largely confined to the Turin–Milan–Genoa triangle in the north. Although in decline, the textile industry remained the largest sector, at least through the war. Much of the labour in textiles had been piecework, something women in particular could accomplish at home. In the face of progressive industrialization in the second half of the nineteenth century, this became increasingly less possible; work shifted to factories located in larger urban centres. Elsewhere, mine closings in Piedmont and a broad decline in agricultural income exerted a constant pressure on rural residents to abandon their barely subsistence-level farm labour for the promise of decent salaries in urban areas. Even the absence of adequate housing failed to impede migration to cities; in many cases families only exchanged thatch-roofed huts in the countryside for tin and board shanties on the peripheries of expanding cities – but at least in the latter there was a promise of work and the prospect of better housing in the future.

Gradually, industrial development took hold in other areas of northern Italy, especially in the Po Valley, but housing to accommodate the influx of immigrants remained a problem even in smaller cities. The government's initial response to these problems was predictably slow, reluctant, limited to the largest cities and arguably mean-spirited. Although the pressing need for housing was abundantly clear to politicians, the first initiatives were paternalistic or consisted of nothing more than contributions of land or tax relief – in effect, limiting access to moderately prosperous workers. Those who promoted government-sponsored housing did so on the familiar grounds of hygiene, both physical and moral. As Italy's earliest centre of industry, Turin's city administration was already addressing the problem of worker housing in the second half of the nineteenth century, but only a handful of apartments issued from interminable meetings held by various government agencies to deliberate on the matter.

Proximity to factories and distance from the city centre drove site selection, as it did elsewhere. In Rome, Giulio Magni's project in Testaccio was the earliest low-cost residential complex (1910–13). While under control of the papacy, for centuries the area remained devoted to agriculture, especially small-scale vineyards, large expanses of pastureland and many inns and hostelries. In the early nineteenth century, the papacy inaugurated the first infrastructural works: an omnibus connecting the city to the suburban basilica of St Paul, followed by the Porta Portese railway station in 1859, and in 1863 a rail bridge connecting Testaccio with Rome's new Termini train station. The earliest plans for post-unification Rome, in 1871 and 1883, entailed making Testaccio a pole of production and housing, beginning with the Mattatoio (slaughterhouse, 1888–91), followed by the general warehouses (1912), Montemartini electricity plant (1912) and the Market (1921), among others. The housing by Magni located near the slaughterhouse and the river left inhabitants assailed by noise and pungent odours, not only from the slaughterhouse but also from the Gazometro, a storage facility for gasoline, and other light industries such as leather production. In Milan, the city council formed a low-cost housing agency in 1903, initially to erect almost 200 housing units by Giannino Ferrini in via Ripamonti (1906). They consisted of eight three-storey buildings that framed interior courtyards with low-rise communal facilities such as showers, laundries, a library, meeting room and nursery. Balconies overlooked the courtyard and gardens. As in Rome, these early low-cost projects sat remote from the centre on cheap land, but most importantly, adjacent to the rapidly industrializing northern section, where flourishing businesses such as Pirelli and Breda were establishing their headquarters.

Despite the fastidious removal of the poor and the working class, politicians and the bourgeoisie hardly cherished historic structures in their

cities; instead, they viewed the city as terrain open for unbridled speculation. They did not revere antiquity, to the dismay of scholars and lovers of
Italy elsewhere: 'All over the land, destruction of the vilest and most vulgar
kind, is at work; destruction before which the more excusable and more
virile destruction of war looks almost noble. For the present destruction
has no other motive, object, or mainspring, than the lowest greed', raged
an article in the *North American Review* in 1886.[32] Over the strenuous
objections of archaeologists and other advocates, the putative protectors
of order and hygiene successfully eviscerated the Jewish ghettos in

40

Florence and Rome and sliced new streets through historic medieval and Renaissance districts. Once able to banish the existing residents, the new government installed the theatres, cinemas, department stores, offices and administrative buildings deemed essential for a successful and bourgeois modern city. After the hiatus of the First World War, attention shifted from bourgeois facilities to an orgy of monuments dedicated to those who lost their lives in the ill-conceived venture.

chapter two

The Exploding Metropolis

New public and administrative buildings altered the physiognomy of Italy's major cities after 1870, but so did the people who left rural areas undergoing precipitous economic decline to relocate to cities, where they laboured in the new factories and staffed new bureaucracies and agencies. Although in 1881 nearly two-thirds of Italy's population was still bound to agriculture, largely grain production, the percentage declined over time.[1] Recent studies indicate that the decade of the 1880s, far from being a period of economic recession, was instead one of widespread prosperity, even if cut short by the worldwide depression of the 1890s.[2] Well-being was not equally diffused throughout the country, however; greater urban wealth in general countered greater rural poverty. Efforts to modernize the peninsula's cities, encourage the growth of industry, establish new towns in rural areas and to Italianize new and old colonial possessions in North Africa and the Mediterranean basin jostled with ever more pressing needs to provide housing, goods and services for the country's burgeoning population. At the same time that governments – especially the Fascist one – promoted heavy industry as the primary tool for modernization, they also discouraged consumption in the hope of ensuring that capital investments fed industrial development rather than commodity production.[3]

Before settling on Rome as capital, the fledgling government nourished grand ambitions for outfitting Turin for that role. During the second half of the sixteenth century, Savoy dukes began to embellish the city, setting out from the ancient Roman grid, with the goal of transforming the small provincial city to take advantage of the economic hub taking shape even then in the Po Valley. By the nineteenth century Turin had comfortably secured regional prominence. The selection of the aristocratic House of Savoy to be the country's new royal family launched an ambitious challenge to transform a regional capital into a modern and national one. The model to which most European cities looked as the epitome of modernization in the middle of the nineteenth century was Baron Haussmann's Paris, with its broad boulevards terminating in important cultural monuments, new sewerage system, network of parks and elegant bourgeois housing – not to mention its dogged removal of lower-class residents from the historic

Angiolo Mazzoni, housing for railway employees, Bologna, 1923–4.

centre. In Turin, with its Francophile cultural traditions, early visions of a renovated city sprang almost directly from the Parisian model, such as the plans for the Parco del Valentino and its extensive grounds, which became the focus of a lively debate on how to expand and consolidate green zones in the city along the lines suggested by Haussmann's elaborate network of Paris parks.

Fate intervened to spare Turin a major remodelling; once eliminated as the capital, the energy to transform the city dissipated and indeed the population shrank for a time when the new nation's bureaucrats and their families decamped to Florence. In the second half of the 1860s, Turin's city council decided to resolve the consequent economic downturn by encouraging industrialization through measures enacted to entice entrepreneurs to the city: price reductions on consumer goods, coal and transportation, and plans to erect low-cost worker housing adjacent to or near sites planned for industrial growth. Whatever incentives the city offered, however, none was quite as compelling as that of electrification. With an energy source no longer dependent on the rivers (the Dora or the Po), industrialists could now look to other parts of the city, particularly the southwest section. The success of the project is undeniable: the city's population more than doubled within just 50 years and, with Milan and Genoa, Turin became one of the three poles of industrial Italy throughout the twentieth century.[4] By the first decades of the twentieth century, automobile manufacturing was

Parco del Valentino, Turin.

the leading industry, with the Fiat company, owned by the Agnelli family and established in 1899, making Turin its headquarters: the company's plant at Lingotto, built in 1914–26 and designed by Giacomo Mattè-Trucco, was the largest and most avant-garde production facility in the nation, with a widely publicized proving track elevated on the roof of the starkly modern concrete structure. So captivated was Le Corbusier by the audacious rooftop track and its spiral ramp for automobile access as a splendid illustration of the functional modernism he promoted that he illustrated it in his book, *Vers une architecture* ('Towards an Architecture', 1923). With the factory's operation reflecting the importation of efficiency-based, or Taylorized, methods of production, the building itself could hardly do less than celebrate crisp efficiency with an engineering-based profile. Following the closure of the factory in 1982 and a competition designed to elicit proposals for what to do with what had otherwise become an enormous white elephant, Renzo Piano reorganized the structure to insert cinemas, a shopping centre, restaurants and cafés, a hotel and a rooftop gallery to accommodate part of Gianni Agnelli's art collection.

Turin offers a keen illustration of the twin features of post-unification Italian cities: upgraded, modernized and tourist-oriented city centres, and often squalid and unplanned, burgeoning bedroom suburbs. Refashioning urban centres to render them appropriate for the professional and administrative classes, but also to capture the national and international tourist trade, necessitated the removal of unsightly, low-income neighbourhoods; urban policies to widen narrow ancient city streets to accommodate public transportation and automobiles; restoration or remodelling of important historical buildings to emphasize the city's noble history; construction of modern railway stations; and the liberation of important ancient, medieval and Renaissance architecture from the agglomerations of structures that had attached to them like barnacles over the centuries. None of this was possible without demolishing buildings considered unimportant, or simply obstacles, and the consequent dispersal of inhabitants to whatever shelter they could find. The housing alternatives offered by the pre- and post-First World War governments for groups such as these were provisional at best, even if they continued to be occupied for several decades. In general, both the Fascist government and its predecessors enjoyed greater success at addressing the housing needs of the middle and upper classes than those of industrial workers and the urban poor.

The middle and upper classes shared a common concern with public order and security both before and during the Fascist era, principles that underlay most of the decisions by both governments about housing the new urban proletariat. Observers outside of Italy embraced similar views; a correspondent for *The Times*, writing about the widespread urban rebellions

Formia, medieval tower with later building attached.

in May 1898 and their consequent loss of life, urged as a solution 'energy to the verge of brutality if necessary, ruthless repression of political insurrection, and a sounder administration under a practical dictatorship'.[5] Virtually every outbreak of riots and rebellion led to the deaths of innocent bystanders, including children, police and demonstrators; martial law was declared in Como on 11 May 1898, and riots in Rome, Milan, Genoa, Venice and Florence followed a general strike in June 1914.[6] In each case, public transportation came to a halt, factory production ceased, shops were damaged and many people were injured. Even the Catholic Church initiated a grudging acknowledgement of the 'social question' in *Rerum Novarum*, the 1891 encyclical of Pope Leo XIII, in response to the enormous economic transformations under way.[7] Ultimately, the periodic rebellions of rural masses in the nineteenth century, and increasingly of urban masses in the first two decades of the twentieth, slowly persuaded the bourgeoisie that repression alone would not eliminate them, and that providing at least a minimum of decent housing might translate into a reduced risk of uprisings.

To fund diverse housing types for a growing population, city leaders turned to national and international capital, especially banks, insurance companies and large-scale property developers, whose primary concern was profit and whose strategy was simply speculative development. At the same time, where the upper classes had formerly depopulated the old city centre in favour of suburban estates in a pattern common among the peninsula's cities, they now moved back to urban areas with a vengeance, driving out the poor and welcoming banks, insurance companies and corporate headquarters to share the newly upgraded centres. Cities throughout the peninsula inserted facilities such as theatres, cinemas, shopping arcades, department stores and museums for the middle classes, such as the Galleria Umberto I in Naples designed by Emanuele Rocco and Paolo Boubée (1887–92), and the Teatro Massimo in Palermo by Ernesto and Giovanni Battista Basile (1897). In 1906 the engineer Serafino Amici replaced a wooden outdoor theatre on the new via Nazionale with Rome's first building erected entirely in reinforced concrete, the Teatro Apollo (now Teatro Eliseo), to which he applied a Liberty-style facade.

Historic centres began to recover their appeal among the prosperous middle classes almost immediately after unification. The capital city of Turin, formerly the stronghold of the 'most aristocratic Court of Europe', had by 1864 opened its palace gates, both literally and figuratively – 'once so jealously guarded against all those who could not prove that their families had had a virtual right of passage there for many generations' – to 'all who by their own merits or good luck have raised themselves in the political, Parliamentary, official, military, and even the professional or artistic career'.[8] Haussmann's transformation of Paris into a bourgeois capital between 1852 and 1870 represented the model of civic modernity adopted by city leaders throughout Europe; in Italy, planning strategies in larger cities such as Florence, Turin, Milan and Rome in particular evidenced the effort to duplicate the Parisian model. Even the architectural style adopted for many of these new facilities, Stile Liberty, took its cues from designs drawn from France and Belgium. The sinuous iron balconies, floral window and door surrounds and abundant curving lines became the motifs of choice for retail and leisure structures, even in small cities. Some of the most exuberant examples are found in Sicily, where urbanization and new wealth funded fresh and fashionable Liberty-style upper-class housing. Ernesto Basile was responsible for the most elegant late-Liberty and Vienna Secession combinations in Palermo, including the Ribaudo kiosk (1916) and the Kursaal Biondi theatre (1913–14). Less positive was the campaign around the turn of the century to gut medieval and nineteenth-century sections of the city to create a grand promenade, the via Roma, according to the master plan devised by the engineer Felice Giarrusso.[9] Angiolo Mazzoni's magnificent Post Office occupied some 5,500 square metres of a formerly dense, largely fourteenth-century neighbourhood.

The mechanisms adopted to accomplish the goal of cleaning out the poorest districts paralleled those adopted elsewhere in the industrializing world in the nineteenth century: all were linked to health, both physical and social – that is, concerns about infectious disease, worker unrest, crime and vice. Euphemisms such as 'reclamation' (*bonifica*) and 'slum clearance' often simply masked more venal interests in acquiring property. The dynamic pattern of unbridled speculation and removal of the poor in the nation's expanding centres faithfully followed this logic from the

Serafino Amici, Teatro Eliseo, Rome, 1906.

Ernesto Basile,
Ribaudo kiosk,
Palermo, 1916.

second half of the nineteenth century through most of the twentieth, even
if the motives underlying specific transformations varied from city to city.

Once designated the new capital in 1864, Florence began to experience
the first signs of ambitious building programmes, just as Turin had earlier.
Beginning in 1864, the planner Giuseppe Poggi tore down the city's walls

and replaced them with boulevards; but this was only the first of many massive transformations planned for the urban landscape. Demolishing the historic ghetto, with buildings dating back to the fourteenth century, and sweeping away its inhabitants, allowed the formation of a newly regularized street grid with far larger and more expensive speculative neo-Renaissance buildings, a style embraced with no evident sense of irony at the substitution of clearly fake Renaissance structures for genuine ones.[10] An insistently voiced desire to emulate Haussmann's Paris underlay the demolitions and reconstructions, 'while the megalomania which [is] one of the weaknesses of the Latin race [led] them to try to "go one better" in mad projects for the adornment of the resultant demolition'.[11] Perhaps the most infamous enterprise in Florence was the replacement of the city's old market and other buildings in the centre with a huge ceremonial piazza framed by new buildings, today's Piazza della Repubblica, its immense triumphal arch trumping the old city gates, the only fragments of the demolished city walls still standing.[12] This manifestly speculative enterprise ushered in an even more ambitious plan in 1897 by the city's mayor, the Marquis Raffaele Torrigiani, to raze the entire area between Porta Rossa and Palazzo Pitti, in effect an effort to transform central Florence along the lines of Haussmann's Paris, destroying palaces, churches and towers.

The gutting of the city proceeded at breathtaking speed, but Florence escaped some of the planned demolitions, in part because in 1871 the capital of Italy shifted to Rome and in part due to Florence's privileged position on the historic Grand Tour route of northern Europeans. An active and educated cultural elite of residents and visitors from England, led by the outspoken British author Vernon Lee, cherished the city's picturesque districts and fought aggressively to preserve them. They were often successful: Lee helped found an organization, the Associazione per la Difesa di Firenze Antica (Association for the Defence of Old Florence), to marshal and focus the outrage of expatriates and intellectuals against Torrigiani's plans in favour of retaining the city's rich and diverse architectural patrimony.[13] Lee particularly excoriated the demolition of the centre, including the old market, Vasari's fish market, several churches, palaces and guild headquarters, and a lively array of medieval streets. The centre, Lee charged, 'was not cleared or ventilated, or drained, or otherwise sanitated, but simply swept off the face of the earth, not a trace of it remaining in the group of commonplace and inappropriate streets, and the ostentatious and dreary arcaded square which arose on its site'.[14] The organization drew attention especially to the late medieval and Renaissance parts of the city; so successful was its propaganda that the city and its surroundings underwent a neo-Renaissance revival in the late nineteenth century that lasted through the onset of the Second World War.

Despite the favourable resolution for some parts of Florence, escaping the wrecker's ball was not common in the years after unification. An ancient and densely inhabited quarter in the heart of Milan disappeared to make way for the spacious piazza in front of the Duomo and for the Galleria. Similarly, in Rome the architecturally rich district around the Capitoline Hill fell to make way for the monstrous, grossly inappropriate Vittoriano, the monument to a singularly undistinguished royal family and specifically to the Savoy king, Victor Emmanuel II. Euphemistically called the 'isolation of the Capitoline Hill', the enterprise started with demolitions in the nineteenth century but continued after the First World War under the supervision of Armando Brasini and Antonio Muñoz. This was but the tip of the iceberg: rampant speculation underlay the destruction of the ghettos of Rome, Florence and other cities, not primarily to open their gates (already abolished in most cases several decades earlier) but to carve new traffic arteries and erect new office buildings. Not every instance of flagrant destruction was aimed at removal of the poor; many members of the Roman aristocracy happily destroyed old family villas and carved up their gardens into residential and office blocks. Emblematic was the fate of the Villa Ludovisi, adjacent to the Villa Borghese. This gracious villa, the glory of papal Rome with its spectacular gardens of pine and bay trees, also hosted a remarkable aviary that included nightingales and peacocks. The city purchased the grounds for 3 million florins, immediately demolished

Domenico Primicerio,
low-cost housing,
Duca d'Aosta district,
Naples, 1913–39.

the villa and gardens, and by 1888 speculators were filling the site with housing blocks.[15]

The one Italian city already a crowded metropolis by the time of unification was Naples, a long-standing, teeming population magnet. For centuries under various monarchies, most recently the Bourbon, aristocrats congregated in the city and with them all of the servants, soldiers and public employees who serviced their households and the state. Its port also drew a fluctuating population of sailors and a full complement of labourers and enterprises associated with commercial trade.[16] Noticeably absent were centres of production; the overcrowded city depended upon the court and its status as capital of the Kingdom of the Two Sicilies (1816–61) to survive. Joseph Bonaparte initiated Napoleonic reforms after 1799 in an attempt to gain the support of the peasants by making land available and reducing taxes, fundamentally by attacking the feudalism still regnant in the then Kingdom of Naples. After a law of August 1806 abolished the personal and jurisdictional rights of the barons while leaving intact their landed rights, the government attempted to compensate for this by giving over ecclesiastical properties seized in the wake of the revolution.[17]

With one stroke, on unification in 1860 the court and the capital disappeared, throwing the city into a crisis it never entirely overcame, economically, socially or politically. That the new government was unable to deal with Naples's problems was soon apparent. 'What hope was there for a municipal government that spends millions on public festivals', wrote

Romano Manebrini in 1864, 'and abandons a city where everything has to be created, and a population of which two thirds lives in a social hell, shadowed by ignorance, rendered brutish by hunger?'[18] Although the mercantile elite continued to enjoy record profits, a growing impoverished underclass fiercely competed for scarce employment and ever declining resources. In this environment, the state was reluctant to invest in low-cost housing, but as elsewhere, promoted housing for the middle and upper classes along the bay to the north and west, in flagrant violation of the city's master plan. Industry developed to the east and south, also the zones densely packed with the city's burgeoning urban proletariat. Post-war films recounted the stories of struggling Neapolitans in tragicomic style, such as those starring Antonio De Curtis, known as Totò (1898–1967), including *Napoli milionaria* ('Side Street Story', 1950), *Operazione San Gennaro* ('The Treasure of San Gennaro', 1966), *Il medico dei pazzi* (1954), *I ladri* (1959) and *L'oro di Napoli* (1954), in which 'Naples's gold' is the patience of its inhabitants, their willingness to pick themselves up after yet another blow and to keep going.

Conditions in southern Italy and Sicily differed in significant ways from those of central and northern regions. Even in the waning months of the Second World War, Italian agriculture in the south was still shockingly primitive, as a United States military attaché wrote: 'In contrast to the neat and, for Italy, modern buildings on the farms are the retarded methods of cultivation. In the spring fields are tilled by men and women walking behind bovine-powered single-share plows or swinging broad hoes endlessly

. . . Hand harvesting and threshing are . . . common, and are almost invariably used for legumes and minor cereal crops.'[19] What scholars and politicians have long defined as 'the Southern problem' described political, social and economic circumstances generally termed backward, as applied to the regions south of Rome known as the Mezzogiorno – circumstances substantially different from those typically associated with northern Italy. Land tenure and agricultural policies, as well as a governmental tradition based upon the Bourbon monarchy, government officials argued, had conditioned a society that was unable to keep up with the industrially driven economies of northern cities. Recent scholarship emphasizes that there is no single Italian 'south' but several souths, each with its own particularities. For example, in the provinces between Rome and Naples, resident agents managed *latifondi* (vast agricultural landholdings belonging to Roman and Neapolitan aristocratic families and cultivated by tenant farmers), which were largely devoted to cattle raising. The *latifondi* in western Sicily similarly were great estates worked by tenant farmers also owned by the nobility; by contrast, here the owners traditionally eschewed diversification in favour of cereal cultivation as the most rapid source of the immediate profits necessary to maintain their social status. But cereals were far more vulnerable to declines in agricultural prices and competition from North America; this form of agriculture resulted ultimately in only economic stasis and emigration.

By contrast, the Bourbon monarchy invested significantly in infrastructure to serve landholders throughout the south and to encourage diversity, a strategy rejected by the post-unification liberal government, which viewed such tasks as the responsibility of the individual landowner rather than of the state.[20] Likewise, landowners and farmers along the southern coasts over the course of the nineteenth century shifted to citrus fruits and olives, producing by the end of the century some of the highest rates of return anywhere in Europe.[21] In short, by contrast with the image presented of the south for nearly 150 years, many regions responded rationally to changing economic conditions. Instead of industrial development, trade and the brokerage of goods produced elsewhere dominated the southern economy, and have continued to do so at the beginning of the third millennium.[22] Because the liberal state focused on industrial and capitalist development as the key to modernization, these forms of economic and social activity simply did not figure in their calculus, so the new Italian state attempted to force its own version of capitalist modernization on the south, all the while ignoring the specificity of conditions in different parts of the region – a strategy pursued with remarkable consistency in the face of stubborn resistance on the part of southerners. Not surprisingly, many voted with their feet, either leaving the country altogether or heading for the factories of northern Italian cities. The twentieth-century 'economic miracle' of the post-Second World War period indeed drew its strength largely from the migration of southerners to the north.[23]

A much longer tradition of a distant monarchy in the south also led to a concept of the state as one in which the individual needs to develop a network of hierarchical connections so as to ensure the economic survival of the family. Best known in the version that emerged as constituent characteristics of organized crime, this economic and social system centred on commercial activities and often ended up reinforcing the poverty so characteristic of this region.[24] As recent scholarship argues, all three post-unification governments based their policies upon viewing the south as a backward dependency of the north – and all of the programmes the three successive governments developed along those lines failed miserably despite the oceans of money tossed at the problem of grinding and persistent poverty.[25] Naples, once again, proves a case in point. Its sewer system remains the one constructed in 1888 when the city was a fraction of its present size, and even a major cholera epidemic in 1973 failed to prompt significant change. As we shall see in future chapters, whether the problem was sewers, earthquakes, rubbish or inadequate housing, every planning effort has been reactive and inadequate.[26] As elsewhere in the south, 'The weak economic base of the south Italian city results in high levels of unemployment and under-employment and an inflation in the tertiary sector in a form of hyper-urbanization more commonly associated with the Third World.'[27]

As I argued in chapter One, industrial development, high on the agenda of governments both before and after the First World War, saw factories cropping up throughout northern Italy, from Turin in the west to the Po Valley in the east, compellingly illustrated in Mario Sironi's paintings of the industrializing periphery of Milan. Light industry also clustered around the outskirts of cities, such as the Peroni beer factory in Rome also mentioned earlier. What the politicians and upper classes had not counted on, however, were the changes to cities generated by the presence of the masses of workers needed to operate the factories and their families. In fact, the brutal suppression of the Milan riots in 1898 made it clear that the liberal majority 'did not want to open its eyes to the reality of a society undergoing a wave of social changes'.[28] For their part, 'bourgeois entre-preneurs decidedly opposed reality, refusing to accept the link between the modernization of economic structures and the political and economic demands of workers'.[29]

Electrical, chemical, metallurgic and mechanical industries fuelled econ-omic development in the Turin–Milan–Genoa triangle in the decades prior to the First World War. Although in decline, the textile industry endured as the largest sector at least through the war. Workers fled their villages and the countryside for cities, where salaries were higher, even though they encountered persistent and severe housing shortages, precisely in the industrial triangle in the regions of Lombardy, Piedmont and Liguria. Gradually, industrial development took hold in other parts of the north, especially in the Po Valley, but housing for the influx of immigrants remained a problem even in smaller cities. Workers arriving with no income, no savings and no access to housing even when they found jobs, established squatter camps (*baracche*) on the peripheries of the nation's largest cities. Exemplary in this respect was the Borgata Gordiani, adjacent to the Gordiani villa on via Prenestina, the ancient Roman consular road. Here in 1870 immigrants from the Abruzzo, Campania and Marche provinces settled in tin-roof shanties no different from those on the peripheries of cities in developing nations today, with no lights, no water and no transportation. Although soon decried as disgraceful, unsanitary and visually unappealing, the squatter camps remained, and even when city governments finally started producing low-cost housing they could not keep pace with the pent-up demand. Borgata Gordiani, for example, saw the shanties replaced by masonry houses in the 1940s and '50s, but even today some *baracche* remain in the area, for example on the grounds of the abandoned SNIA Viscosa factory near the via Prenestina and Largo Preneste. Nonetheless, governments from the end of the nineteenth century through the late twentieth century energetically cleared out such camps, usually on the grounds of hygiene, both physical and social: they were considered 'moral pestilences' in which vice and crime thrived.[30] Whatever their problems, in rapidly expanding cities such as Turin, Milan and Rome, *baracche* formerly on cheap land on the city's edge eventually succumbed to the bulldozers as land values skyrocketed and only the shanties blocked the speculative fever of developers.

By the late 1870s, workers' movements began to organize institutions to erect their own housing, such as the Building Society for Worker Housing in Milan, which managed to erect a handful of housing units near Porta Vittoria. Milan's city council only formed a low-cost housing agency in 1903, first with the goal of providing around 200 units in via Ripamonti, a development which, by contrast with the typically small rental housing usually erected for the working classes, included communal facilities (see chapter One). These early low-cost projects on sites at the time remote from the centre and on cheap land, facilitated rapid industrialization in the northern section, where flourishing firms such as Pirelli and Breda were establishing their headquarters. They needed workers readily available, unencumbered by the need to travel long distances to work, hence the appeal of public housing projects near the factories. Nonetheless, a typical feature of these and virtually all low-income projects even following the Second World War was the absence of public transportation, a tactic aimed at reducing the risk of restless urban masses mingling in the city proper. Projects such as Secondigliano and Ponticelli, erected in Naples after the Second World War, were 'built to minimal standards and with limited infrastructural provision'.[31]

No post-unification government took on the problem of housing with determination prior to 1920. The workers so necessary to man the country's factories came with little education, no money and a growing penchant for taking political action – a disruptive gesture in a country where political activities had always been the province of politicians, aristocrats and members of the upper bourgeoisie. So profound were the fears of government officials that shortly after Rome became the nation's capital, finance minister Quintino Sella convincingly argued that the city should be kept free of industrial development precisely to eliminate the danger of concentrating the working class in the capital because of the threat officials believed its members posed to social and political order.[32]

> I believe that the direction of the supreme interests of the country should be in Rome . . . but I have never wanted there to be great concentrations of the working class. [Rome] should be the place where many intellectual questions should be treated, which will require the labour of the country's intellectual resources; popular impulses of huge quantities of workers would be inappropriate [for this]. I believe such an arrangement would be dangerous . . .[33]

Deep fears about the revolutionary potential of uncontrolled urban masses, in part fomented by the succession of urban revolts in Paris and elsewhere in the nineteenth century, and the assassination of King Umberto in July 1900, led to a plethora of hopelessly conflicting policies. On the one hand, state and local governments reluctantly sponsored housing projects for low-income workers; on the other, efforts to prevent migration into cities persisted and even strengthened under fascism. The massive emigration from Italy to North and South America after 1890 received tacit and, ultimately, open support from government officials: 'Italian statesmen . . . regarded emigration as a necessary evil, for it had rid the nation of the poor and discontented and provided a 'safety valve' to insure domestic peace.'[34] In the early 1920s, Mussolini still believed that emigration was necessary to maintain social order. The loss of poorly educated lower class and rural Italians certainly did not concern him. In the post-First World War years, they were no more welcome in the United States than they had been at home, where Italians and other southern Europeans were deemed 'racially inferior, morally deficient, and impossible to acculturate':

> Italians were considered among the worst of this 'inferior' group ... Italians were stereotyped as uneducable illiterates and willing slum dwellers. They also carried the stigma of political radicalism and were considered innate criminals ...[35]

Indeed, the U.S. Senate passed the Johnson Immigration Act in 1924 despite the active opposition of Mussolini and the Fascist government.[36] After the previously open door to the U.S. ended in 1924 with a radically transformed immigration policy that largely excluded southern and Eastern European immigrants, emigration to South America continued unabated throughout the interwar period. Only in 1926 did Mussolini begin to rethink his emigration policy: rather than promoting it as a safety valve, he decided to launch a campaign to present it as a means of promoting 'Italian economic, political and cultural expansion'.[37]

Back at home, although the pressing need for housing was abundantly clear to politicians, the first initiatives were paternalistic in inspiration and usually consisted solely of contributions of land or tax relief. Only in 1903 did the government pass a law laying the groundwork for *case popolari* (low-cost housing), followed five years later by an inclusive law addressing several types of subsidized housing.[38] Almost immediately after Rome became the capital, officials had devised an orderly programme to transform the land between the Aventine Hill and the river Tiber into a mixed, light industrial district. Events quickly overtook the plans, including alternating periods of economic crisis and speculative fever; with few exceptions industrial development did not occur until many years later, and construction ended up consisting primarily of residential blocks. By the time Giulio Magni designed his public housing in Testaccio, the slaughterhouse was already in place (1888), as were facilities for treating waste (Fabbriche Mira Lanza, 1899). By 1936 light industries peppered the insalubrious surroundings. For these working-class families, the state helped subsidize the construction of primarily one- or two-room apartments with minimal services and no elevators, even in four- and five-storey buildings. By comparison with later constructions, however, Magni's design included elegant decorative elements on the facades and variations in massing among buildings, adding an attractive streetscape even if not significantly easing the lives of inhabitants. As the city grew around it, by the late twentieth century Testaccio, no longer remote from the centre and spurred by the transformation of parts of the slaughterhouse into a university campus, mutated into an area of trendy clubs and concert venues. The

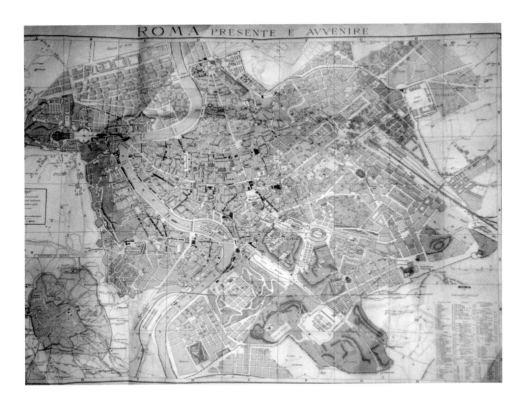

ROMA PRESENTE E AVVENIRE

Rome, master plan of 1883. The plan envisions the new monument to Victor Emmanuel II at the foot of the Capitoline hill, and the development of the Prato area adjacent to Vatican City. The plan envisioned the future shape of the city, demolitions and transformations included.

old crowded housing, too small for the large families of the first part of the century, is now ideal for the much smaller households typical of late twentieth-century families. While it is difficult to determine precisely what groups of people moved into all of these apartments originally, one thing is certain: most residents acquired their units as a result of political patronage, and even residents of shanty towns often had to pay to purchase the right to move into government-funded, low-cost units.[39] In any case, only the smallest and least desirable apartments were available to the poorest Italians; most of the public projects were destined for workers in government or para-government institutions.

Other than the *case rapidissime* cheaply assembled as basic shelter for those displaced by urban renewal programmes, the least expensive, most minimal residences were *case popolarissime*, or very low-income housing. Found primarily in larger northern cities and funded by the Istituto per le Case Popolari (ICP, Institute for Low-cost Housing, later IACP, or Autonomous Institute for Low-cost Housing), these usually consisted of two- to three-room units, without balconies, in five- or six-storey buildings, on the cheapest land available. One typical example in Bologna, although unusually

Franco Albini and
Renato Camus,
Giancarlo Palanti,
low-cost housing
in via dello Scalo,
Bologna, 1934–7.

Giulio Magni,
working-class
housing, Testaccio,
Rome, 1910–13.

Gazometro, Rome, 1935.

well maintained, evidences the denuded facades typical of these inexpensive units. Such massive residential blocks excited considerable public comment; of comparable building in Rome one commentator remarked, 'The frightful blocks of new houses, the hideous new streets, the filthy tramways, the naked new squares, are all made by foreign speculators who purchase the right of spoliation from the municipalities as the private owners of the soil.'[40] Nonetheless, at least Rome had a millennial tradition of multi-floor tenements for the lower classes: Cicero lamented the Rome he saw 'suspended in the air' by contrast with 'Capua lying comfortably down in the plains of Campania Felix.'[41]

City and state employees at all levels fared better than lower-class families. The state railways, banks, insurance and pension organizations, ministries and other organizations all began to erect housing blocks for their employees, the apartments sized according to the grade and status of their future inhabitants. Kitchens, storage facilities, complete bathrooms and separate rooms for sleeping and entertaining featured prominently in these units. More generous spaces also meant higher ceilings, larger rooms, more windows and better quality floors and fixtures, in general marking

Umberto Nordio,
minimal housing,
Piazza Foraggi,
Trieste, 1926.

them as superior to working-class housing. Moreover, the locations of these complexes typically sat closer to the central districts, or if not, at least in areas already serviced by adequate infrastructure. For example, the owner of a cotton factory near the gates of Collegno and an adjacent rail line planned the Leumann Workers' Quarter in Turin for his employees (1896–1911), with housing organized hierarchically according to the status and income of the workers. Among other housing estates erected by factory owners for their workers were those of SNIA Viscosa on the northern outskirts of Turin (Vittorio Tornielli, 1924), and in the country's northeast in the province of Udine, at Torviscosa (1938–40).

The middle and upper bourgeoisie instead could avail themselves of developments such as Piero Portaluppi's classicizing office and residential complex in the form of a triumphal arch on Corso Venezia in Milan, an exuberant example of the response of traditionalists to the need for dignified designs that expressed the inhabitants' high status. Unlike the working class, people from these groups could turn to private builders for their apartments, and indeed the overwhelming majority of housing erected during the first 50 years of the twentieth century came from private builders and speculators. Overall, the housing produced by public or semi-public agencies ended up being distributed according to an age-old class system, with the upper classes enjoying good infrastructure, spacious apartments and privileged access to central locations, while the lower classes made do with minimal quarters.

Piero Portaluppi,
housing on Corso
Venezia, Milan,
1926–30.

chapter three

Architecture and the Fascist State, 1922–1943

In his book celebrating the public buildings erected during the first ten years of Benito Mussolini's premiership, Minister of Public Works Araldo di Crollalanza cited Nicholas v, the fifteenth-century pope responsible for initiating the project to enlarge St Peter's Basilica, as an explanation for why the Fascist government accorded such significance to public building:

> [the beliefs] of people ignorant of letters [would] . . . gradually collapse over the course of time . . . unless they are moved by certain extraordinary sights. But when that vulgar belief is continually confirmed and daily corroborated by great buildings . . . it is forever conveyed to those both present and future, who behold these admirable constructions.[1]

The shattering reality of the First World War, with the country's war-mongering elites still stinging from the ignominious defeat at Caporetto in 1917 and the subsequent failure to reclaim Istria during post-war negotiations, meant that any government had to assert its legitimacy anew. During the war, as prices rose and profiteers and black markets flourished, returning soldiers found no work and no aid, and since matters failed to improve following the peace treaty in November 1918, it became progressively more difficult for the government to justify itself. Angry Italians, tired of vertiginous price increases following the war, seized and sacked grocery stores in 1919 in cities as far apart as Genoa and Palermo, but the flashpoint of the struggles were Tuscany and Romagna.[2] In October 1920 during a general strike, serious riots broke out in Milan, including bombs being thrown at the hotel hosting a British government delegation, and deaths from rioting were reported in Milan, Bologna and elsewhere.[3] The strikes, factory occupations and urban unrest in the streets during the war years, but especially between 1919 and 1922, led to a demand for a return to order that Mussolini and his fascist companions promised to achieve once they took over the reins of government.

An ambitious construction programme therefore became a key component of the new Fascist regime when it came to power in October 1922.

Adalberto Libera,
Palazzo dei Congressi,
EUR, Rome, 1938–41.

At the same time, the building campaign also attempted to address one of the most disturbing issues to emerge at the end of the war: the reality of nationalism. The landless proletariat and peasants who provided the manpower – cannon fodder, if you will – for the armed forces during the First World War returned from the battlefield posing the same kinds of questions that young Russian officers had after the Napoleonic Wars a century earlier: for whom, and what, had they fought? While rulers had pressed peasants into involuntary military service for centuries on the Italian peninsula, since the Middle Ages the community and persons for whom they fought had been reasonably clear, if not always fully visible: the local authority, whether secular or religious, and the citizens of a particular city or region, that is, one's neighbours. Things were not so clear in 1918: what loyalty did these young men owe a distant king who did not even hail from their part of the country, or even more potently, what did they owe to an abstract idea of a nation that provided them neither with land nor, in many cases, with sufficient resources to support their families? Benito Mussolini famously acknowledged this every time he repeated Ferdinando Martini's comment 'We have made Italy: now we need to make Italians.'[4] As we will see later, the Fascist regime addressed these concerns in several ways: by erecting new towns and giving land to the landless; by constructing low-cost housing throughout the country; by erecting infrastructural showpieces such as the Autostrada; and by erecting public buildings that at once symbolized national (and Fascist) power and yet targeted not the elite but all classes.

Public Building

The pre-war government had focused on erecting structures of presumably national significance such as ministries, national museums and libraries, urban and national infrastructure such as roads, railways and tramlines, and the apparently inevitable monuments to the Savoy dynasty, but the accomplishments outside the largest cities such as Rome, Milan and Turin remained relatively limited. To assert the primacy of fascism, hence also that of Mussolini and the Italian state, a far more extensive building campaign was in order after 1922. To reiterate, politics proceeds according to images of reality, and buildings provide exquisite images of desired realities, not only through style but in their actual purposes. Choices about what to construct mattered more than the choice of architectural language, a notion architects generally resist vigorously but which Mussolini and the Fascist state fully understood. Mussolini once commented that twentieth-century Rome faced 'the problems of essential needs and the problems of greatness. The greatness', he said, 'could not be faced until the needs had

been solved.'[5] The appropriate administrative apparatus was also essential. Within two months of assuming the post of prime minister, Mussolini initiated a thorough administrative reform and consolidation. Where formerly, individual ministries had controlled construction within their areas of competence, now the reconfigured Ministry of Public Works incorporated all public works, from schools to sewers, within the country's regions. The reorganization straightforwardly aimed to synchronize logically linked construction enterprises: the new ministry would tie irrigation schemes to reforestation and erosion- and flood-control projects, and low-cost housing to road networks, schools and other infrastructure. The regional offices ceded control to the central government in a further reorganization in 1924, following which one office now directly controlled all planning for public works.

The modernization programme initiated during the country's first 60 years now gathered momentum. If Italy was to compete in international markets along with countries industrialized a century earlier such as Britain, the u.s. and Germany, then massive infrastructural works were of critical importance. Indeed, the largest percentage of funds went to hydroelectric, hydraulic and reclamation projects, and to maritime works and the building of aqueducts, roads, highways and railways. Utility was the key to these projects, but this did not limit concerns strictly to function. Roads, Mussolini proclaimed in 1929, were fundamental to the fabrication of

Viaduct over the
Stura, Cuneo.

national unity, for the facility of travel between cities and to and from villages was a necessary prerequisite to substituting national for local loyalties. *The Times*'s correspondent in Rome noted that 'Signor Mussolini once confessed to having "an almost Roman passion for roads"'.[6] Di Crollalanza proudly proclaimed that the barriers within and among regions were crumbling, and he believed that Italians were already joined into a single, national family. Given the eruption of separatism in northern Italy during the 1990s and in Sicily after 2000, it is safe to say that he was overly optimistic, but in any event, huge sums of money poured into the effort to achieve unity in spirit as well as in actuality.

Relative to that spent on roads, reclamation and other infrastructural projects, buildings commanded a comparatively small percentage of total public works funding, with expenditure particularly limited in the south. Between 1925 and 1932, for example, buildings accounted for only 5 per cent of public works expenditure in Abruzzo and Molise, 10 per cent in Campania, 2 per cent in Calabria and 4 per cent in Sicily.[7] By the late 1930s, the government nonetheless spent nearly one-sixth of all public works funding on the construction of schools, hospitals, courthouses, police and customs offices, post offices, train stations and libraries. In contrast with the buildings for Rome, Milan, Turin and a few other large cities commissioned by the pre-war government, those constructed during the two decades of fascist control blossomed in cities and towns of all sizes, so that the national government could manifest its presence throughout the country. New hospitals and schools, as published in weekly newspapers and photographed for the Istituto Luce newsreels after 1926, also enjoyed a visual impact far exceeding that of a new road or a reclamation project. Overall, the building programme intended to address the demands of modernization: a more educated and healthy workforce and a more efficient bureaucracy. Then, as now, buildings dovetail representational and symbolic needs with the operational goals of a specific programme such as that of a hospital or school.

Although groups of architects representing many positions argued for a Fascist style to give coherence to the national building programme, the government wisely chose to ignore this pressure and to recognize that the question of what a modern and Italian architecture might look like could profitably remain unsettled. Among the groups competing to define a new, fascist architecture were the traditionalists, or Accademici, the Novecento group in Milan and a comparable group of moderates in Rome, and the Rationalists. The first group included nationally known figures such as Armando Brasini, Cesare Bazzani, Carlo Broggi, Piero Portaluppi and their spokesman Ugo Ojetti, who promulgated a continuation of nineteenth-century eclecticism and unaltered neoclassicism. The moderates in Rome and Milan, including Marcello Piacentini, Pietro Aschieri, Giovanni Muzio and Gio Ponti, proposed a simplified version of the academic style as a prelude to devising an original and quintessentially Italian synthesis of modern and traditional architecture. The Rationalists defined themselves as the avant-garde and in varying degrees drew upon the currents prominent in northern European modernism, especially in their celebration of extensive glazing, flat roofs and unadorned surfaces. Or, as at the parking garage adjacent to Piazzale Roma in Venice designed by Eugenio Miozzi and Alberto Magrini (1931–3), alternating open and closed horizontal strips in the vein of Ludwig Mies van der Rohe's projects of the early 1920s. The fascist revolution in Italy pre-empted the driving impulse of modern architecture elsewhere in Europe – that is, its revolutionary pretensions, which left it up to Italian architects to elaborate a programme based not upon triggering a revolution but the far less potentially disruptive challenge of identifying an architecture that could exemplify the fascist revolution. The unique circumstances in Italy, then, involved defining

Eugenio Miozzi and A. Magrini, car park, Venice, 1931–3.

not a revolutionary architecture but a fascist one; the various strands of modern architecture that developed over the Ventennio (twenty-year period of fascist control) competed on a linguistic terrain founded on a consensus about the political and social principles of fascist modernity.[8] Exponents of all groups sought to have their versions of modernism become the representative style of fascist architecture.

Edoardo Persico, among the most trenchant of the era's critics, recognized that the debates among the various factions were purely formal, and indeed, he criticized the Rationalists for advancing an architectural programme distinguished purely by abstraction.[9] While he was not favouring historic architecture, he deftly pinpointed that the core problem underlying the architectural debates during the Ventennio was that it left the factions essentially competing for prizes rather than vision. Captivated by the modernity of structures such as Fiat's Lingotto building and by factory labour itself, Persico reflected long on the moral implications of modernism, industrialization, Rationalist architecture and Catholicism. Of aristocratic origins and himself a Catholic, Persico could not avoid bringing moral concerns to the table when discussing modern architecture, and a conviction that the social dimensions of Catholicism were as revolutionary, and as pertinent, as those of industrialism itself. A profoundly modern structure such as the Lingotto, with its rooftop proving track, at once testified to industrialization and prophesied the future, and not only of architecture.

In the aftermath of the Second World War, historians defined the diversity of approaches as evidence of confusion or contradiction among architects faltering in their struggle to deal with the new political reality of fascism, or indeed viewed it as evidence of the cynical manipulation of building styles by the regime to enhance its status. Both may be true to some degree, but a more convincing argument emerges simply by shifting the historical perspective. A broad consensus on political grounds allowed groups of architects to pressure government figures to select their particular brand of modern architecture as that which best embodied the principles and revolutionary appeal of fascism.[10] Although difficult for architects and critics of the Ventennio then and later to accept, in 1922, 1932 or even 1938, no one could anticipate which version of modernism was going to dominate – that is, which would be crowned by subsequent historians and patrons as the modern architecture *par excellence*. For several decades after the war, only the most putatively avant-garde, Rationalist architecture merited the label 'modern'; critics and historians dismissed everything else as irrelevant or mistaken, or worse, tarnished by association with fascism. The campus of the University of Rome, master planned by Marcello Piacentini but with individual buildings completed by several architects in styles ranging from Rationalist to stripped classicism, nicely illustrates the problem. Historians resolutely distinguished between the Propylaea (Arnaldo Foschini) and Piacentini's Central Administration building, both in a severely neoclassical style, from the ribbon windows, continuous stone moulding and graceful, glass curtain wall of Giuseppe Capponi's Biology and Chemistry Faculty. The former purportedly represented the epitome of fascist architecture, while the latter was a 'daring display of modernity' and 'the very antithesis of the lithic solidity of Piacentini's Administration building'.[11]

The logical gymnastics required to airbrush Giuseppe Terragni's Casa del Fascio of the taint of fascism but to damn virtually everything by Piacentini as fascist were inventive, but ultimately flawed. If the Fascist state commissioned a building, it must therefore constitute a testimony to that regime.[12] While this is not all there is to say about the many public buildings erected during the Ventennio, it remains one of their significant and inescapable features, and recognizing this helps us step out of the vicious circle of assessing a building's significance solely in terms of style. There is no 'fascist' style, any more than there is a democratic or communist one, but there are buildings patronized by specific governments. In fact, a comprehensive review of building under fascism reveals that overall, the public works funded by the Fascist state evinced a commitment to continue but significantly expand on strategies initiated by the previous government, and to which the new regime added a wide variety of other buildings to accommodate its own political and social initiatives.

One of fascism's singular contributions was to confront the disregard of popular culture and the masses so characteristic of the nineteenth-century liberal government, as exemplified by Crispi's arrogant disdain for the lower classes. Ventures ranging from theatrical productions to state-sponsored exhibitions, such as the biennale in Venice (begun in 1895) and the triennale in Milan (begun in 1918), for the first time brought the rural and urban working classes into the orbit of bourgeois culture made available to people throughout the country by means of discounted train fares.[13] At the same time, state institutions affirmed the significance of popular culture through sponsorship of local and regional exhibitions, not to mention the opening of a national museum for the purpose of exploring and documenting the many varieties of Italian popular culture. Even though all of these ventures reeked of propaganda on behalf of the regime, and arguably cynical manipulation, there is no gainsaying the belated acknowledgement they gave to groups of Italians the previous government ignored unless required to provide police power to suppress them. The state also began to challenge the barriers erected to favour high culture by subsidizing and celebrating new media such as film, through the Istituto Luce and through the construction of Cinecittà, a district in Rome dedicated to the film industry. Sponsorship of guides for tourists, weekly publications celebrating Italy's cities and regions, and cinematic documentaries on Italian cities and villages also aimed to diffuse information about the peninsula's cultural and artistic heritage. Where the response of the government to the urban and rural working classes in the decades after unification had often been violent repression, the Fascist state now opened up a range of programmes that in one form or another engaged ever larger segments of the population. Whether these programmes helped weld people to the party is questionable – but along with an expanded police presence, they certainly helped prevent the kind of urban unrest that characterized Italian cities at the turn of the century and in the immediate aftermath of the First World War. Mussolini shrewdly recognized that simply oppressing the labouring classes was no longer an option; they had to be made to feel part of the nation, and this the Fascist Party worked hard to accomplish.

A second major interpretive problem historians confront concerning the architecture produced under fascism has been their own preference for a dominant stylistic unity and discomfort with aesthetic diversity. In this respect they tend to mirror the aesthetic ambitions of Adolf Hitler – who resolutely sought a single, neoclassical language as that which best expressed Nazism – more than those of Mussolini, who evinced openness to a variety of architectural languages. All of the groups competed to develop a state architecture, and all, including the Rationalists, argued, as critic and museologist Pietro Maria Bardi did in 1931, that the Fascist state needed to control and give unity to architecture as the quintessential expression of civilization. Bardi intoned:

> We declare that the state has an interest in controlling the delicate question of architecture according to unifying and dictatorial criteria, as well as in setting out the general character of building programmes . . . The one proposing this is not asking for a State architect, but for a State that establishes definite and strict norms for architecture.[14]

Historians echoed this position when they lamented the failure of the regime to enforce unity on Italian architects, or, alternatively, when they celebrated what they believe to have very nearly been the triumph of Rationalist architecture over the traditionalist model; as one historian happily noted, 'Until 1937 modern Italian architecture had seemed the official representation of the fascist regime.'[15] In their focus on the public battles waged among proponents of various versions of modernism,

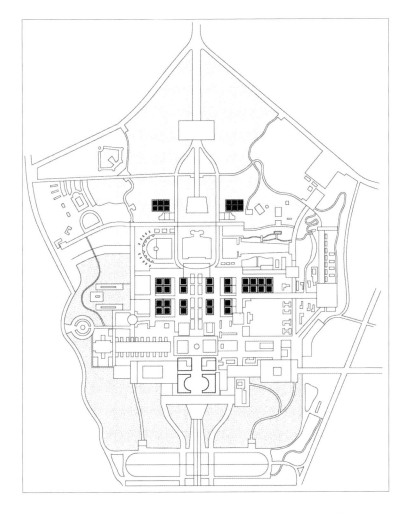

Marcello Piacentini, EUR, plan, 1937–43 (redrawn by Joseph Flynn).

historians often used the polemics presented by the various factions as devices to illustrate presumably deep ideological battles among architects somehow conditioned by the uncertainties, moral ambiguities and profound flaws of the Fascist regime, at other times as evidence of a vital, if hidden, rejection of fascism, but in all cases as somehow providing evidence of the moral failings of fascism itself and, by implication, the moral superiority of modernist architects. As an analytical tool this approach leads nowhere. Although rarely posed in these terms, only the exercise of significant control from above, by the Fascist Party or the state, could have achieved the desired unity; in effect, this argument ends in criticizing a totalitarian state for failing to be sufficiently totalitarian.

Paradoxically, critics reserved their greatest criticism precisely for the period they often claimed offered the greatest unity of style: the years between late 1935, with the Italian invasion of Ethiopia and the declaration of the new Italian Empire, and 1943, when Mussolini fell from power. Giorgio Ciucci's analysis of the plan and buildings for the EUR (Esposizione Universale di Roma, originally E.42, 1937–43, the exposition that was to be the regime's most eloquent showcase) offered a case in point. Despite celebrating the University of Rome campus as evidencing, 'for the first time, full agreement . . . between the various tendencies, under the auspices of Piacentini . . . and [Giuseppe] Pagano', Ciucci wrote: 'in contrast to the unity that existed in the planning of the Città Universitaria, the compromise between the various factions was short-lived'.[16] Historians claimed that the architecture of the regime's last eight years became retrograde, more similar in style to Nazi monumentalism than to Rationalist architecture.[17] Adalberto Libera's stunning design for the Palazzo dei Congressi e Ricevimenti (initiated 1938) at EUR is only one of many projects to give the lie to this characterization of the architecture of the regime's last eight years, for the state in fact continued to patronize the diverse architectural styles proposed by Italian architects within the broad framework of fitting the

Giuseppe Terragni,
Casa del Fascio,
Como, 1932–6.

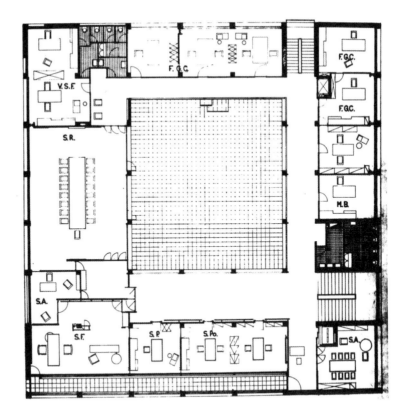

elegance and monumentality of the architectural language to a building's functional and symbolic purposes. It is true, however, that some architects perceived Nazi-inspired monumental classicism and planning to be the wave of the future, the new modern design as opposed to Rationalist, or International Style architecture. They erred, but the state neither forced this style on them nor discouraged them from utilizing it. Many other buildings bore little if any resemblance to Nazi monumentalism, including Gaetano Minnucci's Ente EUR building (1937–8).

In any case, the standards of historical judgment have shifted uncomfortably between criticizing fascist culture first for being too eclectic, and then for being too controlling, with neither attitude providing much analytical muscle or indeed explanations for the mass adherence of architects to fascism. Lodovico Barbiano di Belgiojoso (of BBPR) remarked that just as architects moved en masse to support fascism by 1932, so too they shifted to the Communist Party in 1968, and he confidently anticipated that they would shift to follow the axis of power in the future – as indeed many did in the 1980s, aligning with the then-powerful Socialist Party, and in the 1990s, with Berlusconi's Forza Italia. This phenomenon of ideological suppleness is known in Italy as *trasformismo*, indicating thin ties to specific ideologies but an affinity for power, whatever direction it takes.

The consensus on political affiliations, cynically adopted by some and expansively embraced by others, explains why the Fascist government endorsed all of the groups and delivered commissions to exponents of widely different styles. What it fails to explain, however, is the extraordinary flowering of high-quality design. No other twenty-year period, either before 1922 or after 1943, saw such a prodigious output of overall architectural originality and excellence on the peninsula. From the most academic to the most avant-garde, the architecture of the Ventennio abounds with examples of fine design, much of it for public buildings commissioned by the Fascist state or by the Fascist Party. Among the most well known and widely publicized is the work of Giuseppe Terragni, especially his Casa del Fascio (Fascist Party Headquarters, 1932–6) and the Asilo Sant'Elia kindergarten (1934–7), both in Como. Deeply committed to fascism, in the Casa del Fascio Terragni sought an ideal synthesis of modern and traditional that would give expression to the highest ideals of fascism. Terragni employed high avant-garde language to interpret the traditional Italian town hall type, by rendering its configurational elements – rusticated tower, arengario (balcony from which a party official summoned citizens to meetings or issued important announcements), loggia, monumental staircase, great hall, crenellation – in a modern and fascist key. He reduced the tower to a simple, un-fenestrated block; the arengario to one of three corridors set behind the regular grid of the facade; the open loggia to a set of sixteen doors that opened simultaneously onto the interior court; and the monumental staircase to a glass-lined passageway.[18] The extensive use of glazing symbolized fascism for Terragni, who believed that 'Fascism is a house of glass into which all can look.'[19] Evidence of the enduring power of Terragni's designs can be found in the fact that a building such as the Casa del Fascio can be recognized for its symbolic political goals as well as its explorations into the language of modern architecture, without diminishing the significance of either. Terragni exploited the principles of Rationalist architecture to develop a new type of light and open school complex for the Asilo Sant' Elia, unique in its approach to facilities for early childhood education in Italy at the time, which had not yet solidified into a particular building type.[20] Pursuant to the notion of binding language and symbol, in the kindergarten Terragni conceived of Rationalism as providing the architectural form, but the spiritual content as deriving from the noble goals of education. Although modifications altered some parts of the complex, a recent restoration allows the elegance and purity, and Terragni's originality, to emerge.

Giuseppe Terragni, Asilo Sant'Elia kindergarten, Como, 1934–7.

Marcello Piacentini,
Rettorato, University
of Rome, 1934–5.

Gio Ponti, School of
Mathematics,
University of Rome,
1932–5.

opposite:
Arnaldo Foschini,
University of Rome,
entrance, 1932–5.

Giuseppe Capponi,
Biology and
Chemistry Faculty,
University of Rome,
1934.

Like many of his contemporaries and most subsequent architects, Marcello Piacentini was content to occupy a position of great power granted by the regime, to dole out favours and commissions to architects of all political persuasions, as is evident both in his project for the University of Rome and in the plans and buildings for the EUR.[21] A gifted architect responsible for some of the most emblematic public buildings of the interwar period, Piacentini favoured a moderate version of modernism in which buildings with different purposes received designs appropriate to their place in a hierarchy of public buildings. The Rettorato, or administrative building of the University of Rome (1934–5), for example, boasted a central tower raised on a high podium, with its entrance recessed behind tall, square piers rising the full height of the structure. He considered such a monumental elevation appropriate for the most significant building in the complex, just as the magnificent Palaces of Justice he designed for Messina and Milan received comparably grand treatment, in acknowledgement of their important political and social functions.

The contrast between the two palaces of justice illustrates the broad transformation Italian architecture underwent during the interwar period. The former is an elegantly and linguistically correct neoclassical structure with a monumental Doric pronaos erected according to the new anti-seismic building codes, while Piacentini articulated the equally monumental law courts in Milan in a more modern vein, with a classicism stripped of details such as capitals and architraves. For less symbolically loaded public buildings, such as those for the various academic departments at the University, Piacentini sought quite different architectural languages, including the non-monumentalizing style favoured by the Rationalist architects. After drafting a master plan, Piacentini brought in moderate and avant-garde architects to design individual buildings, such as Giuseppe Capponi for the Biology and Chemistry Faculty, with its ribbon windows and twin glazed towers on the facade, and Gio Ponti for the extraordinary School of Mathematics (1932–5), with its grand, traditional entrance on the front elevation contrasting with the sweeping curves and syncopated fenestration of the classrooms on the rear.

Beyond the political and functional objectives that inhered in any public building, architects explored the poetic and expressive possibilities of new materials and technologies, the relationship between modern buildings and ancient cities, and the design possibilities of new building types. No subsequent government commissioned as many and diverse new public buildings as the Fascist state did; it may be that the magnitude of the enterprise – the sheer number and diversity of commissions – energized architects and challenged them to develop new solutions for both old and new building types. Adalberto Libera's exuberant Scuola

Adalberto Libera,
Raffaele Sanzio
Elementary School,
Trento, 1931–4.

Carlo Savonuzzi, Ada
Costa Elementary
School, Ferrara,
1932–3.

Elementare Raffaello Sanzio in Trento (1931–4) embodies these complex and interlocking objectives. The goal of extending literacy throughout society demanded new schools, but Italy in the early twentieth century had no established tradition of building types for mass education to draw from, leaving the development of new designs in the hands of architects. Libera met this challenge with striking originality, taking account of the specific context. Situated adjacent to the medieval Buonconsiglio Castle on an irregularly shaped site, the school consisted of rounded, lateral tower blocks in a deep Pompeian red intonaco (stucco revetment) that responded to the castle's rounded bastions in an entirely modern vein. Behind the street wing, two classroom wings formed a square with canted sides joined by a narrow, sinuous wing at the rear. The front elevation consisted of tripartite, giant windows divided by travertine mullions set on a high podium; between this block and the towers is a recessed entrance topped by a perforated dark-grey block. The school evinced many of the themes Libera explored in his subsequent projects, such as using staircases as poetic elements, gridded perforations, sweeping rounded forms and extensive glazing on facades set within sober travertine frames. It also offered a bold new approach to the treatment of a facade in a city with one of the most striking medieval and Renaissance piazzas to be found in the entire peninsula.

An equally bold venture in modern architecture appeared in a district of Ferrara newly planned by Girolamo Savonuzzi, with several buildings designed by his brother, Carlo. The highlight of the complex is the Ada Costa elementary school (1932–3), whose sleekly curved and glazed corner block reflects contemporary developments in Italian Rationalist architecture, while the library tower, with its elegant brick pilasters, harked back instead to the brick elevations typical of early Dutch modernism, not to mention Ferrara's own decorative brick traditions. Savonuzzi, one of many gifted architects practising during the interwar years with a strong local base, received scant recognition at national and international levels.[22]

The Fascist government developed new institutions such as the Opera Nazionale della Maternità ed Infanzia (ONMI, founded in 1925 to provide prenatal and early childhood medical care to women and children); the Opera Nazionale Balilla (ONB, a youth organization); and the Opera Nazionale Dopolavoro (OND, providing leisure facilities for workers); as well as for other still new institutions such as post offices. Angiolo Mazzoni, architect and long-time head of the engineering office of the Ministry of Communications, left probably the largest and most distinguished building legacy of any civil servant in the first half of the twentieth century, with striking and original post offices and railway stations erected throughout the country. His earliest projects, such as for the Post and Telegraph office in Ferrara (1927–9), exemplified a refined and exquisitely detailed interpretation of nineteenth-century design strategies on the street elevation, while the rear boldly picks up the evolving forms and motifs of Italian Rationalism. Only a few years later, for the Post Office in Sabaudia, Lazio, Mazzoni gave free rein to an exuberant interpretation of modernism garbed in blue tile, unfortunately not maintained and left open to the ravages of time. While he spent the early years of his career working in the office of Piacentini, Mazzoni considered himself a member of the Second Futurism movement, retaining strong ties with post-First World War Futurists throughout the interwar period and frequently involving them in the design and decoration of his public projects.[23] Such was the case for his Post Office in Palermo (1928–34), where Benedetta Cappa Marinetti painted five enormous panels dedicated to a poetic exploration of the synthesis of terrestrial, maritime, air, telegraphic, telephonic and

radio communication (1933–4), and Bruna Somenzi designed curtains to outfit the walls of the conference room.[24] The building's monumental grey colonnade on via Roma towered over its surroundings, its intercolumniations opening to nine arched passages into the barrel-vaulted entrance portico. As in many of his other projects, Mazzoni challenged what he saw as the sterility of modern architecture by enlivening the spaces with rich chromatics, such as the deep orange vaulting at the entrance and the Moroccan red of the chairs, along with a bold use of materials such as copper (including for chairs in the administrative offices) and expensive, wood-inlay Futurist motifs by Paolo Bevilacqua for door panels. Mazzoni defined Rationalist architecture as a branch of Futurism, which itself was more lyrical and poetic than Rationalism. The latter, in Mazzoni's view, because of its origins in northern climates, 'though congenial and powerful, lived without the sun . . . and [so] our genial and lyrical creativity could heat [it up]'.[25] Unconstrained by historical precedents for these new building types, architects' experimentation with building forms and poetics could achieve remarkably fresh syntheses. For these regime agencies, in part through careful attention to scale, architects, although freed from

Angiolo Mazzoni, Post Office, Palermo, 1928–34.

the constraints of tradition nonetheless managed to design buildings that fit comfortably into even dense historical settings.

The only major organization sponsored by the state unique to women was the ONMI. An extremely high infant mortality rate lay behind the decision to focus on maternal health and the care of newborns, but of course this centred attention on women in their roles as mothers. Little other space existed for them in fascist mythology. Women participated in fascist organizations parallel to those of the men, such as the women's section of the Party (Partito Nazionale Fascista, PNF), but were clearly secondary in status. Women in Italy had been struggling to acquire a public voice since at least the beginning of the century. Led by prominent figures such as Maria Montessori and the socialist Anna Kuliscioff, suffragettes vigorously pressed for female suffrage as early as 1903, an objective not achieved until January 1945. Official approval for women to enter all professions, from medicine to law to architecture, had been granted in 1919 following the First World War, but access nonetheless remained limited by age-old, deeply ingrained prejudices about women as wives and mothers, and the architectural profession still today remains one of the most resistant to the participation of women. The ONMI facilities only reinforced the importance of women's roles as mothers; nor did women receive commissions to design these buildings.

Often these new Fascist agencies could be erected in settings where fitting into an existing urban environment was not an issue. In the Lido di Ostia, for example, Libera's Casa del Balilla (1934), with its rounded portico and crisp white stucco volumes, recalls the simple white forms of coastal villages throughout the Mediterranean Basin, here employed on behalf of an institution only recently founded by the Fascist state and for which building types had yet to be developed. The Balilla organization for children, founded in 1926, was similar to international Scouting and to Catholic youth organizations and included recreational and instructional activities. By contrast, an earlier Casa del Balilla in Rovigo, in the Veneto region, with its pedimented entrance, quoins and high podium, recalls the school buildings erected by the post-unification government in styles ranging from neo-Renaissance to neoclassical.

Perhaps the most ubiquitous of the new buildings planted in towns throughout the peninsula was the Casa del Fascio, or Fascist Party headquarters. With all of its institutions, the Fascist state aimed to emphasize the immediacy and totality of its presence, but this was especially true of the Case del Fascio. In the early years of the regime, the party simply adapted existing buildings to the needs of its headquarters and tacked an appropriate quote on to the walls to indicate the building's role; at Incisa Valdarno the chosen quote read: 'We say that only God, never men and things, can bend the Fascist will.' Lacking any features specifically linking them to fascism, such structures did not fulfil the party's representative aspirations. By the early 1930s, the Casa del Fascio had taken on typological

Franco Manzoli and Alberto Gagnani, Casa del Balilla, Rovigo, 1932.

Casa del Fascio,
Incisa Valdarno.

form, and the form chosen was a modernized version of the northern and
central Italian medieval town hall: rusticated tower, arengario (balcony
from which the podestà, officials, could summon citizens), large interior
meeting hall, ceremonial staircase, battlements and portico. The Casa del
Fascio gathered these elements, with the exception of the battlements, but
assembled them in a modern language, such as in Giovanni Lorenzi's
Casa del Fascio in Trento. Borrowing the symbols of medieval communal
power before towns lost their autonomy to strongmen or aristocrats

without actually vesting authority in the community was a long-standing tradition in Italy, as in the Palazzo Comunale (town hall) of Montepulciano. Likewise, PNF headquarters clearly identified the source of power as Rome, and the proliferation of Case del Fascio with the same configurational elements reinforced this authority.

All of these structures sustained important roles in diffusing ideas about how society should operate and the roles of individuals within the collective. PNF headquarters usually included places where local groups could meet, play cards and listen to the radio and, by the late 1920s, where they could also watch films and Istituto Luce newsreels. Since most people could not afford radios, this brought one of the most significant new technologies of the early twentieth century to an expanding audience, fusing indelibly modernity and fascism in the minds of many Italians. Not all programmes broadcast on the airwaves concerned politics; many were informational while others brought news of the country's football teams right into small villages, including the national team's spectacular success in winning the World Cup in 1932 and 1936 – victories tailor-made to unite Italians behind the national team and, the government hoped, behind the Fascist state.

As permanent additions to Italian cities, institutional buildings such as the OND and ONB were daily reminders of the presence of the Fascist Party in the lives and public affairs of the community. But like its predecessor, the Fascist state also promoted public spectacles as part of the culture of mass engagement in the regime. Grand celebrations greeted both the initiation and the completion of buildings, roads, dams, reclamation projects and the foundation of new cities. In this, the Fascist regime followed centuries-old traditions: in Italian cities even during the Renaissance, full-scale temporary triumphal arches constructed for the arrival of important visitors stood sheathed behind scaffolding and drapery until presented to the public with great pomp on the day of the event. Other deeply rooted traditions the regime adopted and adapted are some of the most criticized, such as the practice of attaching the fasces, designated the official state emblem in 1926, or an M for Mussolini on new constructions as well as old. Popes and princes in Italian cities from antiquity onwards, and especially following the Renaissance, considered it absolutely normal to place their coats of arms, initials and names on everything from the walls of family palaces to those of stables and, wherever possible, replacing those of earlier powers, thereby branding them for the present and future as their property or accomplishment – just look, for example, at the entablature on the facade of St Peter's cathedral in Rome.

Reminders of power were coordinated with activities that more directly engaged the broad public, for the challenge, as the political activist and theorist Antonio Gramsci recognized, was to gain consent. Oppression alone would not suffice; consent springs in large part from involvement. Expositions promised to entertain and involve large swathes of the public while at the same time touting the accomplishments of the regime – bread and circuses, as the ancient Roman rulers astutely acknowledged. Politicians and intellectuals on the national and local level planned them, architects erected structures to accommodate them or designed the displays, but everyone could enjoy them. From the late 1920s onwards, party organizations mounted a regular sequence of exhibitions throughout the peninsula, covering subjects from the history of the fascist revolution to the celebration of imperial conquests in the Mediterranean and North Africa, to after-work clubs (OND). The Mostra delle Terre d'Oltremare (Exhibit of Lands across the Sea, 1940), mounted in Naples in 1940, celebrated the African and Mediterranean colonies labouriously acquired by the new nation since the beginning of the century.

The output of inventive design over the twenty years of fascist rule is striking, but the sheer number of commissions alone cannot explain it. Certainly the openness of the Fascist regime to a wide range of architectural languages helped, as did the diversity of commissions available. A third factor cannot be discounted. Overwhelmingly, architects practising in fascist Italy, as members of the upper middle class, especially the urban bourgeoisie, often enjoyed inherited wealth; Adalberto Libera, for example, son of a prominent lawyer and descendant of the aristocratic Pallavicino and Sforza families of Parma, came from a family in which work was more hobby than economic necessity. Whatever else there is to say about their class affiliations, the freedom from the need to work also granted architects freedom to experiment. Other factors included energetic engagement with the other arts. Class affiliations led architects to rub shoulders with peers who were artists, graphic designers, actors, directors, poets, writers and musicians, many of whom were also experimenting with new forms, new materials and new approaches in their fields, including being influenced by the work of Mexican muralists to develop polemical and socially inspired murals for public buildings throughout the country. These artists often shared a view of the arts as closely linked, and most of them were designing or writing on behalf of the Fascist state. Carlo Belli, often described as the father of Italy's abstract art movement, wrote one of the most important tracts on the avant-garde in Italy, the book *Kn* (1935), in which he summarily dismissed Cubism, Dada, Futurism, Expressionism and Purism, leaving Surrealism as the only true art worthy of the appellation 'avant-garde'. But he sang the praises of Rationalist architecture, which he saw as the most important of the artistic activities of the time – the one that illuminated the path for all of the other arts and which therefore also demanded comparable results in other fields.

Muralists and painters were experimenting with new technologies, sculptors with new materials and, buoyed by consistent institutional patronage from the state, produced art for the new buildings and for the many publications that arose to document and disseminate information about the activities of the many new fascist institutions. The prints and drawings of Duilio Cambellotti, for example, came to constitute the quintessential expression of the grand reclamation project in the Pontine Marshes in publications of the ONC throughout the 1930s, such as the journal *La Conquista della terra* ('The Conquest of the Earth'). His training and early fascination with Art Nouveau and Stile Liberty reflected his belief in them not simply as styles but as examples of art with a social and moral imperative, as design strategies that reject historicism, much as his contemporaries the Futurists had done.

Many of the architects themselves also wrote, painted or created sculptures. The energy that coursed through the arts and enlivened specific disciplines also crossed the boundaries between them, fertilizing one another and perhaps more importantly, helping trigger the outburst of creativity that characterized all of the arts of the period. Magazine and journal covers, advertisements and posters, temporary exhibitions, sculptural reliefs: all were nourished by the same bursts of sustained creativity that flowered in architecture. Often the work depicted architecture, such as the travertine relief illustrating the building of Rome at EUR (1939), or was integral to a building, such as Gino Severini's mural at the Post Office in Alessandria (1940–41). In those exciting times, for members of this prosperous profession, there were commissions for everyone, some permanent, some temporary, and there were competitions and prizes; it would have been surprising if there had not been a cascade of challenging and vigorous art and architecture.

Arguably one of the best laboratories for collaboration between architects and artists was the most famous exhibition of the era, the Mostra della Rivoluzione Fascista (Exhibition of the Fascist Revolution, MdRF) of 1932.[26] Opened on the tenth anniversary of the Fascist March on Rome (28 October), the exhibit occupied Piacentini's Palazzo delle Esposizioni in Rome, but with a reconfigured facade that rendered the building all but unrecognizable. In response to Mussolini's charge to make something of 'today', modern and audacious and without melancholy memories of past styles, Adalberto Libera and Mario De Renzi designed a massive 30-metre-high, deep red cube to sheathe the central part of the palazzo's facade, from which projected four massive fasces of pop-riveted burnished copper. Stripped of decoration and historicizing elements, the powerful imagery

Publio Morbiducci, 'The Building of Rome', detail of travertine relief on EUR Headquarters, 1939.

Gino Severini, 'The History of the Post and the Telegraph', 1940–41, detail of mural, Alessandria.

and crisp chromatics of the front elevation signalled the rhetoric of the interior displays. Organized chronologically and in a processional sequence beginning with the foundation of Mussolini's newspaper *Il Popolo d'Italia* in 1914, the exhibit's sequence of spaces documented the war years, the foundation of the party and continued through to the Sacrario, a monument to those who lost their lives in defence of fascism. A range of artists, many with loose affiliations with the Novecento Italiano group, received commissions to design individual rooms, including Marcello Nizzoli, Guido Mauri, Amerigo Bartoli and Mino Maccari, each in turn teamed with an individual responsible for the historical exhibits in the room. Of these, the most famous was Mario Sironi, a Sardinian painter who moved to Milan in 1920 and became famous for his haunting industrial and urban imagery. Sironi received the unusually large commission for the exhibits in the P, Q, R, and S rooms at the Mostra, recounting the March on Rome, the Room of Honour and the Gallery of the Fasces, totalling nearly one-quarter of the first-floor exhibition space. Three-dimensional figures, sculpted architectural features and powerful graphic components with photomontages and sharp reliefs constituted some of the most visually powerful spaces in the exhibit.

Perhaps most intriguing of all the rooms was the design by Giuseppe Terragni for the Sala O ('O Room'), commemorating the year 1922 and the months leading up to the March on Rome. Terragni ruptured the static 19 × 9-metre room by thrusting strong graphic and iconic elements into the space, such as a diagonal 6-metre-high wall with profiles representing Fascist flags in black, Italy in silver and finally that of Mussolini in metallic black; behind this wall another convex surface erupted into the space. The complex composition of solids, voids, overlapping graphics, three-dimensional imagery and spatial interpenetration signalled a dramatic departure from the Rationalist principles of Terragni's architecture, but cohered with his sensibility as an artist and painter and, perhaps more important, with the rhetorical intentions of the Mostra as a whole and its imperative to give powerful and energetic representation to the themes of fascism. For example, a metallic cobweb descending from the ceiling and draping over a complicated mix of scaffolding symbolized industry ensnared by a web of worker strikes; while in perhaps the most famous image, whirling turbines emerged from a dense photomontage of crowds that transformed into a sea of hands leading to Mussolini's signature. The title explained the imagery: 'Mussolini's thought-action attracts the Italian people like a turbine and renders [them] fascist.' The effect Terragni sought was that of lightness and a sense of floating, conveying the 'rapid succession and simultaneity of events' of the year 1922, something he accomplished by attenuating all stable reference points and creating a sense of weightlessness, aptly described by Persico as 'a seismic fantasy'.[27] Not surprisingly, critics lauded the audacity and inventiveness of Terragni's design, describing it as 'a masterpiece of propaganda art', and even while recognizing that it transformed the tawdry little March on Rome in 1922 'into an event of mythic proportions' credited it with being a sign of 'progress . . . being made in the campaign to modernize Italian architectural practice'.[28] Though José Quetglas celebrated the Sala O as a great piece of theatre, consistent with theatrical elements in other designs by Terragni such as the Casa del Fascio in Como, in the process he fixed on the formal elements and claimed that its subject was not political, but architecture itself.[29]

The Mostra constituted the first great exhibition the Fascist Party mounted, and one directed not to an elite audience but to the masses, educated and uneducated alike; in this it followed the tradition of the great nineteenth-century expositions, which began with the Great Exhibition in London of 1851. What separated the Mostra from its predecessors was the audacious and compelling combination of graphics, architecture, photomontage and interiors rendered in stylistic languages that were fresh and innovative. As such, it served as the model for subsequent exhibits in which the premier architects and designers of Italy freely experimented with techniques, language and style to celebrate Italian aeronautics (Milan, 1934); sport (Milan, 1935); summer camps for children (Rome, 1937); and state-sponsored after-work clubs (Rome, 1938), among many others.[30]

Despite great success at inserting new buildings and building types into cities throughout the country, the Fascist state was less successful at doing so in the capital city, Rome, where bitter polemics halted the construction of several of the most famous Rationalist designs of the period, including the competitions in 1934 and 1937 for the Fascist Party headquarters (Palazzo del Littorio) and Giuseppe Terragni's Danteum (monument to Dante, 1938). Although entire districts, or *fora* – devoted to government (EUR), intellectual activities (Università di Roma) and sport (Foro Mussolini, now Foro Italico) – blossomed on the urban periphery, construction within the capital became surprisingly difficult at the very time that it was becoming easier in smaller cities. Setting these important symbolic institutions on what was then the city's perimeter emphasized directions for growth, but also allowed architects the freedom to experiment with their designs far from the complicated historic urban fabric of the ancient city centre. For the Foro Mussolini, for example, Luigi Moretti designed the Accademia di Scherma (Fencing Academy, 1933–6). This stunning exercise in Rationalism joins two wings, a library and the fencing hall with a cylindrical element and a portico set behind a reflective pool. With all of the relationships governed by subdivisions of the golden ratio, both in plan and in section, the building achieves an extraordinary equilibrium against a backdrop of green hills and the elegant lines of Raphael's Villa Madama. The serene marble revetment and fenestration strips conceal an innovative structure of two reinforced concrete semi-vaults, slightly displaced from one another and which admit diffused light into the interior. Badly damaged from years spent as the setting for high-security judicial proceedings against political radicals and organized crime figures, and hence long unavailable to visitors, the Accademia is currently undergoing restoration. The other remarkable facility at this site is the Stadio

Luigi Moretti,
Accademia di
Scherma, Foro
Mussolini, Rome,
1933–6.

Enrico Del Debbio,
Foro Mussolini,
Rome, 1928–32.

dei Marmi (Stadium of Marbles), a twentieth-century recreation of the ancient Roman circus, with marble seating and enormous travertine statues of athletes looming over it. The entrance to the Stadio dei Cipressi (Stadium of Cypresses, 1937, now the Stadio Olimpico) developed by Luigi Moretti perhaps best illustrates the brilliant interlacing of ancient and modern. Leading artists designed mosaics for the path leading from the obelisk dedicated to Mussolini in the Piazzale dell'Impero to the stadium, including one representing a plan of the entire complex. Lining

the path on either side, monolithic travertine slabs carried inscriptions celebrating Mussolini's res gestae, in the manner of an ancient Roman emperor.

Monuments to the fallen of the First World War or to the victory constitute the last group of structures that mushroomed throughout the peninsula. As with the buildings, viaducts, highways, dams and other constructions it commissioned, by

94

Enrico Del Debbio,
Stadio dei Marmi,
Foro Mussolini,
Rome, 1928–32.

the late 1920s the state branded these monuments with the fasces, symbol of the PNF, thereby associating the party with the soldiers' valour and with the victory, as in the triumphal arch designed by Piacentini at Bolzano, in the Alps near the Austrian border, the Monumento alla Vittoria (1926). Placing a monument to the First World War there, one of the great irredentist areas during the nineteenth-century Risorgimento, constituted more than just a gesture honouring the fallen: it was a polemical reminder to the German-speaking population that while Italy may have given up its claims to this terrain in favour of Austria in 1882 as part of the Triple Alliance, it never quite relinquished the dream. Following the Second World War Italy reasserted its authority and reclaimed the area, along with the nearby region of Venezia Giulia.

Much the same is true of what is probably the most powerful of all the First World War monuments, Giovanni Greppi's military memorial at

Redipuglia, in the province of Gorizia (1938). As much a work of landscape architecture as architecture, it consists of a massive, open-air flight of stairs ascending a gentle hill. The names of 40,000 soldiers killed during the war engraved in bronze line the steps, along with the word 'Presente' (the Fascist response to roll call). At the summit stand three crosses and a spare chapel, their mute elegance memorializing the 100,000 Italian victims of the war – but it also constitutes a reminder that Italy reclaimed an area that in the nineteenth century had been the property of Austria in the nineteenth century, an assertion of national presence in a previously disputed zone.

Interwar Cities and Housing

Coming to power as he did after several years of searing street battles, labour unrest, general strikes, smouldering working-class antagonism and bourgeois fears of disorder in their city streets, it is no surprise that Mussolini made housing one of his major and most widely publicized initiatives. In general, the Fascist state simply followed the strategies already developed under the previous government, but increased both the number and visibility of each new complex. Modern Movement architects, sociologists and political theorists inherited beliefs from the nineteenth century about the capacity of decent housing to resolve festering social

Marcello Piacentini, Monumento alla Vittoria, Bolzano, 1926.

Giovanni Greppi,
Redipuglia
Monument, Fogliano
Redipuglia, Gorizia,
1938.

ills and produce a tranquil, hard-working and loyal populace. These were
the years of major investigations into housing, health conditions and rural
settlements for what they revealed about the standards of living of the
nation's poor.[31] The need for more housing was clear; the only questions
were who would finance it, where it would be built and what the appropriate formulas were for complexes dedicated to each class in the social
hierarchy.[32] Promoters of low-cost housing destined for Testaccio between
1883 and 1907, for instance, celebrated it as relieving a chronic housing
shortage by erecting buildings that squeezed between two and five people
into each room.[33] But the profits associated with middle-class and bourgeois development clearly did not accrue to low-cost housing, so the
task fell to the government or to a particular industry under fascism, as
had been the case in Italy's first 50 years, while private developers and
cooperatives saw to more profitable ventures.

How the Fascist government framed the problem drove decisions about
what and where to build. In cities, for example, the government argued
that the problem was overcrowding: too many people crowded into too
few rooms, too many housing units in too small an area. Armed with statistics showing high densities and high numbers of occupants in few rooms,
the government embraced the official policy of decentralization – that is,
clearing out crowded, presumably squalid inner-city low-income housing and moving families to new, low-density suburbs, or *borgate*, on the
city's edge. Apart from the fact that urban density does not cause squalor,
poverty does – as the example of Manhattan makes abundantly clear –

decentralization and de-urbanization policies led on the one hand to new working-class suburbs and on the other to a series of government-constructed new towns. Mussolini proclaimed in 1928 that it was essential 'to impede migration to the cities and mercilessly decongest them and to facilitate this with any means, and where necessary, even coercive ones'.[34] Contradictions riddled such strategies: for one thing, de-urbanization went hand in hand with efforts to industrialize and modernize the country, a feat that could only be accomplished through the construction of factories, which in turn had to be manned by low-paid workers.[35] Despite the inconsistencies, the Fascist government pursued both policies with equivalent rhetorical flourish.

The first line of defence in blocking migration into cities was to prevent people from moving in the first place, a task made easier by Italy's traditions of citizenship and residency. At least since the Middle Ages, one was a citizen of a city, a privilege acquired either through birth or through special request after a prolonged period of residency. Outsiders needed to obtain permission to live in a city, and citizens wishing to move to another city also had to pursue a series of bureaucratic procedures before obtaining permission from both cities. The mechanisms for controlling the movement of individuals from rural areas were already in place, then, when the Fascist government began to strengthen police and bureaucratic pressure to halt migration into urban ones, a practice known as 'disciplining internal migration'.[36] From repatriating people to their home towns to establishing rules in low-cost housing complexes to prohibit new arrivals from renting, the government aimed to staunch the flow of people from countryside to city, an effort destined to fail both in the long and the short term. Agricultural prices remained low, living conditions continued to be desperate and young people found nothing to tie them to the land when only cities offered jobs or, at the very least, opportunities not available in the countryside – forces over which no government, much less Mussolini's Fascist one, had much control.

The Master Plan for Rome, the work of Marcello Piacentini and a committee of dignitaries in 1931, renders fascist ideas about urbanism abundantly clear in the manner in which it specified the construction of housing for government employees at all levels, as well as for those in the public service sector. The planners ordered housing by hierarchy:

> upper levels were concentrated in the Prati, Trieste, and Parioli districts; midlevel managers in the Verbano and Janiculum districts; junior civil servants in Monte Verde Vecchio and Nuovo; railway employees and tram and bus drivers in San Lorenzo, Santa Croce, Porta Maggiore, and Testaccio. The final element of the

policy was the preservation of the historic centre for the middle- and upper-level bourgeoisie and the consequent construction of *borgate* (suburbs) on the outskirts of the city where inner-city lower-class residents would be transferred.[37]

Architects generally shared this view; Giuseppe Nicolosi, the gifted designer of many housing projects, affirmed in 1936 that the *borgate* solved 'the urgent problem of moving the lower classes to the outskirts [of the city] so as to give the central city areas they currently occupy more appropriate destinations'.[38]

Names for low-cost projects – *case popolare* (popular housing), *case rapide* (fast housing), *casa minima* (minimal housing), *case per tutti* (houses for all) – proliferated, but they simply masked the reality of a deeply classist approach. The poorer the future inhabitants, the more meagre the project; so corridors, foyers, pantries and anything deemed not strictly necessary could be eliminated. Nonetheless, arguably relatively little truly low-cost housing was erected during the Fascist period, for as with the previous government, considerable reluctance surrounded state activities in the construction industry. The laws noted above, and an additional one in 1923, all sought to promote low-cost housing primarily through public and private agencies and tenant cooperatives, via incentives such as land donated by the city, immunity from taxation for anywhere from ten to 30 years and even state subsidies.[39]

Housing developments in Rome, Trento and Milan illustrate typical approaches to low- and moderate-cost housing in the first 70 years of unification. The earliest efforts of the pre-Fascist government involved housing projects consisting of anywhere from six to ten rooms – apartments clearly destined for the relatively prosperous lower middle classes and not for low-wage workers – such as San Saba in Rome by Quadrio Pirani and Giovanni Bellucci (1906–14). Designed for 2,500 inhabitants employed in various light industries, including the city's transportation network in the nearby Testaccio district, San Saba was the first important realization of Rome's Istituto Case Popolari (ICP). The first phases offered residents duplexes, but eventually more cost-effective apartment blocks anywhere from three to four storeys high became the norm. The quality of the design (particularly the delightful and original detailing), landscaping and materials made this early twentieth-century middle-class housing district increasingly attractive to upper-income groups over the course of the century, and what once sat on the city's perimeter now firmly occupies a prime niche in the highly desirable zone within the ancient walls. Such is also the case for the low-cost housing in Trento (ICP, 1919–27), once on the fringes of the city and now close to the centre. Completed

ICP, San Giuseppe quarter, Trento, 1919–27.

Innocenzo Sabbatini, 'suburban hotel', Garbatella, Rome, 1927–30.

in several phases over eight years, this complex illustrates a higher-density version of many of the same principles found at San Saba, although with generally smaller apartments and no duplexes or small villas. It envisioned communal interior gardens and appealingly diverse street elevations. Good maintenance has kept this formerly peripheral housing

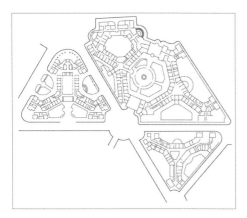

Plan of temporary housing, Garbatella, Rome.

consistently attractive, and the interior gardens have helped create cohesive communities among its inhabitants.

A comparable ICP project erected in Rome, for the most part during the Fascist period, was Garbatella (Gustavo Giovannoni and Massimo Piacentini, 1920–), which explicitly attempted to create an Italian version of Ebenezer Howard's garden city, with little *villini*, duplexes and fourplexes, each with private gardens. Located on the edge of the city not far from Testaccio and also destined for workers in this growing zone of light industry, these much smaller houses contained up to three rooms, often spread out on two floors and enriched with picturesque architectural treatments in a style that came to be called *barochetto*, or the 'little baroque'. As construction continued over the next fifteen years, densities and building heights increased, including in the development of hotels for families dislodged from their homes by demolition and construction projects in the historic centre. Intended to provide temporary housing, the *alberghi suburbani*, or suburban hotels, at Garbatella (1927–30), designed by Innocenzo Sabbatini, soon became permanent apartments because insufficient affordable housing for the city's lowest paid workers was being erected. Unlike subsequent low-cost projects, for Garbatella a range of service structures including public baths and a theatre were soon in place. In pre-First World War Milan, the ICP-erected housing at Ripamonti, Spaventa and Lombardia embodied a generous if Socialist vision of low-cost housing: two- to three-room units, collective services such as showers and baths, kitchens, laundries, nursery schools, libraries and community meeting rooms. Not surprisingly, over time most residents carved out private baths and kitchens. In the few years between the end of the war and the arrival of fascism, the ICP planned four large districts of duplexes containing anywhere from one to five rooms per house (Baravalle, Campo dei Fiori, Gran Sasso, Tiepolo) with large kitchen gardens and private baths and kitchens, lacking therefore the community services common to the earlier developments.[40]

The suburban hotels and *case rapide* (houses built rapidly in the *borgate*) in Rome served as the only refuges for poor inner-city residents evicted to make way for new public buildings, upper-class housing (*case signorili*) or wider streets. Although they were either low rent or free, inhabitants did not get much of a bargain. At Tor Marancia, 700 rooms housed 4,000 people; Gordiani's 1,000 rooms were destined to house 5,400 people; and by some estimates, 30,000 people lived in makeshift hamlets such as

Primavalle, Acqua Bullicante and Sette Chiese in Rome.[41] No paved streets, bus lines or other amenities moderated the remoteness of these settlements, and neither did minimal modern amenities such as baths render the apartments themselves more habitable. Designed to last only a few years, many survived into the 1970s before finally being demolished.

In general during the Fascist period, housing erected for the poorest groups sat either at the fringe of an urbanized area, such as the Istituto Autonomo per le case popolari (IACP), or Autonomous Institute for Low Cost Housing quarter on Corso Racconigi in Turin (1927–8), where residents could take advantage of nearby transportation and other services, or far removed from it and hence from urban services, such as was the case with the low-cost housing in the *borgata* of Primavalle in Rome after 1937.[42] Certainly in the case of Rome, isolation from the city and from other *borgate* made solidarity with others in the same situation more difficult, and it also facilitated various forms of control, including police control. It is easy to forget just how extensive police control was during the Fascist era. The secret police maintained an extensive network of spies throughout all levels of society, many of whose reports still repose in state archives. Attentiveness to providing public spaces in government projects of the Fascist era must be taken with a grain of salt, because, for example, laws forbade more than two people to walk and talk together due to the danger of conspiracies or even criticism of the state – so how 'public' could public space truly be?

Again, by contrast with the previous government, the Fascist state sponsored leisure facilities throughout the peninsula to make available to the broad public the kinds of facilities historically reserved for the upper

Swimming pool, Bologna.

Angiolo Mazzoni,
Colonia Rosa
Mussolini,
Calambrone di
Tirrenia, 1932.

classes. Swimming pools and seaside and mountain summer camps for
low-income urban youths blossomed along the coasts and in most cities.
The government also claimed to have erected 3,000 stadiums, from the
very small to the grand stadium at the Foro Mussolini in Rome. Although
driven by the larger goal of gaining consent for the Fascist state, these facilities nonetheless offered possibilities for the urban proletariat and the lower
middle class unheard of in the past. While political control and propaganda
remained constants, the summer camps and swimming pools opened up
for the first time new worlds for large segments of the population.

The meagre, ill-served housing erected for the poor stands as counterpoint to some of the most extraordinary architecture of the first half of
the century: private housing for the upper classes in cities throughout the
peninsula. Three exceptional examples can stand for the many units built
for the prosperous bourgeoisie: Giuseppe Terragni's Novocomum in Como
(1927–9); Adalberto Libera's Casa Malaparte on Capri (1938); and the
design by Gio Ponti and Emilio Lancia, Casa Torre Rasini in Milan (1933–
6). The first, which Terragni presented to the city of Como's building commission as an ordinary bourgeois apartment complex just off the lakefront,
remained hidden from public view throughout construction. When the
scaffolding came down, city officials were shocked to find a Rationalist,
even Constructivist design, with sleek rounded corners, curved windows,
brilliant blue and orange details, and glazed cylinders erupting through the
corners. Interior detailing and other elements remained faithful to local

Athletics field,
San Remo.

building and material traditions, but the sleek and bold modernist expression now brought the principles of Italian Rationalist architecture right into the centre of the city, with all the detailing and massing typical of residential housing on the peninsula swept away in favour of a stripped, starkly modern look. The city commission opened an inquest into the building to determine whether 'the house constitutes a disruptive element in the area, and eventually whether it would be susceptible to modifications, and if so, which ones, so as to harmonize with the surrounding environment'. Nothing came of the commission's investigation; indeed, Terragni pursued the same strategy for the design of his Casa del Fascio, with the explicit support of the podestà.[43] Como's citizens promptly baptized the Novocomum Il Transatlantico (because it resembled an ocean liner); it signalled the onset of a radically new approach to the public face of residential blocks, its denuded exterior setting an explicitly modern standard for elegant austerity. Although exquisitely detailed, the upper-class apartments within broke no new ground, in implicit acknowledgement of the bourgeoisie's willingness to accept modern images but reluctance to change the patterns of daily living in the privacy of their homes. Terragni's design therefore repeated conventional plan types. The Novocomum did not generate imitations; rather, it opened the door for designers to introduce sleek, modern elevations for housing for all social classes. Even Terragni himself did not follow the Novocomum with similar projects: his efforts in subsequent apartment blocks such as the Giuliani-Frigerio house (1942) explored the new, Rationalist architectural language in a substantially different, more abstract fashion.

In his project for the Malaparte house on Capri, isolated in every way from other buildings, Adalberto Libera confronted quite a different set of issues. Terragni explicitly set out, in 1927, to design a definitively modern structure in dialogue with other examples of European modernism. Libera's task instead was to satisfy an exigent client, the journalist and writer Curzio Malaparte, who had his own strong ideas driven not by the desire to make a polemical statement but to accommodate a personal desire for privacy and the enjoyment of a spectacular site. Indeed, Malaparte appears to have played as equally important a role in crafting the design as the architect did.[44] Set on a rocky outcrop in a remote part of the island, the architect carved away the simple rectangular block on one entire elevation to form a monumental staircase leading to the roof, which in turn became an essential living space in the mild Mediterranean climate. The deep red

Giuseppe Terragni, Novocomum apartments, Como, 1927–9.

of the stucco facing and the simple massing synthesized with the extraordinary site and the blue sea beyond into a breathtaking panorama that, from above, appears to have emerged almost without human intervention. Even more than the Novocomum, the Casa Malaparte is a singular design which generated no progeny, although to be sure, that a client would receive permission to build a house on a similar site is, at least theoretically, unthinkable today. This of course makes Casa Malaparte even more unique, and perhaps precisely for this reason, the house came to be seen as one of the two or three most important works of Italian architecture of the first half of the century. Something of its fame emerges in the starring roles it played in Jean Luc Godard's film *Le Mépris* (1963) and Liliana Cavani's *La pelle* (1981).

Even if no image can capture the essence of either of these buildings, both yield consistently stunning photographs; the same cannot be said for the Casa Torre Rasini, and yet this housing block represents a remarkable example of bringing together the two dominant architectural styles of the 1930s: the streamlined modernism inspired by Rationalist principles, and the more moderate Novecento style characterized by diverse materials, massing, and traditional elements. The two architects, Ponti and Lancia, joined two quite different apartment blocks, the lower one faced with marble and modulated by a series of projecting balconies, and the adjacent tower revetted partly in travertine, partly in brick, with a rounded bay window projecting from the main street elevation. The smaller building echoes Rationalist notions of horizontality, austerity in ornament and simplicity in massing, while the tower is a lively combination of recessed porches slotted into part of the rear elevation, intersecting horizontals and verticals, elegant brickwork, windows set close to the corner, a penthouse tower framed by two small tower blocks perched on the top and an almost polemical emphasis on verticality. Despite being rather indifferently maintained in the years since – the revetment has crumbled, parts have rusted and exposed the iron – the way the architects carefully integrated each detail and surface of the interior as well as exterior is still apparent. Even the projecting balconies sport a distinctive diamond pattern on the underside, an area normally ignored by designers. This attentiveness to detail and openness to diverse architectural languages was one of the distinguishing features of Gio Ponti's designs, and indeed those of Marcello Piacentini, even though they were often less bombastically contentious than their Rationalist contemporaries. Such was the case with the design by Giuseppe Pagano and Gino Levi-Montalcino for Riccardo Gualino's Palazzo Gualino (1928–9), where the architects excited comment for having substituted a polemically charged flat roof for the pitched tile roofs common to the city.

Adalberto Libera,
Casa Malaparte,
Capri, 1938.

In a design otherwise carefully stitching together the modern – with
the horizontal windows of the centre block, for example – and the traditional – the dark heavy cornice and the high granite soccle – the two wings
of the Torre Rasini, one five storeys, the other seven – the flat roofs
bespoke an early Rationalist challenge to the standard design approach
to urban offices as well as housing. Such ventures were not limited to
northern Italy, for the prosperous, modern bourgeoisie throughout the
peninsula looked to architecture as one device to assert its modernity.
The Villa Baratta (Luigi Centola, 1935) in Battipaglia, Salerno province,

Balcony detail, Casa Torre Rasini.

Luigi Centola, Villa Baratta, Battipaglia, 1935.

with its flat roof, art deco decorations and curved elements, exemplifies this even in a largely rural area well outside the Rome–Turin–Milan axis. The owners engaged in food production, particularly tomatoes, migrated south in the early twentieth century and transformed the sleepy hamlet into a bustling city. Unfortunately, most of the buildings erected after this villa brought no distinction to the growing city.

New Towns

With King Victor Emmanuel III, his wife Queen Elena of Montenegro and a full complement of Fascist dignitaries in attendance, officials of the ONC (Opera Nazionale dei Combattenti) inaugurated the new town of Sabaudia that rose from the former Pontine marshland with pomp and ceremony on 15 April 1934.[45] Aeroplanes buzzed overhead and marching bands played as the 6,000 labourers and future residents celebrated the church, theatre, hotel, town hall and dwellings that had appeared with miraculous speed only eight months after Mussolini laid the foundation stone. Conspicuously absent was the prime minister himself, who generally avoided upstaging – or being upstaged – by royalty at such events. Yet he was responsible for the other aspect of fascist housing schemes that distinguished the interwar years from the first 50 years of unification: the construction of new towns, particularly on previously unavailable land such as the former marshes of the Agro Pontino south of Rome, but also in Sardinia, Sicily and the nation's African colonies.[46] Launched with massive public relations campaigns and grand opening day ceremonies, the Agro Pontino new towns represented the most visible of the government's efforts to send families away from crowded cities into the countryside and to attempt the revival of an increasingly non-competitive and struggling agricultural sector. Visibility helped provide a sound measure of public image, but most of the towns did not achieve the hoped-for economic success until long after the interwar period, and often not for the reasons originally imagined. Sabaudia, for example, though intended primarily as an agricultural centre and only secondarily as a tourist destination, by the early 1960s had become a wealthy seaside resort community for prosperous Roman families eager to avoid the masses at the beaches closer to Rome. Pomezia became a pole of attraction for light and medium industrial development; Aprilia and Pontinia remained tied to agriculture, while Latina grew into a prosperous provincial capital with a diversified economic base. Instead of compromising the integrity of the original enterprise, the subsequent success of these communities provides telling evidence of the appropriateness of the conceptions and architectural designs that underlay their planning.

Like other industrialized and industrializing nations hit hard by the prolonged and worldwide depression, Italy needed to put people to work, and it needed to do so in ways from which maximum publicity could be drawn. In Italy, building new towns enjoyed a history that reached back to the ancient Romans, who first established military camps and then towns throughout their empire, a practice that continued in somewhat different form during the Middle Ages and the early modern period. In the delicate balancing act of the traditional and the modern that the Fascist state sought to maintain, constructing new communities could represent obeisance to the past and promise for the future, and the first salvo in the town-building enterprise was at Mussolini's own birthplace, Predappio, in Emilia-Romagna, in early 1923. Because Dovia, the fraction of Predappio in which he was born and raised, sat below the hill town and was therefore the target of jokes from the residents of the town proper, Mussolini evidently nourished a long-standing grudge against them; becoming dictator and having the town suffer from erosion and landslides gave him the opportunity to do something about it.[47] Many of the rationales deployed in support of the new town campaign of the 1930s could be found in Predappio: chronic unemployment, geographic conditions warranting a construction programme and a new location better

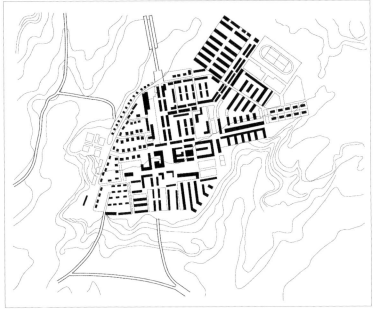

suited to transportation links than the old site had been. Of course, because the reasons for founding a new Predappio were eminently personal, absent from the discourse about this particular hamlet was the argument found elsewhere about decongesting cities by moving inhabitants to new rural settings. Despite the fact that he did not show for Sabaudia's inauguration, the prime minister did visit the building site in December 1933, conveying in his speech to the workers the importance he attributed to new town construction:

> I am pleased to speak to you from high on the scaffolding constructed to make your labour easier. You have been granted a great privilege, that of constructing a new town. I am informed of your work conditions, and have decided that your labour will be fairly compensated, both for you and your families. When all these buildings are finished, when people occupy these houses, when the territory is populated by farmers, you will be able to say that we, with our labour, have been the founders of your town.[48]

Mussolini was not the only Fascist official to refashion his hometown; emblematic in this regard was the town of Tresigallo in the Po Delta, massively transformed in the twentieth century by its most famous son, Edmondo Rossoni. 'The poplar lined road from Ferrara . . . turns toward Tresigallo, a milestone of the Fascist era, a citadel of work and industrialized agriculture', lauded the Union of Corporative Enterprise's periodical in 1936.[49] For centuries little more than a tiny agricultural hamlet, Tresigallo during the 1930s became the object of Rossoni's ambitious plan to halt the exodus from the countryside to the city by exploiting the area's agricultural resources through industrial development, such as a factory for distilling alcohol from *barbabietola* (sugar beets). To avoid local and national opposition to his ambitious enterprise, Rossoni worked quickly and quietly. He wanted to have

> in the shortest time possible, not just an idea, but a completed example to give greater weight when he countered his interlocutors in the debate under way in those years on the shape of the society that Fascism should promote and make its own.[50]

As Minister of the agency dealing with agriculture and forests, Rossoni certainly enjoyed the power to deliver resources to Tresigallo, so in short order he saw to outfitting the town with a sports centre and football pitch, elementary school, dance hall, a facility providing assistance to retired workers, two hotels, including a luxury one, state police headquarters and barracks, and more. With the exception of the larger roads, Rossoni's plan obliterated the pre-existing town and replaced it with a series of axial roads: an orthogonal one delimiting the industrial zone; a central axis lined by major public buildings such as the kindergarten, Fascist Party headquarters, cinema-theatre and the youth organization's Casa

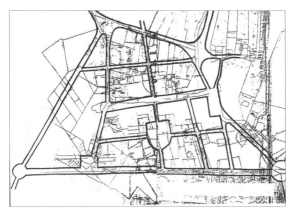

Tresigallo, plan showing overlay of new roads over the old (redrawn by Rebecca Pasternack).

del Balilla; and a monumental central piazza. The north–south axis linking the town to the industrial zone terminated at the town's massive new cemetery, in turn dominated by the monumental Rossoni family mausoleum. The heart of the city was in any case its factories, which Rossoni had negotiated before initiating his project; he planned the road network, he wrote, specifically to service the factories.[51]

Although scholars did not recognize Predappio and Tresigallo as Fascist new towns for decades, there was no mistaking the campaign that took place in the vast swamps of the Pontine Marshes. After the Romans destroyed settlements in the region nearly 2,000 years earlier, the zone had settled back into a millennial torpor, submerged underwater as much of it was for most of the year. Draining the marshes became the first priority, an intense labour involving an army of unskilled workers; as soon as enough land was available, work began on the construction of Littoria (now Latina), the new province's capital, with the first buildings completed in late 1932. The other four Agro Pontino towns followed in rapid succession: Sabaudia (1933); Pontinia (1934); Aprilia (1936); and Pomezia (1938).[52] The towns were to be the centres of a massive agricultural economy, with individual plots of land, houses and farm structures, tools and some animals being provided to each family, who would then work the land and from the profits pay for their properties over time. Originally intended to be settled by volunteers, the towns' new residents were commandeered with a combination of persuasion and coercion from their home regions instead. On the whole the farms failed to become self-supporting during the 1930s, although the entire area became much more prosperous during the second half of the twentieth century, particularly because some of the communities also became centres of industrial development, which in turn fostered agricultural development. This was made possible not by the farmsteads, but by the towns themselves.[53] No better example of this chapter of Italian history exists than Antonio Pennacchi's award-winning book, *Canale Mussolini* (2010). Pennacchi's engaging narrative follows the lives of a family in the Veneto in the decades before the arrival of Fascism, and their transfer to Littoria in 1932.

The first order of business was settling on plans for the future settlements. Pressure quickly mounted to follow the newest principles of Rationalist

urbanism – long, straight streets lined with rows of flat-roofed buildings set in plots of greenery on all sides. The Swiss architect Le Corbusier eagerly offered his services to Mussolini, only to find his magnanimous offer to take charge of the project spurned. If nothing else, for this decision the Agro Pontino can be grateful to Mussolini, as so many post-Second World War housing schemes illustrated.

Instead, in general the town plans respected time-honoured urban planning principles outlined by architectural theorists since the Renaissance: Littoria's plan echoed that of Sforzinda, an ideal town devised in a treatise by Filarete (Antonio Averlino) in the mid-fifteenth century.[54] In the first version, north–south and east–west axes bisected the central piazza, with radial avenues stemming from the corners; in actuality, the municipal building occupies the northern flank. A series of ring roads encircle the centre of this modified radial plan, with individual secondary piazzas serving as centres for the Church, police, military facilities and administrative buildings. Towns the Fascist state indeed intended them to be, but small, not large ones, due to the polemical and aggressive position of the government against large cities – a position shared by the architects of Sabaudia. As the architect Luigi Piccinato wrote:

> the establishment of Sabaudia [is] a gigantic step towards the
> achievement of a new socio-economic reality in the agricultural

life of the Nation: not only as a result of the vast scale of the reclamation and resettlement enterprise but also because it represents a concrete and tangible achievement of the new national spirit. The head of the Italian government (Mussolini) by realising the importance of this spirit, by outlining its lines of development and by insisting on its immediate realisation – while in other countries the will to start afresh was wasted in simple research – has in effect pointed the Italian nation in the right direction; this will allow the design of our environment to progress in such a way as to ensure a safe future for our society.[55]

Littoria, aerial view, 1930s. The church is to the left; the town hall, with tower, is in the centre.

Although in theory the outer ring road demarked their limits, in fact over time all of the towns expanded well beyond their original boundaries. Sabaudia was the most celebrated; the designers devised its plan according to the principles of modern town planning but inflected it to accommodate the traditional institutional and social relationships of Italian towns. Two

orthogonal roads also bisect Sabaudia's centre, but the institutions and buildings rotate out from the main piazza asymmetrically, one axis passing adjacent to the Casa del Fascio and terminating at the church and its piazza. Opening and closing spaces and vistas, calibrating varied building and tower heights, rendering all in the crisp and unadorned language of flat-roofed Italian Rationalism, together endowed the town centre, both in plan and in three dimensions, with a poetic vitality that remains potent even today, when the town is an exclusive and expensive summer resort.

The three subsequent Agro Pontino towns, while also crafted with unadorned surfaces, were less audaciously modernist, more sober in their overall effect. Such was the case with Aprilia, with its sombre, un-fenestrated brick tower, traditional pitched tile roofs and heavy projecting cornices similar to that also found in Pomezia, designed by the same team of Roman architects. Giorgio Ciucci's publications on architects and architecture under fascism consistently criticize the effort of the regime, and the architects, to blend the traditional with the modern; an architect who did so, according to him, was 'son of a chameleon, able to wear the garb of tradition and appear modern, or vice versa, to wear modern clothes and respect tradition, ready in every situation to adapt to changing conditions'.[56] Much derided by subsequent critics for their adherence to more traditional models of town planning and architectural form, the towns nevertheless work well precisely because of their traditional plans and their responsiveness to the social and cultural habits, expectations and needs of residents.[57] Pomezia in particular, due to its proximity to the capital, became a nucleus of light industrial development south of Rome, and one of its bedroom suburbs. Designers resolved the relationship between traditional and modernist plans and forms differently in each case, but in all cases in a manner consistent with what Italians expected to find in a small town. Paradoxically, it is precisely this non-dogmatic openness that has triggered criticism along the lines Ciucci suggested.

The League of Nations's sanctions against Italy after the brutal invasion and conquest of Ethiopia in 1935 ultimately led to a shift in emphasis in new town construction. New centres such as Carbonia (1938) and Guidonia (1938) focused on enabling the country to achieve industrial self-sufficiency, the former to provide housing for coal miners in Sardinia, one of the few locations in the country where this essential mineral could be found, and the latter to accommodate the country's main aviation training centre to the east of Rome. Mussolini confronted the apparent divergence from the long-prominent policy of encouraging agriculture and discouraging urbanization with equanimity; the air force needed to secure the skies, he announced, so that farmers could work their fields and enhance their yields in safety.

Rome's ICP oversaw the construction of Guidonia, the design of which took shape under the guidance of a team of architects including members of the Gruppo Urbanisti Romani, responsible for the design of Sabaudia: Giorgio Calza Bini, Gino Cancellotti and Giuseppe Nicolosi. Their plan respected the conventions typical of the earlier ventures, with institutional buildings clustered around a main public square and with secondary squares serving as centres for religious, military and market activities. Situated on gently sloping terrain, Guidonia's roads and main buildings adjust to the variations in level and of importance. As in Sabaudia, the modernist language of the architecture converges with a far more traditional concern for visual relationships and perspectives, so that building placement depends upon sequential vistas and hierarchical ordering rather than upon the indifferent and abstract geometries typical of modern movement designs. Nonetheless, the architects had studied the canonical buildings of northern European modernism and incorporated some of its principles in their architecture, as is evident in the Casa del Fascio located on the main square. Lifted high on pilotis, or columns, the Casa also boasts horizontal windows and flat roofs like most of the town's public buildings, and the detached tower has asymmetrically placed fenestration along one side, all of which constituted contemporary hallmarks of modern architecture. Almost in counterpoint to the serene Rationalism of the public buildings, much of the housing erected for air force officials and staff appeals instead to more traditional housing types; in fact, Guidonia contains a rich mix of housing, the organization of which, as in other cases, followed military status hierarchies. Guidonia represents perhaps the most intriguing integration of tradition and modernity of all the new towns constructed by the Fascist regime.

Historians continue to dedicate considerable attention to the Agro Pontino new towns; certainly less known and studied are the many rural hamlets established throughout the peninsula and the islands, not to mention those in the African colonies. In Sicily alone, twelve such rural villages still dot the island, from Trapani to Agrigento, all designed by different architects and each outfitted with a church, social centre and tavern, post office, clinic and schools.[58] It was precisely their settings far from urban centres that led their designers to respond primarily to vernacular rural building traditions. They have, by and large, fallen into squalid decay, brooding relics of pre-war enthusiasm for new town developments.

Far better known than the communities of the Agro Pontino, Guidonia and Sardegna is the new city centre erected south of Rome for the exhibition Esposizione Universale di Roma (EUR, formerly known as E.42), planned for 1942 but never mounted because of the war. Conceived in

1935 as the brainchild of Giuseppe Bottai as a way of responding to a diverse group of political objectives, from celebrating twenty years of Fascist government to the success of the war in Ethiopia, the project vaunted the nation's economic success despite the League of Nations sanctions imposed after the war. Even the location selected for the exhibition carried rhetorical weight – southwest of the city centre, on a site that straddled a new road, the via dell'Impero, which stretched from Piazza Venezia in the centre to Ostia and the sea – because locally the regime made much of the connection between Rome and the Mediterranean. Unlike most previous international expositions, officials always planned EUR to be a permanent suburban city, outfitted with residences, public and private administrative offices, churches and museums, hotels, a lake and an amusement park. Once again, Marcello Piacentini received the call to prepare the master plan, an enterprise to which he in turn summoned a diverse group of architects, most of whom had stellar Rationalist credentials: Giuseppe Pagano, editor of *Casabella*; Luigi Piccinato, primary designer of Sabaudia; Ettore Rossi, responsible for an important

EUR view, with Palazzo della Civiltà Italiana on axis, 1938–43.

ONMI pavilion at the 1937 exhibit of seaside camps for children; and Luigi Vietti, one of the chief designers of projects for the Palazzo del Littorio competition in Rome. After the first draft of the plan (heretofore the 1937 variant, on which see below), Piacentini relegated this group to the role of consultants, while he worked out the definitive plan with Gaetano Minnucci, chief architect of EUR. For the exhibition, the plan proposed a set of zones wherein pavilions were to be dedicated to science, art, artisan works, the corporate economy, overseas colonies, entertainment and a variety of smaller exhibits. It was to be, in Mussolini's words, an 'Olympics of Civilizations'.[59] Italian civilization and its accomplishments set the standard towards which other nations could only aspire, and the exhibition would showcase the peninsula's history on a breathtakingly monumental scale. The pavilions of other countries, however, would be disassembled after the exhibition. The architecture was to be emblematic of a fascist style; in the words of the general commissioner of the EUR organization, Vittorio Cini:

This great display will enable us to reveal the fascist style fully.
The buildings' style should constitute the basis for the ornamentation of the future city: it should reveal the tendencies of the era.[60]

The initial proposal consisted of building complexes fabricated in
concrete, steel and glass and bristled with the long, straight building blocks
so dear to modernist architects. The second version, the final plan (1939),
more baroque than modernist, consisted of an axial road traversed by three
large cross axes, each of which terminated at both ends with major public
buildings. As one passed along any of these axial roads, spaces opened and
closed laterally, drawing attention to a diverse range of monumental
structures and thereby adding a visual interest largely but not entirely absent
in the more modernist 1937 variant. Although labelled by some historians
a 'celebratory monumentality', several of the monuments nonetheless turned
out to be worth the price of admission, including Libera's Palazzo dei
Congressi e Ricevimenti (Congress and Reception Hall, 1938–42, completed
and inaugurated 1954); Giovanni Guerrini, Ernesto La Padula and Mario
Romano's Palazzo della Civiltà Italiana (Palace of Italian Civilization,
1938–43); the Ente EUR headquarters by Gaetano Minnucci (1937); and the
Museo della Civiltà Romana (Museum of Roman Civilization, 1939–52),
designed by Pietro Aschieri, Cesare Pascoletti, Enrico Peressutti and Domenico Bernardini.[61] The outbreak of the war meant that several structures
planned during the 1930s would never be built, including Libera's grand
arch at the terminus of the axial road leading from Rome, which also
suffered from technical problems that could not be overcome at the time.
In fact, this panorama received its final definition only just in time for
the 1960 Olympics, when Pier Luigi Nervi erected the Palace of Sport
(Palazzo dello Sport, 1960) on the same site.

The Museo della Civiltà Romana was among the first commissioned,
in 1939, by the Turin automobile manufacturer, Fiat. Two buildings mirror one another with monumental entrances and rough, un-fenestrated
dark tuff wall surfaces (*tufo*, a volcanic rock) with heavy travertine cornices above, while the rear, less visible public elevations have a simple stucco
revetment. The massive and elegant Egyptian-style travertine columns at
the entrance, projecting out towards one another, also serve as an elaborate backdrop for the parades and other ceremonial events planned to take
place in front of the structures. Inside, the artefacts assembled for the
exhibit dedicated to Augustus were to be on permanent display, and
indeed have been since 1955.

Only one major structure at EUR faithfully followed the principles
of Rationalist architecture: the Post Office designed by BBPR (Gian
Luigi Banfi, Lodovico Belgiojoso, Enrico Peressutti and Ernesto Rogers,

Gaetano Minnucci, EUR headquarters, 1937–8.

1939–42). Rationalists and post-war advocates of modernism have consistently praised the building, in particular for the second, rear edifice's moveable wooden panel interior walls, and the clear distinction on the exterior between the load-bearing, reinforced concrete pilasters and beams and the non-load-bearing walls. Nonetheless, the structure is certainly one of the least interesting aesthetically and urbanistically, with its indifferent and relentlessly gridded rear elevation, whatever its other merits as architecture. After the passage of more than 70 years, it is fair to say that the instincts of those who resisted the reductive modernist glass-and-steel buildings monotonously aligned against one another have held up over time; in fact, we can probably be grateful that several other modernist buildings slated for EUR never saw the light of day.

The Palazzo della Civiltà Italiana, affectionately known to Romans as the Squared Coliseum, Colosseo Quadrato, and much derided for decades, has now come into its own as an original and engagingly rhetorical structure, with its simple cubic shape lifted aloft on a high podium with stairs on two sides, identical elevations on all four sides, and sleek surfaces and rows of nine arches on all six floors. The statues of the Dioscuri at the

Pietro Aschieri,
D. Bernardini and
Cesare Pascoletti,
Museo della Civiltà
Romana, Rome, 1941.

corners and the assorted inscriptions celebrating Roman genius now often serve as backdrops for advertising photo shoots.

The building that has best stood the test of time as an example of fine architecture, independent of arguments about style, is without doubt Libera's Palazzo dei Congressi. In the first phase of the competition, Libera proposed a round structure, but when he developed the second phase project, he chose a design with a square, umbrella-domed hall fronted by a colonnaded portico and with a glazed one to the rear. The colonnade across the facade is a good indicator of some of the theoretical issues that bedevilled the architects at EUR. By the late 1930s, architects pursuing a modernist aesthetic found themselves embattled in Europe and the United States; the avant-garde charge that powered the movement early on now came up against forces that instead supported a return to classical architectural principles, or some modified version of them. There were good reasons to question many of the most famous modernist icons in Italy, to be sure: not all of the materials were holding up well, such as the revetment of Terragni's Casa del Fascio in Como. Terragni had employed thin but large marble panels glued into place and had insisted that nothing project, that the panels be identical and that the reveals be barely visible, if at all. Not surprisingly, there were struggles over his refusal of panels with any slight variations in colour, and within a few short years the revetment needed to be redone because, as a party official lamented in a letter to headquarters in 1940, 'Many of these panels, because of freezing [weather] are mashed, and others are broken and threaten to fall.'[62]

But the challenge to modernist design did not depend upon materials or technology, but rather on aesthetics and symbols. Scholars debate what caused the generalized shift away from public buildings designed according to modernist principles: was it increasingly conservative governments in Italy and Germany (although this explains neither Soviet Russia, nor the United States), or was it due to greater exercise of power by older and more conservative architects tired of being confronted by angry young architects (but at EUR, for example, Rationalist architects also served on the juries)? Whatever the case, no one could know which styles history would deem iconic, and the greater the significance of a public building, the less uncertainty government officials were willing to tolerate in response to the debates about the relative merits of new styles. At EUR, for example, officials expected the buildings destined to be permanent to sport columns and other historicizing features. The polemics in Italy about columns and arches dated back to the 1920s, engaging the rhetorical

Adalberto Libera, Palazzo dei Congressi, Rome, 1938–54.

skills and passions of Marcello Piacentini (pressing for more modern designs) and Ugo Ojetti (trumpeting the virtues of traditional architectural elements for public buildings). In the version that took shape around EUR, the League of Nations sanctions led to a shortage of steel and other expensive materials, thereby helping advance the cause of columns and arches. Contemporaries and post-war critics accused the architects who accepted the constraints imposed by the Ente EUR of having collaborated, or of having been co-opted – as if designing in something other than a rigorously modern style was a sin rather than a personal choice with far less significance, say, than the purposes and uses of the buildings.

Libera's slender colonnade, projecting out before Achille Funi's mural of the goddess of Rome, is set at one end of a large rectangular volume subdivided into two counterposed ones, each with its own entry – one for receptions, one for conventions. Certain features surface in many of Libera's projects, such as the glazed portico graced by elegantly tapering mullions and the rhythmic pattern of the lateral stairs (he designed similar stairs a few years earlier for the Post Office on via Marmorata, 1933–5). Others are his ingenious explorations of traditional elements in a modern language, such as the cubic volume of the main meeting hall topped by a shallow cross vault, and glazed lunettes, from which the interior receives raking light. The finely detailed travertine revetment, with narrow bands separating the larger panels, complements the outdoor theatre on the roof, with its travertine block benches, and the dark and light paving of the plaza at either end of the building.

At one end of the major cross axis sits the Palazzo della Civiltà Italiana, and the Palazzo dei Congressi sits at the other; the approach to each initially presents a structure that fills a vista visually compressed by the buildings lining the axis. As one draws closer, the splendid isolation of each structure set in the middle of a large plaza singles them out as distinct, monumental structures. In the post-war period these massive squares became convenient parking lots. Libera's design offers an instructive comparison with the BBPR Post Office, with its monotonous grid and undistinguished elevations, illustrating how an excellent design at least partially inspired by historical principles can be the occasion for a fresh and interesting solution far superior to a banal modern one. Non-architectural aficionados are less kind to the EUR complex, described by English mystery writer Iain Pears as a 'grim suburb, surrounded by office blocks and 1930s architecture and wastelands where nothing much seemed to happen. . . . Only bankers should have to work in this awful place . . . ugly and deathly quiet'.[63] Nonetheless, something about the EUR project captured the imaginations of film-makers in the decades after the Second World War, in surprisingly varied ways. For his adaptation of Alberto Moravia's

1947 fascist-era novel, *Il conformista* (1970), Bernardo Bertolucci used the buildings as indicators of a darkly institutional presence, claustrophobic and depressing for the protagonist, an agent of the Italian secret police agency OVRA. Among the settings he chose was the rooftop theatre of Libera's Palazzo, here transformed into an insane asylum. In Ettore Scola's *C'eravamo tanto amati* (1974), EUR appears as the epitome of economic and social success along the lines of wealthy American suburbs, but where the values of friendship and love have disappeared among the trappings of wealth. Despite the criticism, EUR provided settings for some of Italy's greatest films, including Fellini's *La dolce vita* (1960), *8 ½* (1962) and the episode 'Le tentazioni del dottor Antonio' from his *Boccaccio '70* film series (1962); Michelangelo Antonioni's *L'eclisse* (1961); Vittorio De Sica's *Il boom* (1963); and Dino Risi's *Il mattatore* (1959), *Il sorpasso* (1962) and *I mostri* (1963). Julie Taymor directed the Shakespeare adaptation *Titus* (1999), staged with cars, motorbikes and fashions from the 1930s rather from than ancient Rome, against the backdrop of EUR, with the Palazzo della Civiltà Italiana, garbed in black, serving as the main government building and a lugubrious setting for the bloody, vicious tragedy.

Colonial Expansion

The origins of Italian colonialist ambitions pre-dated unification. Publications such as Vincenzo Gioberti's *Del primato morale e civile degli Italiani* ('Of the Moral and Civil Primacy of the Italians', 1843) affirmed the essential appropriateness of uniting Italy and transforming it into a dominant international force, while Giuseppe Mazzini repeated this view and subsequently called for colonization campaigns in North Africa.[64] Italian prestige was at stake in all of the country's subsequent colonial enterprises in Africa and the Dodecanese; in the late nineteenth century, no nation could realize its ambitions to become a world power without acquiring colonies wherever possible. Sceptical contemporaries disparaged Italian ambitions in Africa, however, noting, as one British paper did in 1911, that with provinces such as Calabria and Apulia, Italy 'need not go abroad for a civilizing mission. Italy has an Africa at home.'[65]

Before the Fascists came to power, Italy already occupied colonies in North Africa. Although Ethiopia inflicted a humiliating defeat on Italian troops in 1896, by 1911 Italy had conquered and claimed Libya, and the conquest of Ethiopia in 1935 rounded out a battery of African colonies that also included Eritrea and Somalia.[66] By the 1920s state-sponsored colonization campaigns were under way. Small new towns proliferated throughout Libya in the 1920s and '30s, and in Ethiopia immediately after the conclusion of the so-called 'pacification campaign'. Following a standard colonial policy of spatial segregation from the indigenous population, the plans for enlarging existing cities and crafting new ones envisioned European districts separate from the native ones, and incorporated contemporary Italian architecture into the network of hotels, administrative buildings, and private and public housing. Animated by the twin goals of establishing self-sustaining colonies and creating venues for selling goods produced on the peninsula, the colonization programme converged with the second primary objective of the building campaigns: the promotion of a tourist industry. To this end the government promoted hotels, restaurants and leisure facilities, and in the homeland, guidebooks, posters and public relations campaigns launched on behalf of colonial tourism aimed to sell North Africa as an appealing tourist destination. The architecture envisioned as appropriate for the new cities was one stripped of ornament, crisp and usually revetted with stucco, in a style described as evoking *mediterraneità* (a concept of Mediterranean-ness). Among the arguments made on behalf of *mediterraneità*, the one that clinched its suitability was that it could be seen as part of a millennial tradition dating back to ancient Rome, with the contemporary examples simply falling into that tradition. The idea of *mediterraneità* was also a rhetorical tool deployed in favour of modern design to counter charges that modernism was international and, by implication, tainted by communist internationalist ideals. More explicit references to twentieth-century examples emerge in the rural hamlets constructed in Libya, which repeated on a smaller scale the forms of the Agro Pontino new towns.

Building in Libya continued over a nearly 30-year period, but the Fascists only held on to Ethiopia for five years, so managed to complete far less in Addis Ababa and elsewhere in the former Ethiopian Empire. Nonetheless, settlements and colonial houses erected for Italians willing to move to Africa to pursue their fortunes remain; the city plan of Addis Ababa proposed preserving an older, native centre as a separate area, distinct from the new enclave to be developed for the European conquerors. Throughout the African colonies, the Italian government erected triumphal arches in symbolic affirmation of its supremacy over the indigenous peoples and as a means of crafting a link between the accomplishments of the Fascist regime and those of the ancient Romans. Visual testimony to this perceived link between the two eras abounded in the colonies, but it also did so in Italy: along the walls of the via dell'Impero, passing from Piazza Venezia through to the Colosseum, a series of panels documented the extent of the ancient empire, with a new one mounted to celebrate the accomplishments of the new Fascist Empire. The Second World War ended the country's imperial aspirations; indeed, Italy lost all of its colonies in Africa as well as those in the Dodecanese.[67]

Florestano de Fausto
and Stefano Gatti
Casazza, Uaddan
Hotel and Casino,
Trípoli, Libya, 1935.

On the mainland, Allied bombs dropped during the landing at Anzio destroyed the centres of two of the new towns in the Agro Pontino, Aprilia and Pomezia, initiating a decline already common to the other new communities that generally continued until well into the 1980s. Scarred by their association with fascism, the public buildings and housing fell into a decay arrested only when functional needs finally trumped ideology and painful memories. Nonetheless, the passage of more than six decades since the end of the war has yet to eliminate the potent political symbolism of the buildings of fascist Italy, even if the relations among the buildings, the architects and the political system remain uncomfortably open questions. The legacy of death and destruction wrought by fascism's wars in Africa and on the mainland, its noxious anti-Semitic laws promulgated in 1938 and the subsequent complicity with Nazi extermination programmes certainly impeded a thoroughgoing confrontation with the legacy of the political system itself. Even a powerfully evocative monument such as that of the Fosse Ardeatine (Mario Fiorentino et al., 1947), erected in memory of Romans (overwhelmingly Jewish) killed by German troops in reprisal for a lethal partisan military action at Gestapo headquarters on via Rasella, summons reflection on the activities of foreign soldiers, not on that of the Italians, particularly intellectuals, who supported the Fascist regime.

Throughout nearly the full two decades of fascist rule, debates raged among traditionalists, Rationalists and Novecentisti, or moderates, about the appropriate style for the new regime. In 1926 the Rationalist Gruppo 7

(Ubaldo Castagnoli, Luigi Figini, Guido Frette, Sebastiano Larco, Gino Pollini, Carlo Enrico Rava and Giuseppe Terragni) vigorously attacked what they saw as a fascination with newness for the sake of newness, but it is difficult to identify the ways in which their own fascination with the avant-garde departed from the attitudes they attributed to their opponents, although the latter did choose a different model.[68] The formal choices of the three groups differed, but no social, political or cultural programme separated them. All laboured to varying degrees to convince regime officials that their aesthetic was the best expression of the Fascist state. Nonetheless, the modernists believed that attachment to modernist forms itself constituted an attachment to the future – to modernity itself – and to a morally acceptable position. Unlike modernists elsewhere, however, many Italian Rationalists never abandoned an interest in the historical antecedents of their architecture – probably because the regime itself attempted to strike a balance between tradition and modernity, and architects adopted this

Umberto Di Segni, Agricultural Village, Bianchi, 1938.

part of the fascist programme along with many of its other features, including the insistence on social, political and cultural hierarchies.

Despite fundamental ambiguities inherent in the interwar Italian version of modernism, two major anomalies characterized the post-Second World War culture of architecture that linked to the earlier interwar period. For many post-war architects, particularly by the early 1950s, modernism still represented the best and surest path to the future, despite lingering associations with the regime. The second anomaly concerned the fact that most of the architects who wielded power in universities, institutions and among politicians during the pre-war period continued to do so after the war ended – just as many politicians and other officials continued undisturbed after Italy switched its allegiance to the Allies in September 1943.[69] Not surprisingly, though the specifics of some of the debates altered, the substance – or lack thereof – remained intact.

chapter four

War and its Aftermath

If the phenomenon of urbanization from 1870 to 1945 primarily concerned northern and central Italian cities such as Turin, Milan, Bologna, Florence and Rome, the post-war period saw the process extend to southern cities such as Naples, Bari, Palermo and Catania, with results no happier than those in the north. The same model of relentless industrialization as that of Turin and Milan characterized the development schemes deployed as a means of lifting the south out of its backward condition, or so politicians and industrialists in the north saw matters.

But any development in the peninsula had first to contend with exponentially greater problems associated with years of war and devastation. Although Mussolini declared war on France in 1940, following the German invasion, he had already launched an Italian war front in Albania in April 1939. On 10 June 1940 he declared war on France and Britain, joining Hitler and Nazi Germany in the vast campaign to subdue Europe. As war fronts multiplied, with Axis assaults on Russia and North Africa, and the bombing campaign against Britain, it became increasingly difficult to supply Italian troops with the minimum food and equipment necessary for survival, and by July 1943 it was clear that Italy's army could not hold up against the onslaught of the Allied powers. On the home front, the age-old problem of grain supply – that is, bread as a basic foodstuff – became a serious problem, beginning in the south in 1942; coupled with the Allied bombing campaign in the autumn of 1942, resentment about the price of the war on the home front exploded throughout the peninsula.[1]

By the spring of 1943 strikes were shutting down factories in even the major northern cities of Turin and Milan, followed by others at Porto Marghera (Venice), Biella (in Piedmont) and in the region of Liguria. With landings of Allied troops in Sicily on 9 July 1943, and much of North Africa already in Allied hands, the bombing of sites in Rome on 19 July finally spelled the beginning of the end for the Fascist regime. After members of the Grand Council of Fascism voted Mussolini out of office in the early morning hours of 25 July, they carted him off to jail. When the news reached Rome and the rest of the country, people spontaneously flooded into the country's public squares, celebrating what they

Mario Ridolfi,
Ludovico Quaroni,
Tiburtino IV housing,
Rome, 1950–54.

believed was the end of the war. They did not realize that the worst had only begun, that the war was about to come to the peninsula with a vengeance. Italy finally signed an armistice on 3 September, only rendered public five days later, after Allied troops had disembarked on the mainland, at Salerno. After German troops organized a daring escape for Mussolini from his prison on Gran Sasso mountain, he announced the birth of the Italian Social Republic (RSI, also known as the Salò Republic) on 18 September. With the nation split in two, with the Allies in control in the south and the Germans and the puppet Salo Republic in the north, the long, slow struggle to liberate the country from Nazi, and Fascist, control began. Mussolini's new government was in reality a puppet state of Germany, and after exacting vengeance on the Fascist Grand Council members who had voted in favour of deposing him (including his son-in-law Galeazzo Ciano) by hauling them up before a firing squad, German troops began the mass deportation of Jews in earnest: of 8,369 Italian Jews deported to concentration camps, only 980 survived.[2]

Many Jews were shipped to Germany or Austria, but Italy also had its own concentration camps. Among the most prominent was the Risiera di San Sabba, on the outskirts of Trieste, for the internment of political prisoners, gypsies, Slavs and Jews, but there were many others across the country. They fulfilled provisions of the Geneva Convention (1929) on prisoners of war, which allowed countries to intern citizens of countries with whom they were at war, and undesirable or politically suspect citizens of their own nations, at sites far from the front but where officials could maintain careful surveillance. Throughout the Fascist period internal exile to such settings became a standard political tool; between 1926 and 1943, an estimated 17,000 individuals were so confined.[3] Among the most famous was the physician, painter and author Carlo Levi, who wrote of his internal exile in *Christ Stopped at Eboli* (1945). Throughout the 1930s, following Hitler's rise to power, a steady stream of Jews fled to Italy, for the most part without any obstacles from the Fascist state until the promulgation of the racial laws in 1938, but especially after the outbreak of war in 1940.[4] Already by early 1940 the Minister of the Interior had divided Italy into five zones and identified sites for civilian concentration camps. Particularly in the early years, most of these camps were in the mountainous regions of Abruzzo, Molise and The Marches, but also in Campania, Puglia and Lazio.[5] At least two southern camps, Solofra in the province of Avellino and Vinchiaturo in that of Campobasso, contained only a specific category of women: prostitutes. Because these women – who may or may not have been prostitutes – had relations with military men, the regime defined them as dangerous and hence in need of confinement.[6]

The small town of Campagna, nestled in the Picentini mountains in the province of Salerno, occupies a special place in the history of these camps.[7] In September 1939 the Ministry of the Interior began to single out prospective sites to use for internment, and in Campagna, officials selected the former Dominican convent of San Bartolomeo to be the sole facility to house foreign Jews in Italy. Among the significant events of its rich past, San Bartolomeo had hosted the young monk Giordano Bruno who, following his ordination as a priest, sang his first Mass in the adjacent church of the Santissimo Nome di Dio (Most Holy Name of God) in 1573. His reformist tendencies and countercurrent philosophies provoked the ire of the Catholic Church, which subsequently burned him at the stake in Rome as a heretic. This early association with controversial ideas became an identifying motif of San Bartolomeo, particularly following the war years and its service as an internment camp. Five large dormitories and twelve smaller ones could house 350 detainees at San Bartolomeo, the Ministry estimated, and the refectory and kitchens were also adequate for that number of internees. The prisoners began to arrive in June 1940 – predominantly artists, musicians and doctors. A shortage of trained physicians led to the regular violation of state laws forbidding Jews from practising medicine; the complicity of officials on all levels was open and untroubled. Internees could roam through the town from dawn to dusk, and they even set up a synagogue within the walls of the convent. Immediately after the armistice on 8 September 1943, and after a visit from German troops demanding that the Jews be locked up day and night until they could be transferred elsewhere, local officials and police conspired to liberate the remaining detainees, hiding them in nearby mountains until the area came under secure Allied control. Former prisoners often remained in southern Italy even after the end of hostilities, refusing to return to their homes because, as one woman reported of her husband, 'He was afraid, you know what I mean, he was afraid that if he returned [to Lodz] he would never be able to return to Italy.'[8]

There is more to this story. The Jews in Campagna did not end up there by accident; Giovanni Palatucci, a police officer in charge of the Foreigners' Office in the city of Fiume, sent them there. Raised as a devout Catholic and a lawyer by training, Palatucci grew increasingly troubled by what he learned about the fates of Jews at the hands of Germans. Using the resources of his department but hiding their true nature under innocuous bookkeeping entries, Palatucci paid the captains of boats to carry Jews to Greek ships destined for Israel or other safe havens. He also arranged to ship new arrivals to Campagna, where his uncle was bishop and could try to protect them, and to help others flee to Israel or to Switzerland; a conservative estimate puts the number of those he and his team saved at about 5,000. But ministerial assessments lamented Palatucci's friendships with Jews, his elevated expenses and the disarray of his records regarding foreign Jews. After the armistice, the Swiss consulate offered him refuge and protection, but he refused, deciding to remain at his post to do what he could to help others. In defiance of German orders, he destroyed all records pertaining to the Jews who had passed through his office and used all available bureaucratic means to obstruct the efforts of German troops to identify the Jews remaining in the city. Arrested in September 1944 by the ss, Palatucci was shipped to Dachau, where he died in February 1945. Palatucci calmly resisted the racial laws, commenting to an associate that 'they want us to think of the heart purely as a muscle and they want to stop us from doing what our hearts and our religion dictate.'[9] San Bartolomeo in Campagna is now being turned into a museum, both to recall the internments of the Fascist era and to celebrate the efforts of a handful of people to resist the persecutions.

Palatucci and others helped spirit Jews out of Italy; others helped hide them, as in the case of the Nobel Prize-winning scientist Rita Levi-Montalcini; while others turned them in to Italian and later German authorities. Most of these people ended up in concentration camps in Austria or Poland, never to return after the war. Some Italian Jews fled the country as soon as the state promulgated the racial laws, such as the Sardinian sculptor Costantino Nivola, whose wife was Jewish, and the composer Mario Castelnuovo-Tedesco, who fled to America where he taught young composers such as André Previn, Henry Mancini and John Williams.[10]

The end of the war brought disruptions only somewhat less violent than those of the war years. Hunger stalked the peninsula; elderly people today still talk about eating weeds, of scouring parks and empty lots for edible flowers and of offering their services to Allied troops in exchange for a little food. People in both the north and the south fled to cities in search of work, shelter and food, even if the latter only consisted of hand-outs from the Allied powers. They found cities shattered by German and Allied bombs; bridges destroyed by fleeing German troops; piles of rubble everywhere; factories bombed out: there was work to do, but little money to pay for it in the short term. Although the most urgent needs consisted of housing for those crammed into temporary shelters, the nation also faced the daunting task of reigniting its industrial base and repairing the massive infrastructural damage inflicted by the years of war.

Even more daunting was the prospect of trying to weld together a nation pulled apart by what essentially amounted to civil war. Although the German army retreated up the peninsula, it did so with as much brutality as possible, punishing the civilian population whenever partisans managed to strike a blow against their troops. The only city where the residents actually rose up in rebellion against the Axis troops was Naples, at the end of September 1943, with the Allies advancing towards the city and the years of suffering too much to bear even for a few more days. Partisans fought the remains of the Fascist government along with the German army, and as Allied forces liberated cities and towns, resentment over the death and destruction laid squarely at the feet of the Fascist Party and its adherents boiled over. When townspeople believed women had collaborated with German troops, they publicly shamed them with the age-old rituals of cropping their hair, tearing off their clothes and pelting them with rotten food.[11] Partisans and long-standing anti-fascists led campaigns to chase down, beat and sometimes kill former officials and sympathizers. While uncomfortable to admit, an undetermined number of these killings were acts of personal vendetta and jealousy masquerading as political retribution. Others were efforts to gain political power at the expense of opposing political groups. The film *Malèna* (2000) grippingly depicted just such acts against women accused of conducting sexual liaisons with the Germans and addressed the complex mix of personal jealousies and resentments that lay behind the reprisals and shaming rituals. Despite the fact that tensions remained high, on 2 June 1946 Italians voted into office local administrators and delegates to a constitutional assembly, and two years later national elections ended the monarchy and transformed Italy into a parliamentary democracy.

The king's decision on 8 September 1943, as Allied troops landed in Salerno, to flee Rome with his family and his ministers and head for Brindisi in the south, cost the royal family dearly: it was this ignominious escape that prompted many Italians to vote against the monarchy in the post-war referendum.

Early Post-war Housing Projects

After numerous false starts, by 1949 the first post-war government had finally implemented a programme to erect low-cost housing, in large part employing the same public housing bodies that had been operating since the beginning of the century: the local offices of the Istituto Autonomo per le Case Popolari (IACP).[12] Other state and quasi-state agencies such as the Istituto Nazionale delle Assicurazioni (National Insurance Institute, INA) also constructed housing, as did banks, the railways and other state agencies, ministries and private companies.[13] At the same time, however, and in parallel with this, a wave of illegal building expanded the perimeter of the country's metropolises at a dizzying pace. Italy's urbanization in the second half of the century cannot be understood without examining both of these developments.

Only in 1946, after the brutal years of war and occupation, did Allied powers hand jurisdiction of northern Italy to the provisional government formed in December 1945. But even as the commission to draft a new constitution undertook its charge, unrest broke out from Venice to the deepest south, as Italians protested unemployment and persistently grim living conditions. In mid-1947 the United States announced the Marshall Plan for economic aid, but its effects registered only slowly over the next decade. In the meantime the police suppressed serious uprisings in Mestre (in the Veneto) in September 1946, in Rome in October, in the entire south in December and again in Rome in April 1947. Under resolute pressure from the U.S. to prevent communists from entering the government, the first national elections of April 1948 saw the formerly resurgent left soundly vanquished by a centre-right coalition amid charges of election fraud. With the new constitution approved in January 1948, the political situation seemed to stabilize and local and national authorities turned their attention to the twin problems of unemployment and housing. In February 1949, the parliament approved Law No. 43, also known as the Fanfani Plan, calling for the construction of low-cost housing (a mandate later called INA-Casa, National Insurance Institute-House), with the double aim of reducing unemployment by vastly expanding the construction sector of the economy and of providing housing for those who had been crowding into the country's urban areas over the previous decade. The entire programme lasted fourteen years. Funded by an ingenious combination of mandated 'contributions' from workers (except for agricultural labourers) and businesses, and with the government subsidizing interest payments, the Fanfani Plan also established a lottery system for awarding apartments to families.[14]

The most generous overall assessment of the residential districts constructed under the rubric of INA-Casa is that they helped spur the building industry and therefore relieved unemployment (the INA-Casa projects annually employed an estimated 40,000 workers in the building trades); to accomplish this, of course, the building programmes relied on labour-intensive practices. They also responded to the enormous need for housing in and around cities both large and small at a time when rural migration to urban areas was vast and continuous (the entire programme ultimately managed to construct 355,000 housing units). As I discuss below, in some cases the experiments architects undertook resulted in residential quarters of enduring quality and significant architectural and urban interest. Following practices honed since the 1920s, building construction consisted of a combination of reinforced concrete and masonry infill. Such technologies both reduced costs and required large numbers of skilled and unskilled manual labourers, thereby increasing employment opportunities. Interesting too are the early guidelines proposed in the manuals made available to designers: produced in three versions between 1949 and 1956, the manuals directed architects' attention to the 'local problem', by which they rejected faithful adherence to the urban principles of Rationalist architecture and instead urged low densities and attention to local traditions, habits, vegetation, materials and forms.[15] The drawings that illustrated what INA-Casa sought in fact departed little from the buildings designed for the Tiburtino IV quarter of Rome by Ludovico Quaroni and Mario Ridolfi (see below).

On the whole, however, little of this was evident in the residential districts constructed over the fourteen-year period, which ultimately proposed urban and architectural forms far more consistent with modern movement principles. Low densities they did achieve in some cases, with buildings rising in splendid isolation in open spaces – in contrast with Italy's millennial tradition of city-building – which, in line with standard modern movement principles, designers optimistically intended to be lush and green, presumably because they assumed compliant residents would maintain them. Usually straining to meet monthly obligations, occupants generally did not, and housing agencies and city governments also abdicated their responsibilities, so residents claimed these undefined and unsupervised spaces mostly for parking – precisely as happened with such spaces in modernist complexes elsewhere in Europe and in the U.S.

The INA-Casa projects also had other significant downsides, chief among which was that they markedly increased urban sprawl, but coming in a close second was their warehouse-like quality, a characteristic found in many of the public projects constructed in the post-war period regardless of which state agency sponsored them. Equally important was that in most cases designers embraced the principle of spatial segregation of shops from housing. As in Torre Spaccata in Rome (coordinator Plinio Marconi, 1961) and at the Harrar quarter in Milan (Luigi Figini and Gino Pollini, 1951–5), architects chose not to place stores on the ground floors of apartment blocks in violation of the peninsula's tradition of Italian city development, and they also chose not to design a piazza. Shops were instead meant to cluster together in a central area, but when business owners failed to set up shop in, for example, Torre Spaccata, squatters occupied them and turned them into apartments, so the district became a dormitory rather than a community. Such deviations from the way Italians traditionally occupied and lived in their cities could occasionally be salvaged by later interventions (a piazza was finally planned in a newer part of Torre Spaccata in 2005), but this was not always the case.

Flush with funding and government support for large-scale projects, architects found themselves summoned to propose housing forms for the new, post-fascist society. But what would those forms be? Returning to the styles of the nineteenth century, many believed, was not possible in the modern era; nor could the architects draft Rationalism to the cause, for as was obvious to everyone, the style was deeply imbricated with the discredited Fascist regime. And yet the latter was the architectural language currently fashionable elsewhere in Europe and in the United States. The years from 1949–65 testified to a search for an architectural language not tarnished by fascism, as Rationalism certainly was, in favour of a style that could offer dignified and decent housing for the people flooding into the cities. Italian architects were not the only ones seeking a formal language distinct from those linked to the totalitarian states. In England the young James Stirling embarked on just such a search in his first projects, including the widely publicized Department of Engineering at the University of Leicester (1960–63). Modernist languages largely prevailed. The quintessential expression of this search, and one of the most controversial, is the combined INCIS-IACP (Istituto Nazionale per le Case per gli Impiegati Statali, National Institute for Housing for State Employees) project for the Tiburtino IV district in Rome.[16] A team led by Mario Ridolfi and Ludovico Quaroni, architects whose work had enjoyed considerable success during the fascist Ventennio, led the effort to build nearly 800 housing units in open fields along an old consular road, the via Tiburtina. The ICP had already erected housing in this area 30 years earlier: Quartiere

Tiburtino II, designed by Innocenzo Sabbatini and Giorgio Guidi (1926–8), semi-intensive blocks with pediments over the windows, arched balconies, pilasters, and pediments along the rooflines. Rationalist architects disdained such traditionally inspired designs, but if ideological reasons precluded Rationalism as a design choice, what were they to do?

The team of architects assembled to design Tiburtino IV (1949–54), led by Quaroni and Ridolfi, found inspiration in the neorealist cinema then sweeping Italy in the films of Roberto Rossellini (*Roma, città aperta*, 1945); Vittorio De Sica (*Ladri di Biciclette*, 1947; *Sciuscià*, 1948; *Umberto D.*, 1952); Luchino Visconti (*La Terra trema*, 1948); and later Pier Paolo Pasolini, with his account of living in the shanty towns and *borgate* on the edge of Rome, *Ragazzi di vita* (1956). The extraordinary poverty and desperate struggles for survival that most Italians experienced after 1944 inspired these directors to represent the vast, not-so-underground world of the excluded in all of its terrible beauty. Paradoxically, their engagement triggered a rebirth of creativity in Italian cinema and led to a reappraisal of, and interest in, the lower classes, perhaps in part because the fascist virus appeared to have infected them least. A similar concern for marginalized groups inspired the architects to emphasize the individuality of apartments and to incorporate elements associated with rural vernacular traditions, which they believed would resonate with the future inhabitants; the very act of employing these references would in turn ennoble them. The architects planned Tiburtino IV as though it were a small town, with high-rise buildings seven to eight storeys high, low-rise units of three to five storeys and row houses (*case a schiera*), interspersed with piazzas, covered passageways, kitchen gardens and ornamental gardens. In other words, they rejected the typology of the anonymous, ever larger housing blocks speculators erected on the edges of the nation's cities – in forms Rationalist architects celebrated during the interwar years, a typology that soon dominated IACP housing as well. Distinctive expressive elements typical of Ridolfi's architecture, such as the unusual geometries of fencing and balconies, enlivened the project, while other features summoned references to rural architecture.

The first residents at least now had a place to live, although they lamented the absence of easy access to public transportation and to other services; but as the city gradually addressed these needs, the inhabitants could comfortably enjoy the varied streetscapes, diversity of housing types and fully serviced apartments. In fact, the care with which residents still maintain the exteriors and the common areas testifies to their pride in their neighbourhood. They could draw comparisons between their own apartments and those that followed, such as the generally long, monotonous blocks – the largest, inflected as a shallow 'V' (with a truss

Mario De Renzi,
Saverio Muratori,
Tuscolano II housing;
Adalberto Libera,
Tuscolano III, plan,
1950–54 (redrawn by
Joseph Flynn).
Tuscolano III is to the
far left.

at the centre popularly known as the 'boomerang'), at Largo Spartaco in the Tuscolano II complex, Rome, by Saverio Muratori and Mario De Renzi (1954–70). Although the seven-storey building's highly visible structural grid broke up some of the visual tedium, the nearly two dozen blocks of Tuscolano II depart radically from the urban forms of Rome. Around the perimeter the architects disposed a series of ten-storey, cruciform towers loosely based on those Le Corbusier planned for the centre of Paris in 1925. The idea was to delimit the area of low-cost housing from its surroundings – as if the design itself had not already done the job. Such towers were a megalomaniacal, wildly inappropriate and arrogant gesture then for Paris, and they were equally so for this Roman suburb. The entire enclave engages architectural issues of language and form utterly remote from the way Italian cities had developed over time or the way residents lived in them even as recently as ten years earlier; they simply packed large numbers of people into tight spaces, leaving between the structures the much discredited no-man's-lands such as those so beautifully dissected by Jane Jacobs in her *The Death and Life of Great American Cities* (1960), and more generally by Aldo Rossi in his *L'Archi-tettura della città* ('The Architecture of the City', 1966). Nonetheless, in designing projects according to adamantly modernist principles, the architects followed the then-internationally approved approach to urban and architectural design.

Another good counter-example from twenty years earlier, on viale XXI Aprile in Rome, is Mario De Renzi's Palazzi Federici. Best known as the setting for Ettore Scola's film *Una giornata particolare* (1977), the 442-unit complex includes modern elements such as glazed and rounded staircase towers but at the same time responds to local building traditions in its colours, materials and architectural details, and in its interior courtyards with porticos and fountains as well as 70 shops on the ground floors. At nine storeys, the buildings exceed the scale of older residences but the massing and setbacks reduce the impact of the greater height somewhat, and the apartments line the block in a manner consistent with Roman urbanism rather than in response to abstract, modernist dictates that insisted upon anomalous long blocks set within parks, such as those at Tuscolano II.

Only Adalberto Libera's unusual, low-rise complex at Tuscolano III (1950–54) departed from the high-density modernist squalor of Tuscolano II. A *tufo* wall (tuff, a soft volcanic stone) surrounds the entire complex, the result of the architect's search for an intermediate scheme between the single-family home and the residential block of apartments. Each interlocking, one-storey apartment enjoys a private garden, three of which form an L-shaped opening around which the units cluster, while the designer shifted a fourth patio to one corner for maximum solar exposure. In a complex marked by chromatic variety, abundant greenery, benches and overhangs, the small paved passageways connecting the units echo the narrow streets of rural Italian villages. A single four-storey block contains one-room units that open off the single-loaded *ballatoi* (exterior corridor balconies). To be sure, the urban planning here also did not take account of Rome's urbanism, but nonetheless, Libera demonstrated how to house 250 people per hectare and provide most units with private outdoor space while avoiding the monotonous Corbusian blocks proposed for the rest of Tuscolano II.

Unfortunately, Libera's project remained an isolated example but for a few exceptions, such as the much later, elegantly stepped low-rise complex in Bergamo by Giuseppe Gambirasio and Giorgio Zenoni (1976–9). Most building has followed the exasperated modernism of Le Corbusier's model – of long, denuded blocks set in parks in contrived forms – such as the IACP project at Vigne Nuove to the northeast of Rome, designed by a team led by Lucio Passarelli. Dating from 1971–9, the design aspired to achieve standardized – that is to say, identical – units collected in enormous repetitive sequences of buildings interrupted only by a sequence of cylindrical circulation towers extruded between every other apartment. In effect, this too was an enormous warehouse indifferent to the particularities of its future inhabitants.

The architects selected to design new working-class housing generally believed that they knew how the lower classes should live, and what appropriate apartments for them should be like. As the influential critic Bruno Zevi wrote in 1953,

> It was evident: [architects' new] clients of manual labourers, farmers, clerks, had neither the culture nor the financial possibility to hire professionals; they just wanted a house, any house . . . They were clients, yes, but elusive, anonymous, inarticulate characters in search of an author.[17]

Such an attitude indicated that it was unlikely that architects would consult the future inhabitants about the form, character, disposition or design of their residences, let alone about how they lived; on the contrary, the culture of the expert as the only person qualified to make decisions dominated relations between residents and designers, and not only in Italy. The inhabitants of publicly funded low-cost housing projects had no say in design, details, spatial organization or anything else, let alone the choice of an architect. And even had they been allowed to consult on their future homes, Zevi's comment, unfortunately an all too typical expression of architects' views, implicitly and even explicitly devalued the habits, desires and living patterns of residents. It is therefore no surprise that the exteriors and outdoor spaces of many residential high-rises are so degraded; the vast green spaces suited an abstract idea of how buildings should relate to the landscape, but had nothing to do

Adalberto Libera,
Tuscolano III, 1950–54,
view of alley.

Adalberto Libera,
Tuscolano III, 1950–54,
view of roofs.

with how people would actually live in them or what they could afford to maintain, either with their time or their money.

Just as neo-realist films such as those of De Sica and Visconti directed attention to working-class Italians' struggles to survive in the misery and poverty of the post-war period, so the documentary shorts produced under the auspices of Americans in the Economic Cooperation Agency (ECA) and Italians in the Centro di Documentazione (CD) information agencies aimed to counter these distressing images with more optimistic ones.[18] The documentaries (or pseudo-documentaries, in many cases, since they often consisted of fictional narratives) begin with stories or events similar to those found in films such as *Ladri di biciclette* and *La terra trema*, but with very different resolutions or, more precisely, with happy endings. Shorts, such as *Aquila* (1949) and *Tiriamo le somme* (1953) depicted the resolution of problems of poverty, isolation or unemployment through governance by a protective state and a coherent national programme of organizing the family as emblematic of the state, within the terms of a generalized effort to modernize Italy – modernization understood therefore as industrialization along the lines of that in northern Europe and the United States.[19] The films also presented mechanized agriculture, reclamation projects, industrial development and public works projects as examples of the successes of the Marshall Plan for economic recovery. As the Cold War hardened, the short films also included persistent doses of anti-communist themes. Presented much like fascism's newsreels, the information agencies' new documentaries played in theatres and public squares prior to the screening of feature films, so that the audiences covered all ages and all classes, rural and metropolitan. Directing their messages toward Italians of all classes, the film-makers designed their documentaries with the specific goals of demonstrating the accomplishments of the ECA and, more generally, the positive future that awaited Italians under the newly elected Christian Democratic government.

The unintended consequences of many of the residential developments of the immediate post-war period, while invisible to the designers at the time, are excruciatingly apparent today. Such is the case for the various complexes designed between 1951 and 1957 for former residents of the Sassi (cave homes) in Matera by Luigi Piccinato, Ludovico Quaroni and Giancarlo De Carlo. For centuries, the impoverished in this southern Italian city carved out living quarters in the rocks surrounding the town of Matera, entire families living together in caves with their animals as had their ancestors for millennia. As they came to be exposed to public view in the early 1950s, the Sassi became an emblematic symbol of the backwardness of the south and as a consequence the subject of a determined campaign to evacuate the inhabitants and close the caves down. Residents received promises of new and modern houses in exchange for their dark and humid quarters in the mountainside. And in fact, the houses are cleverly designed, particularly the La Martella complex by Quaroni, and to be sure, residents had more space, even including gardens and facilities for small barnyard animals.[20]

What the appealing photographs obscure is that the new housing was erected far from the city. Initially, the Ente Riforma Fondiaria Puglia e Lucania (ER, Agency for Landholding Reform) wanted the housing dispersed on individual agricultural plots, with a small centre for churches and other minimal services, while the architects insisted on a residential quarter that would allow residents to be in close proximity, maintaining their communities. The final project, on a low hill expropriated from the landowner, was probably the best solution possible under the circumstances. Services would consist of a church and a small rural centre planned as adjuncts to the meandering rows of duplexes. Nonetheless, where before residents simply walked outside their homes and found all necessary services and facilities, now they had to traverse several kilometres to gain access to a broad range of urban amenities at a time when most did not own cars and public transport was limited. Planners, politicians and architects simply assumed that the Sassi peasants would prefer a rural lifestyle. Not only uprooting people from the city, the new quarter tore residents from the network of relationships beyond their immediate neighbours that had sustained their families and their communities for

Ludovico Quaroni,
Luigi Piccinato,
Giancarlo di Carlo,
La Martella housing,
Matera, 1951–4.

generations. The publicity surrounding the caves of Matera decried the lack of light, the promiscuity of entire families sharing a single room with animals, the humidity, the dirt, and the absence of hygienic services, sewers, running water and other amenities. Time has brought greater clarity to the situation in Sassi di Matera, for the real issue was not the quality of the spaces themselves, or even the absence of amenities: it was the poverty of the residents. Recent gentrification and tourist developments in Sassi render this abundantly clear, as young people, families and even luxury hotels battle to purchase and move into rock-hewn apartments disparaged as a national disgrace barely 50 years earlier. Even if used only for short stays or weekend holidays, once outfitted with modern sanitation facilities the caves are nonetheless eminently habitable.

Architectural criticism has been considerably less kind to Tiburtino IV than it has to the grandiose blocks of most IACP and INA-Casa projects; locked into ideological critical modes, architects and critics still today attack the project as being nostalgic, figurative, romantic, pseudo-rural – and not modern. Framing projects as neo-realist, hence romantic and nostalgic, implicitly diminishes them by comparison with 'modern' projects. From this perspective, only a rigidly modernist, not to say Rationalist, language would have been appropriate. To adopt this view is to ignore the conditions as lived by architects at the time and their entirely correct perception of Rationalism as associated with fascism. It is also to insist on a dogmatic, narrow vision of modernism and to reject openness to traditional typologies as an appropriate strategy for design – not to mention reinforcing mistaken assumptions about the omnipotence of architects.

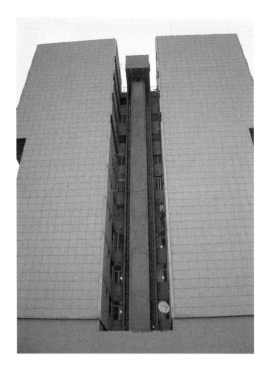

Corviale, detail views.

Mario Fiorentino,
Corviale, adjacent
to goat farm, Rome,
1972–82.

As it turns out, most modernist projects – housing blocks set in green spaces – are anti-urban and they too, in their own ways, romanticize people and environments, such as in the architects' blind insistence on 'green space' without addressing what that space is meant to be, or what people expect in an urban environment. Critics of the Tiburtino project, on the other hand, celebrate the Corviale scheme coordinated by Mario Fiorentino, a 1-kilometre-long housing block remote from the city when built (1972–82), which is squalid and unappealing still today.

In the typical manner of modernist housing estates, Corviale crowns a hilly site surrounded by splendidly open space, or, more appropriately, undifferentiated green space that has certainly not contributed to making the project a better place to live; on the contrary, the ample greenery only stands as a mute reminder of its distance from Rome's urbanized periphery.[21] Every ill-advised conceit of post-war modernist housing complexes found its way into Corviale, from the outdoor amphitheatre to meeting spaces at the foot of flights of stairs and from open interior atria to piloti on the lowest level. Whatever the attractive architectural details and however spacious the apartments, this Corbusian monstrosity-on-steroids is an unrelieved warehouse for over 8,000 inhabitants, with interminably long hallways and lacking shops and services – one in which many of its residents, isolated and anonymous, certainly feel forgotten by the city. Although for some, being ignored is a felicitous development that allows them to grow cannabis in the buildings' interstices.[22] Despite the enormous barrier of what residents call the Serpentone (the Snake), over the years some have managed to form their own micro-communities to establish, among other things, a small library and a room for film screenings and meetings. The arguments of its avid supporters in Rome's architectural community might have more credibility if they themselves sought to rent apartments there; Corviale's residents instead came from the significantly worse *baracche* in the Magliana district, adjacent to the aqueducts and elsewhere, that the city demolished in the early 1980s, and they had no other choice – by contrast with the architects, who celebrate the project but are neither forced nor choose to live in it. It is, as Thomas

Schumacher remarked, a perfect example of the 'abstract, scaleless, streetless, inhumane environments of CIAM [Congres Internationale d'Architecture Moderne] and the early Soviet avant-garde'.[23] Even contemporary archi-star Rem Koolhaas illustrated the failures of modern architecture by reference to Corviale, remarking laconically in a casual aside that it 'may seem ugly to us, but our tastes today are different'.[24] Koolhaas, like other critic-architects, focuses on style, but appears blind to the real problems with this and other projects. The only hope for the Corviale complex is that perhaps it too will one day be engulfed by the rest of the city. Whatever 'works' in this project does so through the Herculean efforts of the priest Don Gabriele and some of its inhabitants, despite rather than because of the architecture.

Other metropolises underwent the same type of development on their outskirts. Perhaps even more explicitly modernist in inspiration was the enormous residential quarter at Forte Quezzi in Genoa (1956–8), under the direction of Luigi Carlo Daneri, celebrated as one of the premier icons of the post-war modern movement in Italy. INA-Casa initiated and bankrolled the project along with contributions from the state, employers and the inhabitants. On hilly terrain, the team proposed five buildings of three to five storeys organized in serpentine curves along the side of the hill, in deliberate imitation of Le Corbusier's Plan Obus for Algiers (1930–33) – a plan, fortunately for the architect's reputation, never realized. The main building, originally projected to reach eleven storeys but subsequently reduced in height, snakes around the flanks of the hill for 540 metres and has an internal street on the third floor, recalling Corbusier's Unité d'Habitation in Marseilles (1947–52). Like Corviale, this complex was supposed to include shops, a nursery, an elementary school, sports facilities, meeting rooms, theatres and a church but, in a pattern common to many post-war housing projects, the city never followed through on its promise to provide these essential amenities. Only the nursery school and the church saw the light of day, the latter some 30 years later. Even at the time it was erected the scheme triggered strong critical responses – celebrated by Bruno Zevi as courageous, excoriated by others who saw it as an uninhabitable and inhuman warehouse.[25] Although touted as a modernist icon, Forte Quezzi constituted yet another example of architects playing with architectural and planning languages in dialogue only with one another – a practice possible only because the future inhabitants were not part of the discussion and had no other choices. Likewise, because low-cost housing is the province of state agencies, architects did not have to confront their projects on the open market, surely a recipe for financial disaster for developments such as these.

Luigi Daneri, INA
Casa Quartiere Forte
Quezzi, Genoa,
1956–8.

A similar scheme characterized the INCIS Decima quarter in Rome (co-ordinator Luigi Moretti, 1960–66), with its series of curved, exceptionally long buildings slapped down in open countryside. Moretti's Watergate complex in Washington, DC, designed with similarly sinuous curves, worked well as a residential base for government employees and other prosperous individuals, but the low-cost version in Rome was considerably less successful. Certainly, civic officials bear responsibility for not providing the promised infrastructure, but we cannot place responsibility for the project's subsequent problems solely on those failures. Perhaps the most devastating critique of the modern movement's approach to working-class housing lies precisely in the fact that architects (and public agencies) willingly experimented on the backs of working-class inhabitants as though their lives, their traditions and their families could be manipulated like chess pieces, and as if their hopes and dreams, by contrast with those of the architects, counted for nothing. If in the 1930s architects sought to fulfil the requirements of *Existenzminimum* – the smallest possible spaces in which families could be squeezed – in the post-war period they too often elaborated the 'grand gesture', out of scale, out of time and out of context. The Genoese compound's plans defied all Italian traditions of community building in scale, in form and in social organization; over time, Forte Quezzi has become yet another of the many isolated modernist ghettos on the perimeters of Italian cities – and certainly not what architects, dazzled by the words, designs and promise of Le Corbusier, thought they were producing.

Luigi Daneri, INA
Casa Quartiere Forte
Quezzi, Genoa,
1956–8.

It is indeed something of a paradox that during the post-war years a generation of young architects passionately sought to confound the experience of fascism by embracing a commitment to the needs of the burgeoning urban masses, adopting a largely left-wing agenda to do so, but ultimately produced housing developments that often amounted to little more than warehouses. Those who entered universities and poly-technic institutes in the two decades after 1945 found the same professors who had been there before the war, their teachings little changed by the twin convulsions of the end of fascism and the bitter partisan battles against German and Italian troops operating on behalf of Mussolini's new base in the Salò Republic. The newly published writings of Antonio Gramsci, a startlingly original Italian cinema culture and fresh possibil-ities for political and intellectual organization after two decades of closure under fascism inspired the younger generations to debate other ways of thinking about architecture, other ways of designing and other roles for architects. At the centre of these debates was the bimonthly Milan-based architectural magazine *Casabella*, reborn in 1954 as *Casabella-Continuità* under the editorship of Ernesto Nathan Rogers.[26] The position outlined repeatedly in the pages of *Casabella-Continuità* asserted the essential for-malist bankruptcy of pre-war Rationalist architecture and at the same time, asserted the moral and ethical imperative of architects to abandon historicism, nationalism and formalism but to be willing to embrace regional inflections in their designs. Architects instead needed to revise their design strategies along the lines of a substantially political and moral response to a new, collective culture with architecture as but one of many elements. Rogers carried his arguments into the university, where he counselled his students not to tolerate accepted dogmas but to bring a critical eye to bear on everything, to question insistently anything pre-sented as established, certain and permanent.[27] Gathered around Rogers in Milan during those years were some who came to be among the most prominent architects of the subsequent decades, including Aldo Rossi, Vittorio Gregotti, Giorgio Grassi, Gae Aulenti, Guido Canella, Giancarlo De Carlo and Marco Zanuso. Stringent criticism of the interwar Ration-alist movement for its icy rationality, its indifference to Italy's historic cities and to how Italians lived in the houses, communities and cities marked in particular the theories outlined by Canella and Rossi during the late 1950s, but they were equally critical of mindless historicism and empty formalism.

The Rogers group did not represent the only view among architects in the post-war period; other groups also adopted positions loosely charac-terized as socially responsible in a shared search for a renewed, non-fascist architecture. Bruno Zevi, who returned to Rome after years in exile in the U.S., where he became fascinated by the architecture of Frank Lloyd Wright, founded the Associazione per l'Architettura Organica (APAO, Association for Organic Architecture), which countered positions characterized as 'academic' and in particular, focused on monumentality, with a human-scaled architecture that responded to the forms of nature. Other groups that took shape elsewhere in Italy, such as the Movimento di Studi per l'Architettura (MSA, Movement for Architectural Studies) in Milan and the Giuseppe Pagano group in Turin, argued for a renewed Rationalism with a social impulse, or for a line somewhere between avant-garde and traditionalist, but distinct from pre-war architecture.

Many of these debates found their homes in architectural publications, but in some respects they also seeped into the buildings designed by the various combatants. Already confronting a building industry newly enamoured of reinforced concrete and precast concrete, architects thus encountered developers who pressed for the cheapest solutions and an industry whose workers no longer possessed the skills and traditional know-how of their predecessors. Architects could no longer draft plans secure in the knowledge that the builders understood how to handle windows, frames, doors, drainage and other technical matters. At the same time, public agencies pushed for the lowest bids – which invariably assured the lowest quality construction. In the small offices of fledgling architects, such as those of Carlo Aymonino, Vittorio Gregotti, Aldo Rossi and others, hiring outside firms to produce working drawings was common. Over time, as they were able to enlarge their offices, most of these firms took on this task in-house.[28]

Casabella-Continuità was not the only post-war publication to press for an architecture of social and/or political commitment; Gio Ponti's *Stile* already in January 1945 polemicized on behalf of the idea of providing a house for everyone, and Luigi Piccinato, Silvio Radiconcini and Bruno Zevi edited *Metron-architettura*, to promote professional practice as rooted in social commitment through the development of an organic architecture. The defeat of the left-wing coalition in the 1948 elections, the intervention of the Marshall Plan and with it the United States government overtly and covertly opposing Italy's left-wing political parties, spelled the marginalization of such optimistic discourses in the bruisingly real world of housing finance and construction, where with few exceptions, right-wing and capitalist economic strategies dictated expenditure, location and ultimately even the form of buildings. In such circumstances, for better or for worse, the quintessentially capitalist figures of Le Corbusier, Ludwig Mies van der Rohe and other modern movement icons, with their monolithic, monotonous slabs punctuated by staircases or balconies, provided the ideal models.[29] Architects such as Libera, Aymonino and others vigorously criticized the massive housing estates their colleagues erected for INA-Casa, but lacked the political space or power to do much more; Libera's intriguing complex for the Tuscolana remained a solitary achievement in the decade after the war ended.

chapter five

The Economic Miracle

The period from 1950 through the 1960s in Italy is known as the 'economic miracle', the era when jobs multiplied and well-being spread to the urban proletariat and even to smaller, rural communities. Even if people found work in the factories, housing was more difficult to come by; this is where the *baracche* and speculative housing spilled out into the countryside. Yet housing for new immigrants in the industrial poles of northern Italy consisted of more than only self-built structures. Factory owners and industrial capitalists made bold attempts to house and educate their workers. We have seen how in the pre-war period, SNIA Viscosa housed its workers near Turin and in Udine, and on the periphery of Rome, Roberto Nicolini designed a workers' village at Piazza Siderea for the employees of Breda both before and after the Second World War (1940–42 and 1947–8).

Among the post-war leaders of company-sponsored enterprises to provide housing and services to employees was Adriano Olivetti, owner of Italy's most successful company (producing office equipment) and in the immediate post-war years the president of the Istituto Nazionale di Urbanistica (INU, National Urban Studies Institute) and financier and director of the magazine *Urbanistica*.[1] In line with the ideas of Lewis Mumford and others, Olivetti envisioned a world in which thoughtful planning well in advance of building guided the development of entire regions; from the 1930s onwards, Olivetti advanced master plans for the Aosta Valley region (1936), for the Canavese (a region of Piedmont near Ivrea, 1952) and for Ivrea itself (1938 and 1952), but only completed parts of the Ivrea plan. Olivetti believed passionately in the important role industrial development played in its social, cultural and physical environment, ideas that he put into practice in the network of services he developed for his factory in Ivrea but which he also made available to the entire community. In significant ways, Olivetti followed in the footsteps of earlier industrialists who sought to both employ and house workers. Nonetheless, Olivetti's ambitions were markedly greater.

Olivetti was also a dedicated patron of modern architecture both before and after the Second World War, summoning some of the most prominent

Roberto Gabetti and Aimaro Isola, west residential complex, Olivetti, Ivrea, 1971, garden elevation.

modernists to design buildings for his factories in Ivrea and elsewhere, including hiring Luigi Figini and Gino Pollini in the late 1930s to design a nursery school and worker houses near the factory (1939–40) and later, seven blocks of housing (1940–42), with an additional 26 residential units completed after the war by Marcello Nizzoli and Gian Mario Oliveri (1948–54). In line with his belief that a full range of services housed in structures of the highest architectural quality ought to be readily accessible to employees and others, Olivetti continued to commission significant buildings by prominent architects, including a cafeteria and recreation centre designed by Ignazio Gardella (1953–9); an elementary school by Ludovico Quaroni and Adolfo De Carlo (1955); and a nursery school by Mario Ridolfi and Wolfgang Frankl (1955–63). Olivetti turned to Figini and Pollini again for the expansion of Olivetti's main factory on via Jervis (1955–7) and for a cultural and social services centre (1954–8), all in Ivrea. Following his death in 1960, the company continued to hire top designers for important new buildings, such as housing by Roberto Gabetti and Aimaro Isola (1967–75) and later a new office wing for the company's headquarters by Gino Valle (1985–8). Just what made the long, curved block of the Unità Residenziale Ovest in Ivrea by Gabetti and Isola reasonably successful when a similar design for Genoa turned into a virtually unlivable ghetto is not readily apparent; perhaps it was less the design itself than the fact that the inhabitants chose to live there, were employed in relatively well-paying jobs and were part of a larger community. The complex of mini apartments set with an earthen berm and single glazed wall facing the garden provided temporary housing for recent college graduates and new Olivetti employees. The units are still occupied today, though they are less temporary than originally planned.

Almost as provocative are the projects he commissioned and then rejected: these include some by premier designers Marcello Nizzoli and Daniele Calabi. Olivetti emphasized the environment and context over an individual building, and the comfort of workers and people in general over the sometimes fantastic visions of a single architect. The signature of a specific architect was never sufficiently persuasive for him to erect a structure that jarred in its surroundings or that failed at the human scale, despite his commitment to modern architecture. On the one hand, such a position could be dismissed as middle-of-the-road; on the other, seen as one that recognized that the whole was greater than the sum of its parts. Notable in this respect is the plan of the Olivetti complex in Ivrea, which historian Fulvio Irace brilliantly identified as an evocation of Hadrian's Villa (Villa Adriana, Rome) far more than an expression of modern Italian urban planning.[2] With its local symmetries and rich anthology of contemporary design deployed along the displaced axis of via Castellamonte,

West residential complex, Olivetti, night view of apartments from garden; watercolour showing half-moon shaped building in context.

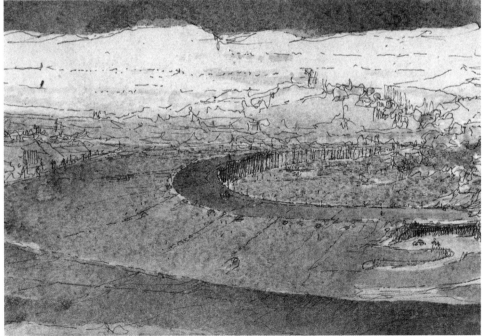

in plan and topography it is light years away from the mono-functional and rigidly rational modernism of industrial complexes such as the Pirelli factory complex at Bicocca in Milan (1907). Further testimony to Olivetti's focus on the workplace as a humane environment for workers with a rich and unpretentious connection to its setting is Luigi Cosenza's design for the Olivetti factory in Pozzuoli (Naples, 1951–4), a distinctly modest, elegant and low-scale complex that snakes down verdant terrain that slopes gently towards the Bay of Naples.

Similar enterprises developed by owners or corporations tended in general to trigger criticism for being paternalistic and forging an unhealthy link between employment and the right to a house – which could be ruptured at the company's discretion. While this seems to have been a correct characterization of many such enterprises, Olivetti's facilities in Ivrea appear to have broken the mould to the degree that high-quality and abundant services enhanced living conditions in Ivrea generally, not just for employees and their immediate families. Like the decaying factories of Milan and other cities, those of Olivetti lie abandoned and are now being converted for other uses.

However problematic many of the enterprises turned out to be, the degree to which the elite protagonists of these and other adventures in urbanism sought to enrich their understanding of the cities and towns involved engaging with other disciplines, especially literature and philosophies of knowledge. This enormous curiosity to know and to understand, too often failed to lead to workable, operational syntheses. An intense fascination with the technical tools of planning and housing design did not encourage an effort to confront problems of governance or of how people wanted to live, in particular when it came to thinking about how to administer the new districts and reconfigured regions these designers envisioned.[3]

In the 1950s, Milan's suburbs expanded and swallowed up neighbouring communities such as Sesto San Giovanni, Monza and even Pavia. Industrialization drove expansion as factories began to regain stable production rhythms after the damages and closures of the war years. Many of the labourers who now manned the assembly lines had emigrated from southern Italy; known as *terroni* (southerners), swarthy and with heavy southern accents, they met hostility, incomprehension and exclusion. Over the next two decades, poverty and criminality came to be associated with some of the new, low-income quarters such as Comasina, Quarto Oggiaro, Gratosoglio and Gallaratese. Some leading architects received commissions to produce housing in these areas remote from the city centre; but even the most attractive, avant-garde architecture could not resolve the problems of poverty, alienation, racism and marginalization, even by the most attractive, avant-garde architecture.

Carlo Aymonino headed the team of architects responsible for creating the Monte Amiata housing complex; one of the buildings, known as the Gallaratese and designed by Aldo Rossi (1969–73), became an icon of the neo-Rationalist movement of the 1970s and 1980s. The contrast between this straightforward, four-storey project and those by the rest of the team could not be greater. Constrained by tight budgets and lacking control over construction (public projects are usually bid for separately for design and construction), Rossi nonetheless managed to produce an evocative complex, with housing on two or three of the storeys, held aloft by gigantic cylinders and narrow concrete slabs. Less than half the length of Corviale, the Gallaratese falls within the general category of modernist design but escapes its worst features precisely because the archetypal geometries and simple purity of lines render it dignified without becoming monumental – and radically opposed to the tortured and busy banality of other buildings in the complex. As happened with most public housing of the time, residents of Monte Amiata complained about a lack of services, public transportation and of the project's distance from the city. Fortunately for the residents, time eliminated these problems; when erected (1970–73), Gallaratese stood isolated in fields of weeds, but after nearly 35 years, trees, gardens and good maintenance have softened the structure's sleek lines and rendered it more rather than less distinguished, and the city, with all of its services, has grown around it.

Studio Gino Valle, tower and row houses at DUC, via della Barca, Bologna, 1992.

The city of Bologna in northern Italy, with a tradition of left-wing governance and significant attention paid both to historic preservation and the production of low-cost housing, established a programme entitled Disegno Urbano Concertato (DUC, Planned Urban Design) in the early 1980s, focusing in particular on housing to be developed in the area west of the main train station, along via Stalingrado. In terms of aesthetics and housing, two projects beautifully illustrate the approaches that dominated in the late 1980s and early 1990s. On the one hand, the tower by Paolo Portoghesi on viale della Repubblica boasts the chromatic and decorative excess so typical of other projects that deliberately rejected modern architecture during the 1970s and 1980s. Oversized crenellation on the roofline, a vaguely cruciform plan with projecting balconies in the centre and a revetment faintly recalling local traditions, with defined string courses and a ring of perky little spires (or minarets?) on the roof make for a jarring, not to say garish, contrast with just about everything else in the surroundings. Nearby, Gino Valle's studio produced a collection of tower residences and row houses on via della Barca (1992). Despite its clearly modern matrix, the diverse fenestration patterns, simple massing and traditional revetments of white stucco and brick also offer subtle links to local traditions, even though

160

Valle too found himself hamstrung by modernist-inspired requirements. The green space here is no less problematic than in the earlier examples, even though the Valle solution neither concedes to the strident expressivism of the Portoghesi project nor to the stark modernism of much post-war housing. Nonetheless, the DUC project suffers from the same shortcomings as most post-war government sponsored housing. During the same years, Valle produced an even more elegant, richly varied and beautifully detailed residential complex for Venice's IACP on Giudecca island (1980–86).

Urbanization in Palermo, Sicily, had a somewhat different history. In 1970 its mayor, don Vito Ciancimino, apparently reached an agreement with Salvo Lima, the Christian Democracy party representative in Sicily, to undertake what is known as the Sack of Palermo: the plunder of the city's parks and periphery through an orgy of building. In a vicious network of Mafia, bribes, cement and politicians, Ciancimino's government issued building permits for sites supposedly off-limits to builders; in one night alone, individuals who lent their names to the enterprise (*prestanomi*) but who were clearly fronting for the Mafia and the politicians who collaborated with them, collected 5,000 building permits. Ciancimino finally

Gino Valle, IACP Giudecca housing project, Venice, 1980–86.

Vittorio Gregotti,
ZEN complex, Palermo,
started 1969, overall
view.

went to jail in October 1984, but the devastation of Palermo was already largely complete.[4] In contrast with the rampant speculative building and exasperated modernism of most of Palermo's public housing of the time, Vittorio Gregotti produced the ZEN quarter, with the explicit goal of incorporating traditional urban and architectural strategies. Four parallel low-rise housing blocks form three residential complexes based loosely on the ancient Roman *insulae*, with interior courts and porticos, higher towers at the corners and three tiers of services – none of which were completed as planned. Poor maintenance and terrible social conditions, exacerbated by poverty and organized crime, have unfortunately given ZEN a reputation as one of the most dangerous and troubled districts in Palermo – perhaps undeservedly so, but nonetheless illustrating the limits of even thoughtful and well-meaning architectural design, unfortunately still evidencing the dominance of modern movement ideas.[5] Squatters occupy many of the public housing units, reinforcing the residents' perception of the marginality of their community with respect to the rest of the city. Never completed as planned, even Gregotti eventually concluded that the best solution for ZEN would be to tear it down and start over, since even the most recent master plans for Palermo offer no proposals to rehabilitate it or to improve the lives of its residents.[6]

Roberto Saviano's *Gomorrah* (2005) and the 2008 film of the same name brought the quarter of Secondigliano, near Naples and the notorious

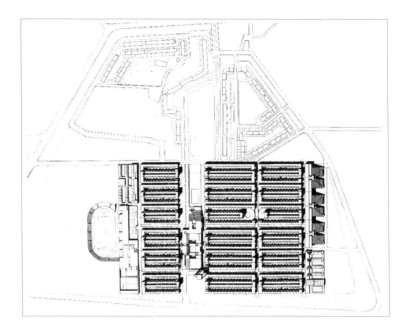

housing project Vele di Scampia (Sails of Scampia), to the attention of the world. Designed and built between 1962 and 1975, this INA-Casa housing project by Franz Di Salvo, with the assistance of Riccardo Morandi for the structural system, has become the perfect illustration of the crime, corruption and squalor of southern Italy, reinforcing the long-standing beliefs of northern Italians about the region. Originally consisting of seven massive apartment blocks, the complex has housed anywhere from 40,000 to 70,000 inhabitants at any one time – all estimates are purely guesswork, since no one has been willing to conduct a headcount. The earliest residents found themselves crowded by newcomers left homeless after the massive earthquake of 1980, and even though the government demolished three of the original seven blocks, an estimated 40,000 people still occupy the badly damaged structures. All of the vices and brutality of organized crime seem to have found a place in what enthusiasts tout as an example of splendid modern architecture. Like Corviale, even Vele di Scampia has its tenacious defenders. Alessandro Castagnaro wrote:

> It is beyond discussion that even if some mistakes were made,
> 'Le Vele' represented avant-garde architecture for the era in which
> they were built, on the model of the excellent examples of masters
> of twentieth-century European architecture, [a list] headed by the
> well-known Le Corbusier, and they have characterized the urban

skyline of [Naples's] periphery, because they were structurally valid and efficient . . .[7]

From the University of Naples, Benedetto Gravagnuolo wrote about how Di Salvo was inspired by 'Le Corbusier's Unité d'Habitation, by . . . Kenzo Tange and other macrostructural models in general, Di Salvo articulated the district's plan with two building types: towers and tents'. Even though Gravagnuolo recognized the 'typological inadequacy intrinsic to the macrostructural model with respect to the housing expectations of the future inhabitants', he nonetheless celebrated the avant-garde qualities of Di Salvo's design:

> If it is in fact true that the technical and aesthetic qualities of the Vele are beyond discussion, it is nonetheless undeniable that they are uninhabitable for reasons beyond the architecture.[8]

Examples could be multiplied without changing the substance of the evaluation: with a handful of exceptions, low-cost housing through the late 1980s became a field for architectural experimentation in which designers deliberately rejected Italian traditions for living in cities and inhabiting housing in favour of an abstract and indifferent, decidedly anti-urban modernism. Exasperated by poor maintenance, lack of services, and poverty, all too often the neighbourhoods and housing became and remained squalid ghettos, whatever the good intentions of the architects. Arguably, formal experimentation is more appropriate for private housing, where the client – whether the builder or the future inhabitant – is able to set out some limits. But even here, some wildly out-scale projects simply carried forward the worst excesses of the public projects: exemplary in this respect was the much criticized satellite city of Sorgane (Florence, 1962–80), a combination of private apartments and state funded low-cost housing. Once the exasperated, over-designed and isolated residential towers of architects Leonardo Ricci and Leonardo Savioli were completed, the size of the scheme fortunately fell from 12,000 to 4,000 inhabitants.

Pre-war private housing ranged from avant-garde Rationalist, such as the crisply modern work of Giuseppe Terragni in designs for the Casa Giuliani-Frigerio (Como, 1939–40) and Villa Bianco (Seveso, 1936–7), to moderate traditionalism, such as Giovanni Muzio's Villa Leidi (Bergamo, 1935), with its arched windows, pergolas and stone podium. Generally modestly scaled and well outside historic centres, these projects became models for private housing in the post-war years. A handful of exemplary projects testify to the extraordinary range of experiments in housing and to some of the most accomplished results.

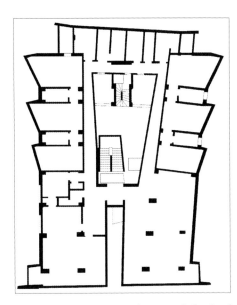

Luigi Moretti, Palazzina del Girasole, Rome, 1950, plan and elevation (drawing by Joseph Flynn).

Certainly one of the two or three most promising Italian architects of the first half of the twentieth century, Luigi Moretti designed some of the country's most memorable and original, and uniquely modernist, buildings of the 1930s, including the fencing academy (1933–6) at the Foro Mussolini in Rome. From this stunning accomplishment, started when Moretti was only 26 years old, he went on to design another extraordinary building in Rome, the Palazzina del Girasole (1950). Working within the basic Roman scheme of base, *fusto* (shaft) and cornice, shops below and residences above, Moretti transformed the type in a thoroughly original and modern key. Each floor contains two apartments distributed as long rectangles with windows that project out to capture the sun. The asymmetrical *timpano* (pediment) at once recalls and negates the classical type, while the front elevation, split by a deep vertical opening, is detached from the building and organized with a series of rolling panels which give a constantly changing and unpredictable appearance to the facade. The building's name, sunflower (*girasole*), refers to the fact that both the elevation and the lateral rooms open out to the changing position of

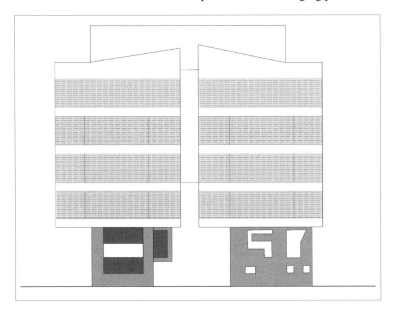

the sun, not with the absolutist rigour of a Corbusian design but with a subtlety that bespeaks the architect's concern for the inhabitants. Moretti cleverly adapted the building to the changing sun through the use of the sliding panels, which permitted the occupants to control views, lighting, ventilation and privacy. After such a striking achievement, the apartment and office building on via Rugabella in Milan is something of a disappointment, jutting awkwardly into the street – even more noticeably after a recent cleaning. Consisting of five structures contained within a unified frame of two distinct building blocks, one nine storeys, the other two, the complex contains a parking garage, apartments, shops and offices. Despite its odd juxtaposition within the neighbourhood, the development nonetheless evidences Moretti's capacity for designing enormously complex structures and linking them ingeniously together.

In the radically different context of Venice and its canals, Ignazio Gardella designed Casa Cicogna, a remarkable variation on the Venetian palazzo building type (1995). Much criticized at the time, it has in subsequent years earned recognition as a dignified but inventive reinterpretation in a modern register of a historic building type, in a daunting setting. Far to

Luigi Moretti, residential and office building, via Rugabella, Milan, 1949.

Ignazio Gardella, Casa
Cicogna, Venice, 1995.

the north in the snowy region north of Turin, Roberto Gabetti and Aimaro
Isola, with Luciano Re, designed the single family Casa Pero (Pino Torinese,
1965–8), with a steeply pitched roof atop shallow arched openings conceal-
ing a richly elaborated series of diagonal and orthogonal interior spaces. And
on a narrow strip of land on the shore of Lake Iseo, Giorgio Grassi worked
with his client in a collaboration similar to that of Adalberto Libera and
Curzio Malaparte some twenty years earlier to produce the Casa Gavazzeni
(Marone Velo, Brescia, 1960), an elegantly modern parallelogram with
ribbon windows and deeply recessed glazed openings on three sides that

Roberto Gabetti and
Aimaro Isola, Casa
Pero, Pino Torinese,
1965–8.

opposite:
Arassociati, Casa
Soru, Sardinia,
2003–04.

offer incomparable vistas of the lake and surrounding mountains. Inside, the rooms open off a narrow hallway running the length of the house. As it hugs the shore, the white volume stands out from its surroundings, but the scale and the simplicity of form minimize any disruption. Finally, for Renato Soru, the founder of the internet company Tiscali and the president of the Sardinia region, Arassociati studio remodelled a pedestrian house, transforming it into a crisply modern structure without altering the volume or adding to the building's mass (Casa Soru, Sardinia, 2004). The project responded to Soru's ideas about avoiding building new structures and adding to the frighteningly large amount of cement flowing onto the Italian landscape, something which Soru fought aggressively during his tenure as president of Sardinia – a programme that earned him the enmity of politicians and entrepreneurs from across the political spectrum, from left to right, and ended up costing him the next election.

Each of these buildings, and some of the public housing complexes, exhibits striking originality and sensitivity to the specific sites and to how Italians live. But they are unique, almost one-off projects that do not tell the full story of the transformation of the Italian landscape over the last half-century. By some estimates, nine out of ten structures in Italy rose within the past 50 years – and altogether too many of these were poorly designed (such as some of the low-cost projects noted above), poorly constructed or produced illegally.

Post-industrialization in Italian Cities

The years of the economic miracle were also the heyday of the trade unions. After the constraints of the Fascist era and the extreme poverty of the immediate post-war years, unions briefly enjoyed a period of enormous power. Negotiating at the national level for public and private employees, the three main unions wrested large concessions in terms of hiring and firing policies, workplace policies, pensions, childcare and such matters as reduced-price train tickets and vouchers for meals. Part of the power of the unions sprang from the willingness of newly politicized workers to participate in massive demonstrations, travelling to Rome and other major cities to fill public spaces with thousands of their colleagues to flex their muscle against the overwhelming power of private corporations and the government. But to obtain a voice at the table, they had to endure more than they might have expected – or than was conscionable. Once the election was over in April 1948 and the Christian Democracy party (DC) no longer needed to worry about inducing labourers to vote DC, the minister of the interior Mario Scelba repressed demonstrations and strikes with an iron fist, to the point that Riccardo Lombardi, a representative in the Chamber of Deputies, claimed: '[treasury minister Giuseppe] Pella creates the unemployed, Scelba kills them'.[9] Indeed, the clashes remained bitter and often violent; police fired on the unemployed in Modena in 1950, killing six demonstrators.

Protests and demonstrations continued through the 1950s and 1960s, and unionists also adroitly used the weapon of the strike, sometimes only for fifteen minutes – just enough to throw a monkey wrench into a production facility or to irritate clients or customers waiting in line. With economists such as Milton Friedman in the United States trumpeting the post-war mantra of free trade, corporations now had a new and powerful weapon in their storehouse of armaments: if unions became, in their view, too demanding, they could simply move their factories elsewhere. Deindustrialization, wherein major industries shuttered their factories in Italy and moved to less expensive facilities with lower-priced labour, usually outside western Europe, took a toll on unions as it did on the working class more generally: the nature of jobs shifted from life-long, protected employment to short-term, flexible work without contracts, often without benefits and without the kinds of protection unionized labour enjoyed. As in many industrialized nations, white-collar employees often saw themselves as closer in kind to management than to workers in the unions' traditionally working-class base; as such they largely resisted unionizing, paradoxically at the very same time that they became more vulnerable to job loss, reduced benefits and pensions. Noteworthy too is the fact that, as in the U.S., when women began to flood into new employment sectors, the long-standing protections by which men guaranteed their positions came under attack. In universities, for example, in many academic fields, as more women than men enter the job market, the concept of the tenured post has been relegated to associate and full professors, where it once extended to researchers as well. Not surprisingly, the impact of this change will fall disproportionately on female researchers who only recently began entering the university system in large numbers. The reforms drafted by then-education minister Mariastella Gelmini in 2010 envision short-term contracts for those seeking academic careers – but without altering the deeply corrupt system of awarding university posts (see chapter Six).

By 1970, northern Italian metropolises began to feel the first faint effects of globalization and deindustrialization – the economic miracle had lasted less than two decades. The dangers associated with the throng of factories in the Milanese hinterland also coalesced on 10 July 1976, when a toxic vapour cloud of tetrachlorodibenzo-para-dioxin (TCDD) rained down on the city of Seveso, a bedroom and industrial suburb of Milan; the area, evacuated for decades, suffered profound and enduring environmental damage. On the most polluted 80 hectares, most buildings were demolished,

the earth cleaned and trees, shrubbery and grasses planted, turning much
of the old suburb into a park, now inhabited by small animals such as
mice, rabbits and foxes.[10]

Over the next ten years, the great factories that employed so many of
Milan's workers, such as Pirelli, Breda, Alfa Romeo and Falck, began to
close their doors as production and assembly lines moved out of Milan
and even outside Italy, to countries with lower labour costs. In 1982, Gianni
Agnelli closed Lingotto, Fiat's premier automobile production facility in
Turin. After an invited competition for ideas in 1983, Renzo Piano received
a brief to transform it into a multifunctional museum and cultural facility; today it is for the most part a vast shopping mall and convention centre,
although at the time of writing the project is not yet entirely complete. The
fate of Lingotto, in its time heralded as one of the most avant-garde works
of industrial architecture, was emblematic of the urban industrial processes of closures and deindustrialization under way that profoundly
transformed the Italian landscape, just as the first phase of industrialization had done only seven or eight decades earlier. After powering the

Fiat Lingotto,
automobile testing
ramp of original
building, renovated
by Piano.

172

Italian economy for decades, Fiat moved production facilities to Poland, Russia, China, Brazil, Serbia and Argentina, where labour costs are lower; half its labour force is now outside Italy and, it is worth noting, in places where environmental and labour controls are less rigorous. In 2010 the company began moving operations to Detroit, Michigan, the traditional capital of automobile production.

At the very time that jobs and factories disappeared from the peninsula, new waves of immigrants flooded the country: Filipinos arrived by the end of the 1970s, and following the election of the Polish pope, John Paul II, thousands of Poles came in his wake. As wars erupted in the former Yugoslavia, Albanians, Montenegrins, Croats, Serbs and Bosnians fled the violence, and as hunger gripped North Africa, desperate Libyans, Ethiopians, Somalians and others took to the seas in flimsy skiffs and made for Italian shores. From the 1980s onwards, Chinese arrived in huge numbers, and Romanians, Russians, Moldavians and others from former Eastern bloc nations also fled to Italy after the break-up of the former Soviet state.[11] The few old-timers still living in Venice suddenly found themselves being served the traditional *spritz* (Prosecco and Aperol or Campari) by Chinese baristas in Chinese-owned bars and cafes. The question posed early in chapter One about Italian identity in the post-unification period took on added urgency as huge numbers of immigrant children filled schools; bars and cafes formed the base of economic growth for Chinese families; and Filipino women staffed Italian hospitals and hospices, not to mention private homes, as nurses and carers. Italians and immigrants alike still struggle to come to terms with a melting pot culture on a scale not known since the Renaissance, and at the end of the first decade of the twenty-first century, answers remain elusive. Among the most compelling evidence of the conflicts and dislocations of Italy's new, diverse population comes from the perspective of the immigrants themselves, as voiced in migrant literature such as that produced by the writers Pap Khouma, Nassera Chohra, Shirin Ramzanali Fazel and many others.[12]

Following the closure of many of Milan's factories from the 1970s onwards, their former industrial properties underwent transformations into offices, high-tech developments and residential complexes, and the older residential districts also underwent transformations. Over time, immigrants from Eastern Europe and North Africa moved in, while the rest of Milan shifted from industrial production to growth-based commerce, in the service sector, financial services, fashion, communications and television industries. Indicative of the changes wrought by deindustrialization is the transformation of the former Pirelli (primarily producers of automobile tyres) manufacturing facilities in the Bicocca area on the northern fringe of the city. Plans for a massive industrial park (about 70 hectares) under the direction of what is now Pirelli Real Estate began with a two-phase competition (1985 and 1988) won by Vittorio Gregotti's firm, Gregotti Associati; construction initiated in 1994, most of which had been completed by late 2009.

By contrast with the rigidity of the manufacturing processes on the Bicocca site, Gregotti's new plans called for an advanced technology centre with structures sufficiently flexible to be adapted to changing future uses. Where the factory had been an enclosed precinct, separate and distinct from its surroundings, Gregotti's project anticipated re-integrating the new facilities with the adjacent city. Otherwise, the initial plan maintained the footprints of the former industrial buildings but inserted large new blocks with interior courtyards linked to one another along a central spine. Among the buildings sited on the east–west axis are those for the University of Milan-Bicocca's scientific research facility (1994–7), with an H-shaped plan and four sunken courtyards within each of the arms. Projecting white metallic bay windows interrupt the surfaces of prefabricated, polished concrete panels punctuated by different types of fenestration; all of the university buildings on the site are distinguished by deep, brick-red concrete. Along the southwestern flank of the Bicocca site Gregotti also designed headquarters for the Consiglio Nazionale delle Ricerche (CNR, National Research Council), a building with sufficient flexibility to accommodate ample space for laboratories of unusual sizes (1992–9). Grey artificial stone revetments adorn the four facades of the closed perimeter block with its low corner towers, while the labs are all accessible to large heavy-loading equipment from the interior court. Like so many other similar projects of this scale, this one has not met with either critical or popular success: it is simply too remote from how most Italians live their cities, or want to live them.

The nearly 1 million cubic metres of industrial property at Bicocca has thus become a multi-use facility, the largest such enterprise in Italy. Gregotti touted the difference between his scheme, which simply involved adapting an existing industrial area, and others that occupy virgin land.

> Areas such as Bicocca are by definition already built up, not green spaces such as those at the Parco Sud [a site city council member Carlo Masseroli targeted for development in 2010]. To talk about dropping cement in a previously industrial site is a senseless banality. Among other things, the Bicocca project is a true example of mixed use, with housing, an extremely important element in new urbanization projects, and yet one found ever more rarely.[13]

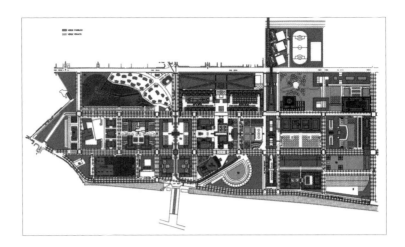

Stung by the criticism of Milan's Mayor Gabriele Albertini, who compared
Bicocca to a Soviet-era district in East Berlin, and by his claim that skyscrapers would have left more green space for the city, Gregotti responded:
'Skyscrapers can be extraordinary, high quality projects only if they are
coherently inserted into the territory. To say that skyscrapers preserve
green space is sheer stupidity.'[14]

Among many other projects, Gregotti Associati also designed housing
in via Emanueli (1993–6), via Sesto San Giovanni (1994–8) and Esplanade
(1993–6), all in Milan, as well as headquarters for the Siemens Group
(1994–2003) and the schools of humanistic studies of Milan-Bicocca university (1994–7). One feature of the scheme was to bring in several different
architects to design buildings; of these, the Deutsche Bank by Studio Gino
Valle (1997–2005) and the adaptive reuse of low-rise industrial sheds by
Maurizio Varratta (2005) stand out.

Bicocca is not the only deindustrialized area in Milan to undergo a
major transformation: LAND (Andreas Kipar and Giovanni Sala) is currently reconfiguring the former industrial facilities of Innocenti-Maserati
as part of a new residential quarter, with tree-lined axial roads in the residential section and a large, wooded park in the area adjacent to the Lambro
river, not far from the eastern part of Milan's ring road, the Tangenziale.
Designers envision reorganizing the spaces beneath the highway to provide skating paths, a reflecting pool and other facilities. The former Faema
facilities also changed between 2000 and 2003, with the transformation of
the factories in Lambrate into a complex for professional offices, housing
and cultural facilities. The project, headed up by Gianluigi Mutti of PP8
(Alfonso Correda and Luisa Olgiati), preserved the height and form of the
existing structures but carved out gardens and balconies and dressed up

the buildings with beautifully detailed industrial finishes and revetments. Expo 2015, to be hosted in Milan, promises to be a grand extravaganza, with silly skyscrapers designed by Daniel Libeskind and Zaha Hadid, and expensive pavilions already looking forward to becoming enormous white elephants, something characteristic of most post-war grand building enterprises, from the Turin International exhibition of 1961 (see below) to the 1990 World Cup facilities (fewer than twenty years after the events, the city of Bari put its expensive new stadium on the market). Few match the outrageously oversized complex (huge hotel, swimming pools and athletic facilities, to name but a few of the amenities) built on the coast of Sardinia, hastened to completion in time for a G8 meeting only to have the location changed at the last minute. The mega-corporation Marcegaglia conveniently stepped in with the only bid to operate the property, paying an annual rent equivalent to about twice that of a moderately priced apartment in Rome.[15] All of these developments promise to dramatically alter large fragments of Milan and other smaller cities, changing both the social and economic complexion of the inhabitants as well as the character of the cultural and service facilities they demand. They testify to the massive shift of industrial production and jobs to locations outside Italy and indeed outside Europe.

New spaces in urban areas have opened up for reasons other than factory closures. Residents of increasingly dense apartment blocks grew progressively intolerant of the smells, traffic and appearance of general markets, fruit and vegetable wholesale warehouses, and other comparable activities – slaughterhouses and *gasometri*. City administrators slowly began moving these businesses further away from urban areas, leaving hulking structures behind on large expanses of land in close proximity to central districts – terrific candidates for speculative building. Such is the case for the former general markets in Rome, which Rem Koolhaas is remodelling as a 'city' for young people. This innocuous sounding enterprise masks some less agreeable underlying motives. In the last decade of the twentieth century and the early twenty-first, Rome became a mecca for young people from throughout Europe; they congregate in the city centre at Campo dei Fiori and Piazza Navona, and nightspots in adjacent areas such as San Lorenzo and Testaccio, or a bit further away in the Balduina municipality, clustering noisily in squares and streets until the small hours of the morning – much to the annoyance of local residents. Setting up an area of clubs and music spots designed to attract young people also promises to contain them in an area less vulnerable to residents' complaints (this is a working-class district) and, perhaps more importantly, easily supervised and controlled by authorities.

Workers and the City in Turin '61

The years of Italy's economic miracle saw the country increasingly linked by new roads and the most technologically advanced means of communication of the time. Even where, as we have seen, large numbers of housing units in the major cities, not to mention rural areas, lacked running water or indoor baths and toilets, the fledgling Italian television network RAI began to spread into homes across the country. The single channel, RAI 1, began broadcasting in 1954, in the evenings only; it gave viewers no options, but the lack of competition made the same experience available to all and in fact contributed to forging links among Italians throughout the peninsula. The first hour, *Carosello*, consisted solely of commercials, followed by news and a range of variety programmes. As an increasing number of families acquired televisions, one could walk the streets on warm summer nights, when windows were open to catch evening breezes, and follow the same television programme from one end of a city to the other. The second state-owned channel only appeared in 1961 and the final one, RAI 3, in 1978.

The opening of new autostrade (motorways), especially in northern Italy and to a lesser degree in the southern regions, and the ready availability of Fiat's cheap automobiles, also helped link Italians to one another as families

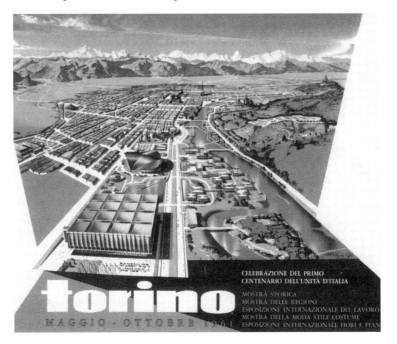

Poster for Turin '61, 1961.

began to travel and to holiday in areas previously difficult to reach by train. Although still expensive, telephones also became more accessible during the 1960s, facilitating links between Italians who toiled in the factories of northern Italy and the families they left behind in economically depressed areas of the country, including but not limited to the south. The great celebration of the nation's 100th anniversary in an international exhibition mounted in Turin, the nation's (brief) first capital city, feted all of these advances.[16] The choice of Turin as the location derived not only from this fact but from its primacy in the nation's industrial development, with firms such as Fiat and Olivetti headquartered in the region. Like other international expositions, the programme included displays mounted by other countries, by the United Nations, and even a 360° circular cinema for a film about Italy that Walt Disney produced and screened.

With pavilions dedicated to the country's history (strategically omitting the Fascist period), to the accomplishments and characteristics of its regions and to the world of work, the project earned the title Esposizione Internazionale del Lavoro ('International Labour Exposition') from the Geneva-based Bureau of International Expositions. Situated along the banks of the Po, Turin '61, as the enterprise was nicknamed, anticipated a range of structures, some temporary, some permanent, to house the individual exhibits. Two of the permanent ones stood out at the time, and still do today: the Palazzo del Lavoro by Pier Luigi Nervi and the Palazzo delle

Palazzo del Lavoro, view of column and radiating branches.

Mostre (Palace of Exhibits, also known as the Palazzo a Vela, or Sail Palace) by Annibale and Giorgio Rigotti, each of which graced the exposition with distinctive and strikingly different forms. In a pattern that persisted in most of the international events hosted by Italy – the 1960 Olympics, the 1990 World Cup, the celebrations for the millennium – buildings had to be erected quickly, all too often without much thought about how to design the permanent structures so that they could be used for other activities once the events concluded. (Such was the case for the new stadium built in Bari for the 1990 World Cup, which the city has recently been attempting to sell.) Contractors successfully completed their commissions on time, but the fates of the buildings after the exhibition belied the celebrations associated with their construction.

The enormous Palazzo a Vela (now Palavela, as it soon became popularly known), with its sweeping, curved concrete cupola tethered to the ground at three points like a sail or a billowing tent, housed an exhibit of Italian customs, fashions and habits, ranging from clothing by prominent designers such as Dior to examples of twentieth-century art and literature,

Gae Aulenti, Palavela,
Turin, 2005.

and a small, circular theatre. In counterpoint to the solid concrete roof,
glass walls enclosed the triangular exhibition space. Contemporary building technologies received exuberant emphasis in the plasticity of the arced,
reinforced concrete roof and offered what organizers hoped was the expression of an architecture projected into the future. By contrast, Nervi designed
the exhibition hall, the Palazzo del Lavoro, to become a centre for professional education at the conclusion of Turin '61. The 47,000-square-metre
rectangular pavilion clearly expresses its structural system: sandwiched
between two flat planes and rendered visible by floor-to-ceiling fenestration, soaring columns hold aloft steel beams that fan out across the roof.
Both of these enormous structures, in other words, emblematically testified
to one of the hallowed principles of modern movement architecture: that
is, the emphasis on structural clarity and transparency. Executed with
remarkable speed, the two buildings suffered a long, slow decline in the years
following Turin '61, and because of inadequate or non-existent maintenance, the Palazzo del Lavoro is prey to rust and the ravages of time.

Although occasionally used briefly for one or another purpose, both
structures almost instantly became white elephants situated on prominent
pieces of property near the Po river. The Palavela finally found a new use
in time for the 2006 Winter Olympics: in 2002 Gae Aulenti received the

commission to transform the Palavela into an ice rink for the games. The breathtaking abolition of any connotation of the building's structural coherence resulted from the retention of the sail-like cupola but the destruction of the ground floor's transparency by the insertion of a weird, chromatically vibrant structure bristling with beams, edges and cantilevers. It might have been better to demolish the structure altogether rather than perform such a morganatic marriage on it. In this as in many other cases, the designer had little choice in the matter, for the decision of what to do and, on the whole, how to do it, preceded Aulenti's selection as architect. Had she refused the commission she would have risked being blacklisted for future projects, and such blacklists are the product of politicians, not corporations or entrepreneurs.

Just as the 1851 Crystal Palace Exhibit in London ultimately signalled the decline of the British Empire, so this exhibit honouring the accomplishments of Italian industry and the skills of its workers almost coincided with the definitive end of the very configuration being celebrated. By the late 1960s, the power of organized labour was in decline, Italian industries were moving offshore – along with much of their capital and their profits – and the wrenching transformations of deindustrialization were well under way. Around this time, Aldo Rossi published *L'architettura della città* ('The Architecture of the City', 1966), a book on which he had worked for several years and that definitively challenged the monopoly of the modern movement on urban theory and architectural design. The modernist dictum that form follows function, Rossi argued, was a simplistic motto appropriate neither for buildings nor for cities, which are not the empty boxes celebrated by modernists but the result of the lives, histories and beliefs of myriad people, generation after generation. Street networks, building types and urban forms constructed in specific places participate in the morphological evolution of cities, and to understand them Rossi proposed not ready-made formulas but a mode of analysis that embraces history, individual stories, traditions and patterns of change. The complexity of actual life and real histories could not be short-circuited if architects were to produce successful buildings and urban designs. Even as Rossi's theories, built upon the radical questioning that characterized some of the architectural discourses of the 1950s, helped supplant those of the interwar period, larger changes under way in Italy and elsewhere in Europe gave renewed energy to his challenges and also helped shift the debate back into the arena of formalism. Student unrest, major public demonstrations, strikes, violent resistance to the centre-right coalition and opposition to the United States's war in Vietnam led, by the 1980s, to different political constellations and to quite different approaches to architecture.

chapter six

Old Cities, New Buildings and Architectural Discourse

Parallel with the erection of new buildings after Italian unification in 1860, a second, equally important development concerned the fate of the existing structures in the Italian countryside and cities. In some cases such edifices dated back to Roman antiquity, but the peninsula also bursts with churches, palaces, villas, houses, and industrial and rural buildings that span the period from the beginning of the Common Era. And that leaves out of the equation the ruins – of ancient, medieval, Renaissance and early modern Italy – whose value to researchers is often inestimable. In the first flush of construction at the end of the nineteenth century, and with little attention paid to their value for historians, politicians and officials summarily destroyed buildings and spaces of the past as part of the speculative fever that gripped particularly the sequence of cities that, however briefly, served as the nation's capital. As noted earlier, among the treasures to vanish in Rome were the Villa Ludovisi and the entire medieval and Renaissance district around the Capitoline Hill, levelled by the Savoy monarchy to make way for its dreadful self-promotional monument, while developers and property owners also ravaged historic districts in Florence, Milan and elsewhere.[1] No ideological or governmental brake existed to halt the destruction in the early phases, but eventually a greater sense of the value of ancient structures prevailed, even if only because of a shrewd recognition of their future value to tourism; unfortunately, this was not before huge swathes of the nation's heritage disappeared forever.[2] Even those that remained did not escape the heavy hands of well-meaning architects. A good example from the late nineteenth century is the restoration of the Castello Sforzesco in Milan in 1893 by Gaetano Moretti and Luigi Perrone. Scholars and architects determined that the castle's tower, though missing since the sixteenth century, ought to be replaced, and in the absence of historical documentation about the tower's appearance, they followed their imaginations – which is, in the end, what the new tower's form and chromatics are: fantasies. But this was not the only instance of invented histories. Two broad strands of historic restoration issues dominated following unification: one involved restorations that aimed to create a picturesque urban landscape,

Carlo Scarpa,
Castelvecchio, Verona,
1956–64.

and the other involved the reconfiguration of old buildings to accommodate new uses.

Arguments about how to handle old buildings were not unique to Italy, and indeed, the broad terms of the debate established in the nineteenth century in France and Britain still dominated discussions in Italy through much of the twentieth century. The French historian and avid restorer of monuments Eugène Viollet-le-Duc's articulation of the challenges posed by ancient structures represented one extreme of the debate.[3] For him, the task of the architect was to make a structure 'whole' again by completing or repairing elements in the original style of the building. While he acknowledged that this also required the restorer to approach each building cognizant of its particularities, Viollet-le-Duc was nonetheless prepared to remove later additions he considered inappropriate and to simulate missing parts so that the building would appear complete. John Ruskin, in dismissing this position as false and misleading, argued instead for allowing a structure to reveal its age and its history without resorting to drastic restoration efforts.[4] In late nineteenth-century Italy, the leading spokesman for restoration was Camillo Boito, who adopted a position that sat more or less between these two, and at times also supporting fully one or the other. When focusing on monuments, he too believed that one should return to the original, and that baroque additions in particular should be eliminated. At the time, the baroque was most unfashionable among intellectuals. For Boito, changes to a structure after its original construction were acceptable only if they themselves enjoyed artistic or historical importance – a judgment reserved to contemporary intellectuals. On the other hand, he argued that all layers of a structure's history were important and should be evident, and where new sections were to be added, they should not imitate the old and indeed should use different materials altogether. All work to be done on the restoration of a monument should be painstakingly documented in photographs, and Boito also called for respect for the entire panorama of buildings in the surrounding environment people laboriously constructed over time.[5] He lamented particularly the destruction of the district at the foot of the Capitoline Hill in Rome and the buildings demolished to make way for the Galleria Vittorio Emanuele II in Milan. Boito's views helped shape those of the subsequent generations of architects and restorers, even if they often lacked the political will, or power, to see them triumph.

Nonetheless, a series of laws promulgated in the early twentieth century aimed to preserve monuments of art and architecture from the mindless destruction so characteristic of the nineteenth century. The first law, in 1902, followed by two more in 1909 and 1913, allowed the state to extend protection to privately owned monuments. A law in 1912 included villas, parks and gardens among the growing list of cultural goods deemed of public interest, and another in 1922 added natural beauties and buildings of particular importance. Passing laws was no guarantee of wise choices, however; a series of new legal mechanisms to assess individual cases aimed to accomplish the goal of making appropriate and consistent decisions.

By the late 1920s, the Fascist government had founded an office to oversee antiquity and the arts within the Ministry of Public Instruction: the Ufficio delle Antichità e Belle Arti (Office of Antiquities and Fine Arts), with an appointed commission of experts impanelled to advise on individual projects, the Consiglio Superiore per le Antichità e le Belle Arti (Higher Council for Antiquities and Fine Arts). The Ministry summoned some of the most prominent scholars, archaeologists, architects and professors to serve on the council, including architects Gio Ponti, Vittorio Morpurgo, Enrico Del Debbio and, most importantly, Gustavo Giovannoni, one of the foremost advocates of preserving not only the most monumental structures from the nation's past, but also the built environment more generally, including minor and humble buildings.[6] Cities and other organizations submitted proposals to demolish, restore or renovate architecture and works of art from all eras; the Higher Council then bore the responsibility for determining whether the proposal met contemporary standards of preservation and whether the projected work should be approved, or modified in some fashion.

While a modern conception of the principles that should underlie restoration or renovation projects was still taking shape in the first decades of the twentieth century, some had already acquired a recognizably modern form, including the idea of retaining original features wherever possible. Specific examples illustrate how this worked – and failed to work – during the Fascist era. The early sixteenth-century unfinished palace in Ferrara, long known as the Palazzo Ludovico il Moro but actually Palazzo Costabili, underwent restoration in the early years of the century.[7] The building's Renaissance architect, Biagio Rossetti, had organized the first-floor arcade with paired bays, alternately closed and open, most likely for a combination of structural and aesthetic reasons. When the restoration effort got under way, Ferrara's dignitaries and scholarly and artistic elite passionately argued to open up the bays that had been closed for some 400 years. Beneath this conviction lay the desire to create what they believed to be a typical Renaissance courtyard, that of Tuscany, the Italian region broadly accepted as having the highest standard of Renaissance architecture: pairs of closed bays did not correspond to any known and accepted Renaissance solution, and the Ferrarese scholars planned to make the building look like a Renaissance palace, in part to attract tourism. An official from the regional body that oversaw medieval and modern arts rejected the proposal, noting that a restoration should not normally depart from the reality of the building and that the pairs of closed and open bays in the upper arcade were clearly original. Over the protests of the Ministry of Public Instruction, local elites nonetheless prevailed and succeeded in opening the closed bays. To compensate for having compromised the palace's structural integrity, an enormous amount of work and money went into shoring it up in subsequent decades.

In the early 1920s, the city of Ferrara also decided to restore the facade of the city's town hall to its late medieval splendour, fixing on the fourteenth century as the ideal moment in the building's past.[8] With neither written, archaeological nor visual materials to guide decisions about how to refashion what had become a nondescript frontage giving no hint of the building's past life, the Ferrarese committee of experts decided to erect a new tower, install crenellation on the roofline, add a new balcony and carve out windows and window treatments. The competition held to decide the exact character of the new elevation did not produce a winning entry, but the chairman of the jury subsequently devised and executed a compromise design that borrowed elements from several of the submissions. Once again, the council rejected the city's planned facade and reproached the city for its proposal, partly on the grounds that the additions and modifications monuments undergo over time should be retained rather than discarded, for they constituted pages in their lives and their histories. Nonetheless, once again, local interests prevailed, and 'renovation' endowed the facade with a clearly faked, generically 'medieval' appearance. Similar instances abounded across Italy, driven by a growing focus on mass tourism.[9]

A second impulse behind the abundant reconstructions was the desire to craft urban settings that met visitors' expectations, whose understanding of the historical topography of Italian cities had been honed by a resolutely Tuscan version of medieval and Renaissance architecture. To the example of the virtual re-fabrication of the Tuscan hill town of San Gimignano we can add the rehabilitation of the town of Gradara, in Marche, famed home of the star-crossed lovers Paolo and Francesca. The castle and medieval suburb of this little town near the Adriatic underwent such a fantastic and heavy-handed restoration by Giuseppe Visconti di Modrone (1923) that critics often call it the 'Italian Carcassonne'. Finally, such projects, whether the falsified reinvention of older structures or the construction of new 'historic' buildings, also spoke to the desire of many intellectuals and artists to provide the new country with a visible architectural identity, both for its past buildings and in its new ones.

In post-Second World War Italy, the most intriguing and thoughtful architect specializing in restoration was Francesco Minissi, who argued that the chief objective of a museum was to celebrate the work of art, and only

Ferrara Town Hall before reconstruction, early 20th century.

Ferrara Town Hall after reconstruction, c. 1924.

secondarily should it serve as a vehicle for diffusing cultural knowledge. For Minissi, a museum comprised not only the building and the artefacts on display therein but the entire setting; as he demonstrated in diverse projects, locating the museum in its relevant context fulfilled both objectives. As in the Museo Archeologico Regionale Paolo Orsi at Villa Landolina in Syracuse, Sicily, Minissi insisted on maintaining the objects in close proximity to the sites where archaeologists discovered them, thereby avoiding the inevitable shortcomings typical of most museums, where the artefacts are far removed from their origins. To this end, Minissi juxtaposed a modern structure against ancient remains, without denying any of their differences but also without yielding to empty sentimentality or historicizing rhetoric. At the Valle dei Templi (Valley of the Temples) near Agrigento, also by Minissi (1960–62), the entrance to the local archaeological museum consists of a long walk around the ancient Greek ruins, through a medieval courtyard and into an elegantly modern building – itself terminating in the remains of the medieval abbey of S. Nicola. The objects on display echo the adjacent archaeological sites as constant reminders to visitors of their original collocations and associations with the monumental temple architecture.

One of the most vexing restoration issues that challenged Italian cities and designers in the twentieth century was how to make use of historic buildings that no longer fulfilled their original purpose and hence needed to be adapted to new ones. Such was the case for the former papal stables (Scuderie del Quirinale) in Rome at the Palazzo del Quirinale, transformed into a museum by Gae Aulenti (1998–9), who earlier completed the successful adaptive reuse of the Gare d'Orsay train station (see chapter Eight) in Paris (1980–86). Since in most cases the commission asks the architect to refashion the old structure to serve new needs, the challenge confronting the designer is among the most difficult: how and when to intervene, and how much to do; how, in other words, to preserve the structure's essence while meeting what are today's often infinitely more complex and technologically sophisticated needs. Among Italy's most successful, and most interesting, instances of adaptive reuse of the mid-twentieth century was that by Carlo Scarpa at the city of Verona's fourteenth-century castle, Castelvecchio (1956–64). His challenge was to give the ancient castle new life as a museum; although heralded widely as the best example of restoration and preservation in Italy, this single work nonetheless barely holds its own against the impressive body of work produced by Minissi in Sicily and elsewhere.

Scarpa has come to be recognized as one of the most unusual of twentieth-century Italian architects despite having produced only a handful of projects, ranging from restoration to new construction; his work at Castelvecchio, at the Querini Stampalia library and gallery in Venice (1961–3) and the Brion Tomb at San Vito d'Altivole (1969–78) secured this well-deserved reputation, however irascible his temperament. Like many buildings in Italy, the castle of the Scaligeri family in Verona underwent numerous alterations throughout its life, including the insertion of military barracks in the courtyard during the Napoleonic era and a misguided restoration in the 1920s. In 1923 the museum's director, Antonio Avena, attempted to fabricate a coherent aesthetic experience, in part by adding a false medieval facade to the early nineteenth-century Napoleonic barracks. Scarpa uncovered evidence that during the fourteenth century, the local lord, Cangrande della Scala, fortified his family against an unhappy populace by closing one of the city's gates and surrounding the castle with a moat, subsequently filled in during the fourteenth and fifteenth centuries – all of which were unknown to historians. In the process of opening the gate and the moat, and hence the connection between the castle and the city, Scarpa also exposed a previously unknown escape hatch that Cangrande constructed for himself in the event he needed to flee the city. Scarpa orchestrated his reconstruction so as to reveal the structure's layered history, including leaving in place the authentic Gothic windows Avena had pillaged from destroyed Veronese houses and inserted into Castelvecchio, but Scarpa added a separate fenestration screen behind the earlier one, emphasizing the latter's fictional character. As in many of Scarpa's projects, there is no attempt to produce something fashionable, nor does any concern to adhere to a contemporary style or architectural language intrude. On the contrary, the highly particular decisions depended upon his close assessment of the problematics associated with the specific site and the challenges it presents. Much the same approach is evident in Giorgio Grassi's sensitive restoration and adaptation of an antique theatre in Spain.

The ancient Roman theatre of Sagunto in Valencia underwent over the centuries various efforts to shore it up, and in other cases attempts to restore it; the latter in particular often produced unhappy results. When the city decided to adapt the ancient structure to contemporary theatrical productions, it opened the question of what to do with the various and usually misguided actions of previous centuries. In his project for the renovation and reuse of the Sagunto theatre, Giorgio Grassi elected to

Giorgio Grassi,
Roman theatre of
Sagunto, Valencia,
Spain, 1985–92.

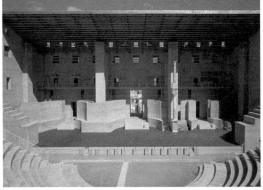

leave in place those relatively modest additions that did not constitute jarring contrasts with the original structure, and to complete the parts that were necessary for the Roman theatre to serve once again as such (1985–92). To meet its structural and formal needs, and taking his cues from the practices of ancient Roman engineers, Grassi intervened only minimally, preserving each piece of the structure but also developing the theatre type as necessary to accommodate modern theatre. To do so he first undertook a detailed study of the Roman theatre, its typology and functioning, and its resolution in other settings. Negotiating this delicate balance, Grassi acknowledged the centrality of the fixed architectural stage set, with its central and two lateral openings, to the Roman theatre, and the hierarchical symmetries it denoted; but large parts of the original stage were missing. Grassi elected to synthesize and abstract the primarily functional antique features on the lower elevation, but the real problem came with the architectural scheme for the upper part of the backdrop. Here he allowed the rear section to become visible – that is, the zone reserved for the mechanisms and artifices necessary to the theatre – and to substitute a purely decorative scheme for the ancient one, thereby illustrating precisely what was absent. The result is a singularly elegant, restrained design in which old and new abut and support one another, without resorting to fakery or false histories.

In more recent times, Italy adopted many of the principles of restoration and historic preservation generally supported in other western European nations, where an approach that gives priority to maintaining original features and recognizing the broad urban landscape in all of its layers and complexities dominates. One fine example in Rome of this trend is the Crypta Balbi museum erected on the site of, among other things, the ancient Teatro Balbi, where curators and architects artfully illustrated each of the site's many transformations over more than two millennia. Nonetheless, principles alone do not resolve vexing questions about how to determine the restoration or renovation of old buildings, in Italy or elsewhere. For example, many Italian scholars and archaeologists focused on and celebrated the importance of monumental buildings such as churches, palaces and oratories. But over the centuries, as cities expanded and grew increasingly dense, individual citizens often erected their own shops or apartments by attaching them, barnacle-like, to such monuments. One of the chief imperatives during the Fascist era was to liberate these monuments from the accretions of centuries, a fate that befell many picturesque structures that had the misfortune to have been constructed adjacent to, or over, a significant building. The most widely publicized and debated cases of the period were the projects that cleared the Roman Forum (and then covered large parts of it up again with roads) and the area around the tomb of Augustus adjacent to the Tiber.[10] To magnify the greatness of the Roman emperor, Mussolini ordered several blocks of early modern buildings cleared out and replaced by a grand new piazza designed by Vittorio Ballio Morpurgo; the scheme also entailed moving the Ara Pacis (Altar of Peace) from its original, ancient location (about 30 metres west of via del Corso and north of the column of Marcus Aurelius in Piazza Colonna) to a site near the Tiber, west of the mausoleum of Augustus (1937–40). The new piazza, refashioned in grandiose style, highlighted Augustus' tomb and the altar that celebrated the Pax Romana Augustus claimed to have brought to the empire. This extraordinary monument sat enclosed in a simple glazed structure with classicizing piers on the corners, and Ballio Morpurgo raised the Ara Pacis on a plinth that left the altar visible to passers-by, while inside, he fashioned a ramp leading up to the famous frieze, permitting visitors a close and unobstructed view.

Over time, however, humidity and pollution damage to the glass box and the altar itself necessitated some new solution. In 1995, Rome's then mayor, Francesco Rutelli (subsequently Minister of Cultural Goods and Activities), decided to take matters into his own hands – rarely a salutary

Museo Balbi, Rome, 1981–2000.

Richard Meier, building for Ara Pacis, Rome, 2006, with exhibition of fashion designs by Valentino, with the Ara Pacis to the left.

development for the well-being of antiquities, since politicians are usually concerned primarily with their own image, such was the case here. Rutelli elected not to hold a competition. Instead, he selected an architect to create a new casing for the Ara Pacis; he chose the American architect Richard Meier, best known for his design of the Getty Center in Brentwood, California. Meier's penchant for white surfaces, only moderated since his design of the Getty Center with the occasional inflection of travertine, appeared an unlikely match for the elegant ancient Roman marble altar. And it was. The structure is beset with myriad problems. With its simple lines and transparency, the previous housing highlighted the altar, the ramp gave good visual access to the frieze and the glazing made it visible to passers-by. Meier's structure quite simply dwarfs the Ara Pacis and, in the absence of anything like the ramp in the old one, the frieze is far more distant and less visible, and furthermore, can now only be seen at an awkward angle. It is, in effect, hostage to Meier's uncompromising modernism. Perhaps the most striking of the many flaws in this structure is that during much of the year, the afternoon sun piercing the grid of glazed windows with their projecting brise-soleil panels reflects on the altar itself, generating an annoying optical effect of zebra-like stripes that also impede a clear view of the altar, a problem found in other Meier projects as well. Unfortunately, image and architectural signature – Meier indeed scrawled his name triumphantly on a travertine slab near the entrance, something even Michelangelo did not hazard at St Peter's dome – trumped function and simplicity.

No longer a simple case for the extraordinary Augustan altar, the structure was now a free-standing building in its own right, destined to function as a small museum with its own auditorium. This was hardly what Rome needed – another museum. But city officials rapidly found a use for it. During the summer of 2007, Valentino (Garavini) exhibited his couture dreses from his 45-year career in the building. With the gowns draped on mannequins that looked like leftovers from Cold War-era East Germany, rows of the giraffe-necked creatures framed and fatally impeded a view of the altar itself in an awesome crescendo of appalling tastelessness. While Valentino acquired status by proximity to the altar, even he scorned the design. In the documentary *Valentino: The Last Emperor* (2009), Valentino remarked of Meier's building, 'You feel as if you are in Macy's department store.'

A second and equally important set of concerns involves the urban placement of Meier's building. Where once the Porta di Ripetta's gracefully curving stairs led languidly into the heart of the city, the early twentieth-century concrete embankments of the Lungotevere indifferently channel traffic along the riverside. Now Meier's steel-and-glass behemoth further blocks vistas into and out of this historic section of Rome. The bright white walls and starkly modern features jar strikingly with the other structures nearby, especially the lovely churches of San Rocco and San Gerolamo, which date from the early modern period; only in spring and summer, when the trees lining the Tiber are in full leaf, does the structure recede into the background, at least from across the river. Karl Friedrich Schinkel's early nineteenth-century urban configuration of Museum Island in the Spree offers an instructive comparison: he did not design the foliage he adroitly deployed along the river in Berlin to obscure the buildings on the island but to offer a carefully calibrated sequence of vistas of his impressive Altes Museum and the adjoining customs facilities. Would that so noble a purpose and elegantly timeless a building lay behind the trees planted along this stretch of the Tiber.

In many ways, the new Ara Pacis encapsulates the broader shifts in Italian architecture, politics and culture that took place in the decades after the 1970s. After the season of student unrest beginning in 1968; the so-called *anni di piombo* (Years of Lead) of the 1970s and the urban rebellion of the Red Brigades; the assassination of the Christian Democrat politician Aldo Moro; the deceptive destabilization programmes engineered by right-wing secret police with the covert support of the u.s. Central Intelligence Agency (CIA); and the first great gasoline crisis, the 1980s ushered in a period of economic expansion and increased wealth and education for wider segments of the population. The historically small Partito Socialista Italiano (PSI, Socialist Party) found itself wielding inordinately large amounts of power in Italy's parliamentary democracy. In a country with two large, but not majority, parties, and many smaller ones, governments could only be formed of coalitions, and the PSI held the balance for more than a decade. Led by Bettino Craxi, party membership grew exponentially, most adherents attracted by the seemingly endless cascade of money (largely bribes from industrialists and business interests) that flowed through party coffers. Even as deindustrialization eviscerated Italy's factories, small businesses and professionals, especially in construction, expanded and flourished. The information, service, fashion and design industries, but especially tourism, became the country's motors. The role and purpose of architecture likewise underwent a change: housing proliferated as before, but the dominance of tourism led to a second wave of restorations, modifications and transformations of existing but poorly maintained historic buildings. In the early post-unification decades, architects and politicians had worried about what an Italian architecture could be; in the decades following the late 1970s, they instead asked how Italian designs could be threaded into an international scene composed of architectural stars and their spectacular buildings. Indifferent to its setting or local architectural traditions, Meier's design slots nicely into the ranks of the global elite, thereby also rendering the Ara Pacis the venue of choice for brand-name fashion giants: first Valentino's gowns, then Bulgari's jewellery.

If leaving such choices of buildings and architects to a politician is unwise, what about holding competitions? In fact, Italy conducts many, with results often no less infelicitous.

The Complications of Competitions

In the early autumn of 1996, Joe McGinniss, author of the best-selling true crime novels *Fatal Vision* and *Blind Faith*, travelled to a small town of 5,000 people called Castel di Sangro, in the Abruzzo region, to follow the seemingly miraculous success of the village's football team. In the space of one short season, the team had made an unimaginable, phoenix-like leap from the lowest rank of football (Terza Categoria, the lowest of ten possible grades) to Serie B – one level below the top. A recently converted football freak, McGinniss followed the team up close throughout the year, coming to know its players and owners, and local townspeople. By the last couple of games of the season, and against all odds, the team had again clinched its Serie B berth; delighted, McGinniss prepared to attend the final game, against Bari. 'Don't go', one of the players told him; 'Do yourself a favour and just don't go.' Puzzled, McGinniss pressed the players to tell him why he should skip the appointment. Only when he overheard the players clarifying the scheme for the game – how and when they should score, and when and how often they should let Bari score – did he realize that having secured their goal, they were now assuring the Bari team of its place in

Serie A. When McGinniss protested to the players, they accused him of being naive; one player explained:

> Some teams that badly need points pay for them. Others to whom the points mean nothing accept. And it is not always only a matter of money. It can be a favour requested or a favour repaid between the presidents of the *Società* [clubs]. It can be many things. In Italy it is called *il sistema*, and for someone who has not grown up with it, I am sure it can seem very complex.

To which McGinniss responded, 'It doesn't seem complex. It just seems crooked.'[11] This has ended up being a more fitting opening to a discussion of architectural competitions than I originally anticipated – competitions whose murky contours resemble those of the football league, have only occasionally been clarified or reversed, and rarely in public.

One example can stand for many. In 1985, as Chair of the second Architecture Biennale in Venice, Aldo Rossi organized an international competition for ideas for ten different sites in Venice and the Veneto region.[12] With the promise of winning one of ten first-place awards and having their project exhibited in a prestigious venue, hundreds of entries from professionals, students and even artists from around the world flooded into Venice. The jury met for a week in April and undertook a preliminary review of the submissions to select about 500 of the 1,500 submissions for exhibition. The second stage of the jury process was slated for July, after the show had been mounted but prior to the official opening. The full jury conducted a preliminary review in April, and nine members of the jury convened only shortly before the official opening for the second and final round, with but two hours available for discussion. Chair Claudio D'Amato opened the session with the announcement that five of the ten awards should go to Roman architects, the logic being that Paolo Portoghesi was President of the Venice Biennale, and from Rome, hence his compatriots should receive awards. Ultimately, the jury rounded up the usual suspects – among them Peter Eisenman, Daniel Libeskind, Raimond Abraham and Robert Venturi – to receive first-place awards, along with three Romans selected by D'Amato, with only the last two going to relative unknowns.

So-called competitions for university posts tend to end with results that the term 'surprising' does not begin to capture: wives, children and partners of deans and faculty members win university posts with one or two thin publications. Historians and architects routinely apply for university posts whose results the faculty decides even before the advertisement appears. By the time the *Gazzetta* officially announces a job and professors choose a committee from the university faculty to select the winner, the result in nearly all cases is a foregone conclusion. Committee members essentially agree to rotate the selection of one another's preferred candidates in current and future competitions. Individual members in turn choose from among former graduate students (when family members are not available), often after years of unpaid service as assistants, to receive the post. Altogether too often, this selection does not depend primarily upon the talent, skill and accomplishments of the candidate, but the years of loyal, uncomplaining service they have given the professor. As a device for maintaining the hegemony of the bourgeoisie in university posts, the system excels. Obviously, only those with family money can afford to donate years of free service on the promise of an undefined future post with remuneration. Every university graduate knows this system. The task of unpaid assistants is to help the professor by teaching classes, conducting research and at times ghostwriting books to advance the latter's career. Foreign scholars marvel at the dozens of books Italian academics publish; this is how many do it. Aspiring faculty members are regularly well past their 40th and even 50th birthdays before their turns arrive to win a paid position at the university. To be sure, not every academic appointment is without merit: many faculty members are accomplished scholars and teachers, including some of those who acquired their posts through family or other personal connections. But how many others of comparable or even superior qualifications never managed to enter the system at all because they lacked such connections, or refused or could not afford – that is, lacked the financial means – to carry some professor's bag, unpaid, for decades?

It is worth noting that the current generation of academics did not invent this system; as Paolo Nicoloso demonstrated recently and at some length, the system was already deeply entrenched during the Fascist era.[13] Not surprisingly, the end of the Second World War did not terminate it; in fact, it continued largely undisturbed through the end of the century and beyond, to the present day.

One might shrug off such concerns by dismissing it as a type of informal welfare system for intellectuals, but the consequences of such rigged competitions are far-reaching. Through such university appointments architects gain the stature and credentials necessary to exert power over competitions for buildings and urban plans, or to become beneficiaries of such competitions, as well as to acquire positions as critics in the nation's magazines and newspapers. Look no further than the world of competitions and culture of favours at all levels in Italy to explain the degradation of the countryside and urban peripheries. In Italy, connections are determinative, and talent and ability only count if a senior professor decides that they do and is prepared to enter the fray on behalf of the candidate.

It is something of a miracle that young architects in Italy enter competitions at all, given the tight network of connections that usually operates to ensure victories. But the situation is even more shadowy than it appears, for the playing field is far from level in other respects. Professors who enter competitions draft putatively legal 'agreements' with their universities to pay meagre sums to architecture students, to produce models for the professors' competition entries. Small architecture offices whose principals do not have university posts do not have access to the same 'benefits' as those with university posts; they are left to pay market rates for their models, including labour costs, which unscrupulous university professors typically receive free because they can coerce the work from their students. To be sure, the situation is considerably worse in the fields of medicine, law and of notary publics (where the financial stakes are significantly greater). A recent investigation by one of the weekly news magazines documented the wives, sons, daughters, lovers and other relatives who fill the faculties of medicine and law in particular. Despite having identified corrupt contests and outrageous nepotism, even pinpointing specific competitions and individuals, the country's prosecutors have had little luck in bringing action against these crimes, and even when successful they are unable to pry the offending parties out of their jobs, much less into jail.[14] Small wonder that so many Italians from all disciplines flee elsewhere in the world to make their fortunes.

After its early prominence in the post-war period, Italian cinema suffered from some of the same ills as did architecture. With a few notable exceptions, Cinecittà churned out films written, produced and starred in by individuals with great political connections but considerably less talent, a practice that quickly transferred to the television networks, where the same individuals host the same television variety shows (or the San Remo Festival) that they did 40 years ago. Some bright lights remained, however; Federico Fellini directed his own quixotic and critically acclaimed films through the 1980s, including *La dolce vita* (1960), his critique of the growing hedonistic culture of the post-war Italian bourgeoisie, with the drifting and self-indulgent journalist (Marcello Mastroianni) apparently oblivious to the depthlessness of a life lived consumed by ephemeral pleasures. Until his death in 1975, Pier Paolo Pasolini challenged the tedious pabulum the industry regurgitated with his own provocative vision of Italy, Christianity, contemporary urbanism and human relationships in films that almost inevitably aroused vociferous debate and often censorship. One of a dwindling number of public intellectuals, Pasolini published poetry and novels and wrote, directed and produced many films and documentaries. His first film (with another young and promising director, Bernardo Bertolucci), *Accattone* (1961), chronicled the aimlessness of young men who were the dubious beneficiaries of the growing post-war prosperity. In later films and in his novels, he told of the *borgate* dwellers inhabiting the shanty towns on the periphery of so many Italian cities, but instead of condemning their squalor he recognized them as representing the extraordinary possibilities that being on the margins creates, a radical openness in violent contrast with Italy's consumerist, post-economic miracle society. Elsewhere, as in *Teorama* (1968), he exposed an alienated bourgeoisie crumbling as it comes face to face with authenticity for the first time.

Rebuilding La Fenice

In 1991, a fire destroyed the opera house in Bari, the Petruzzelli theatre. Subsequent investigation laid the blame on a Mafia don, who allegedly bribed the manager to award him lucrative reconstruction contracts before commissioning the fire; but after nineteen years and three criminal trials, as of this writing there has been no conviction. On 29 January 1996, the venerable Venetian opera house La Fenice (The Phoenix), then undergoing renovation and retrofitting, also went up in flames. By the following morning, only the facade and the building's shell were standing – fire had gutted the entire interior. Initially officials deemed the fire an accident, and charges were filed against all those responsible for the chaotic and dangerous conditions in the opera house, starting with Massimo Cacciari, philosopher and professor at the IAUV University of Venice and then-mayor of the city. Within a few months, however, officials designated arson as the cause, and a year and a half later charged two electricians with having set the fire to avoid paying a fine for being behind schedule with their electrical work for the renovation.

The unofficial word, however, was that other obscure persons were responsible for the arson. Who might they have been: organized crime figures? In fact, some years earlier a local Mafioso recounted to the police that he had once planned to torch La Fenice. Or was it the owners of large construction companies, who expected to get rich on the reconstruction? Or was it politicians who could siphon off bribes from the huge sums of money expected to cascade into the city to pay for the refurbishment? All of these theories floated around Venice and the hinterland in the fire's succeeding months and years. No individual names ever emerged officially, but conspiracy theories abounded. In Italy, as in Roman Polanski's film *Chinatown* (1974), things are not always as they seem. Just one example: politicians attributed a series of high-profile bombings and terrorist activities during the 1960s and 1970s, including one in Trieste in 1972, to leftist groups such as the Red Brigades. After a lengthy, decades-long investigation, it turns out that they were instead the work of a group within the

Italian secret police, a covert paramilitary outfit (Gladio) set up by the U.S. Central Intelligence Agency in 1956 in Italy and elsewhere and entrusted with making preparations for a potential invasion from communist Russia. However Gladio did more than that: its operatives had orders to engage in domestic subversive activities to delegitimize the left; and they were also to state coup-d'états whenever the threat from the left grew to sufficient size (in fact, there were three such attempted coups d'état in Italy, in 1964, 1969 and 1973. Such cases feed the propensity of Italians to see conspiracies everywhere.

Following the fire, Mayor Massimo Cacciari quickly announced that the Fenice would be rebuilt in two years, '*com'era, dov'era*' ('as it was, where it was'). When the city announced the competition to reconstruct the theatre on 2 September 1996, the brief called for construction companies and the architects with whom they associated to submit their qualifications by 11 October, following which the commission would invite ten teams to participate by 20 November.[15] The choice of architect and contractor would not issue from an open competition. As the owner of the building, the city of Venice elected to conduct the selection process by identifying major building companies to compete for the jobs; these firms in turn were to choose architects with whom to work. After extending the invitations to the ten teams to submit bids and projects for the reconstruction, six actually did so: Impregilo (Fiat), with Gae Aulenti and the Venetian architect Antonio Foscari (owner of Villa Foscari, also known as La Malcontenta, a villa designed by Andrea Palladio in the sixteenth century); Holzmann-Romagnoli (Germany), with Aldo Rossi in collaboration with Francesco da Mosto; Carena (Genova), with Gino Valle; Consorzio Cooperativa Costruzioni (Bologna), with Carlo Aymonino; Mabetex (Lugano), with Ignazio and Jacopo Gardella; and Ferrovial (Madrid), with Studio Salvador Pérez Arroyo and Eva Hurtado.

The appointment of the jury, impanelled by the La Fenice reconstruction committee chaired by the city prefect, Giovanni Troiani, lagged behind the competition by several months; Troiani did not assemble it until spring of 1997.[16] The first problem arose when the jury officially opened the bids: it promptly eliminated Ferrovial because of a missing anti-Mafia document (a declaration by contractors and subs that they have no organized crime connections) from one of their subcontractors. Furious, the Spanish team claimed that in fact they had included it as an attachment to their entry but, the team charged, it evidently had been removed sometime after the bid was opened. Although the team filed an administrative protest, they lost. Now only five teams remained.

The number of points that each team accrued in four (un-weighted) categories was the basis upon which the jury would decide the winner of

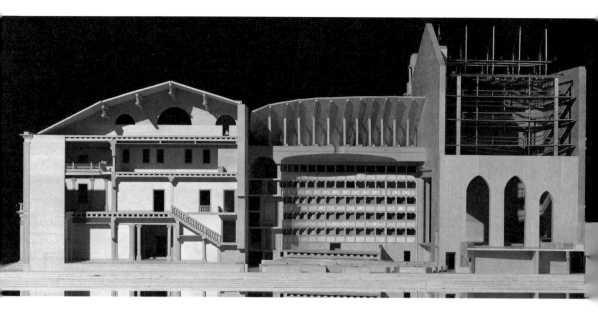

Aldo Rossi, La Fenice
opera house, 1997,
Venice, model
section.

the competition: length of time anticipated to complete construction; construction cost; design and technical quality; maintenance and use costs. When the jury announced its decision on 2 June 1997, they had awarded the points as follows: Aulenti/Impregilo, 70.1; Rossi/Holzmann-Romagnoli, 67.5; Valle/Carena, 62.9; Aymonino/Consorzio Cooperativa Costruzioni, 47.9; Gardella/Mabetex, 10.7. The leftist mayor Cacciari lauded the result, noting that the top two projects were superior to the others but that all were of high quality, and so did the president of Impregilo, Franco Carraro, who enthused that his firm had participated out of passion for Venice and professional prestige.

As Aldo Rossi remarked, adjudicating a competition on the basis of these categories might be appropriate for a highway construction project, but it was clearly a questionable mechanism for determining who would reconstruct a major public building as in the case of La Fenice, which is also a work of art. Nonetheless, so the city of Venice, through Mayor Cacciari, determined what were the appropriate criteria. In fact, Rossi's concern highlighted problems with the results of the competition: Aulenti received more points than he did only in the categories of time (she anticipated finishing two months earlier) and cost (her bid was about €4 million less). Rossi received the highest scores for technical and artistic quality, and for maintenance and use costs over time – categories arguably more important than the other two. When Rossi's collaborator Francesco da Mosto reviewed the competition entries a couple of days after the winner was announced, he made a startling discovery: Aulenti had neither designed nor estimated costs and time for about 1,500 cubic metres on the south wing. Although the competition documents included this wing, most of the structure was privately owned and the owners were recalcitrant about selling. The city had already initiated procedures to purchase that wing in the spring of 1996, but negotiations were still under way at the time of the competition. A few days later, on 30 June 1997, the Holzmann group filed an administrative lawsuit, charging that the jury should have eliminated the Aulenti project because it did not include all of the required design elements, a far stronger reason to dismiss her project than the absence of one minor document, as in the Spanish submission. Indeed, Holzmann's lawyers argued, Aulenti failed to design the entire southern wing; this alone accounted for the lower cost and shorter estimated time frame for her project, because Aulenti's design omitted approximately 1,500 cubic metres of construction costs and time. How could this be? How could a proposal so defective and with such fundamental lacunae win?

In fact, early in the competition Valle's team notified the prefect Troiani about a lack of clarity in the competition rules about the south wing: a red line was traced around some but not all of the floors of the structure on the wing. Troiani in turn notified all the teams that they were to include this wing in their designs, making clear that he meant 'from the ground to the roof'. Five of the six teams designed the entire wing, including the

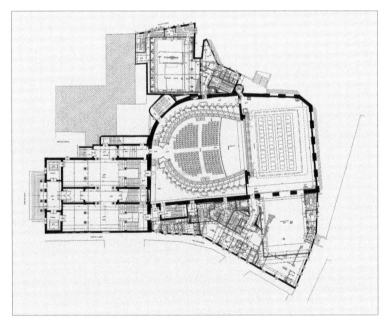

Aldo Rossi, La Fenice opera house, ground floor plan.

floors not yet owned by the city. Only the Aulenti team ignored it. Rossi's decision for this space was particularly brilliant and unique. Instead of simply replacing existing offices as the other teams did, he decided to move the rehearsal hall from the main building to the ground floor of this wing, and to design it so that an entire orchestra could rehearse there. It could also host chamber music recitals or even be used for small conferences, with seating for 164 people. Acoustically isolated and with a separate entrance, it could even be in use for musical performances at the same time that there was a performance at La Fenice without disturbing events in either setting, thereby increasing both capacity and sorely needed income for the beleaguered opera company.

Rossi had already achieved considerable renown for the reconstruction of another theatre, Carlo Felice, in Genoa, some fifteen years earlier. He entered the La Fenice competition knowing, as virtually everyone in Venice and in the architectural community did, that unnamed figures had already selected Aulenti to win the competition. Impregilo is the construction arm of Fiat, the automobile company owned by Gianni Agnelli, then one of Italy's wealthiest and most famous men and a permanent member of the Italian Senate. A decade earlier, Agnelli and Impregilo renovated the Palazzo Grassi in Venice, with Aulenti as architect. Agnelli had a personal interest in the city, in the competition and in architecture; indeed he was one of the permanent members of the Pritzker Prize jury until his death in 2003. There were well-informed rumours to the effect that Agnelli's team would win, and in fact, by some reports, one of the jurors allegedly sought to change the verdict during deliberations but was rebuffed because the decision to go with the Agnelli conglomerate had been made at a much

Aldo Rossi, interior, La Fenice opera house, 2004, Grand Room, Sale Apollinee.

Arassociati, Sala Rossi, La Fenice opera house, 2004, used for chamber music and as a rehearsal room.

higher level. Additionally, artisans and other firms in the Veneto were reportedly already at work producing models for sculptural and other details for Aulenti the summer before the competition was even announced. Aulenti's technical report attached to the design was sketchy by comparison with those of the other teams, especially Rossi's, and she presented nothing like the expensive wooden model, the watercolours or the elaborate details that Rossi and, to a considerable degree, Valle, included as part of their projects. With the fix in, the extra work and expense were obviously not necessary; in Italy, such decisions are rarely, if ever, subverted by compliant, hand-picked juries, let alone by administrative judicial bodies.

Left up to Rossi, the matter would have ended there, for Aulenti was also a friend with whom he had worked on *Casabella-Continuità* in the 1950s and 1960s and so he would never have initiated legal proceedings, but Holzmann, a German firm unaccustomed to such nonsense, was unwilling to drop the matter and filed an administrative lawsuit. In the meantime, Aulenti's construction yard got under way and work began on the foundations. On 31 July 1997, the regional administrative jury (Tribunale Amministrativo Regionale, TAR), chaired by Judge Gaetano Trotto, spurned Holzmann's claim in a sentence deposited on 22 October 1997. Undaunted, Holzmann crafted an appeal directly to the Consiglio di Stato (State Council). To everyone's surprise, on 10 February 1998 the council handed down a final decision overturning the TAR's verdict, withdrawing the commission from Aulenti and handing it to Rossi's team. The

Giovanni Michelucci, Nello Baroni, Pier Nicolo Berardi, Italo Gamberini, Sarre Guarnieri and Leonardo Lusanna, Santa Maria Novella Railway Station, Florence, 1933.

competition rules, and the clarification given by the prefect in regard to the south wing in January 1997, the council affirmed, were utterly clear, and of the five teams, only Aulenti's had failed to complete that part of the competition. The Consiglio rejected the TAR's claim that the motto '*com'era, dov'era*' indicated that the wing need not be designed because it had not previously been part of La Fenice. The judgment affirmed that the opera house could never have been reconstructed just as it was, and anyway, such a motto, however engaging and popular, had no legal standing. Aulenti's project should indeed have been disqualified. The action by the state council overturning the TAR's decision and disrupting the well-oiled machine by which such competitions are decided was not unheard of – but it was certainly rare. The decision stunned everyone involved: Impregilo, Aulenti, Mayor Cacciari and the members of the original jury. Unfortunately, Rossi died in September 1997 of injuries suffered in an automobile accident a month earlier, so did not live to enjoy the victory.

The problems were now multiple – Aulenti's foundation did not match that of Rossi's project, and now Rossi was not around to adjust it; Impregilo had spent several million euros already – who would pay for that? Da Mosto and Rossi's studio, still staffed by people who had worked for him for as long as twenty years (the firm continued under a new name, Arassociati), picked up the reins and saw the project through to completion in December 2003. They accomplished a remarkable feat, for La Fenice came out a spectacular success. The street elevations corresponded to the old ones, the brilliantly illuminated foyer returned in a crisper version, the stage apparatus now included all of the modern requirements for complicated scenographic displays, and the auditorium echoed the original one, with velvets, gilding, figures and festoons richly covering the surfaces and a brilliant glass chandelier suspended above the *platea* (auditorium). With remarkable sensitivity, Arassociati did not conceal the interface of new floors with parts that had been salvaged, but allowed it to remain visible, as a subtle reminder of how today's building came into being. The design included the introduction of state-of-the-art technology, but what meets the eyes and ears of the spectator recalls the spirit, and best of all the acoustics, of the pre-fire theatre.

The decision of the Consiglio di Stato affirmed the corruption of the competition process and indeed of the earlier effort to achieve justice via administrative appeals. It bears remembering that the jury disqualified the Ferroval project because of an absent letter clearing a subcontractor of Mafia connections, but ignored the missing 1,500 cubic metres in Aulenti's submission. Justice prevailed in the end, but at great cost to everyone involved, in both time and money. Alas, such usurpations of fairness and equity in competitions happen in places other than Italy, but rarely with such exquisite visibility.

Over several years one website, www.Arcaso.it, made a practice of exposing the corrosive practices in the architectural profession and academy

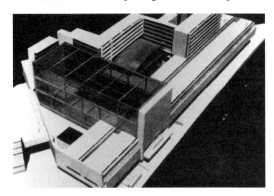

Terragni Group, Solution A, Fascist party headquarters competition, Rome, 1933.

E. de. Debbio, A. Foschini, V. Ballio Morpurgo, Ministero degli Esteri, also known as the Farnesina, Rome, 1939.

with respect to competitions and university appointments; in the spring of 2006 it disappeared, perhaps shut down because it had hit far too close to home. The many honest individuals disgusted by the deeply corrupt processes whereby competitions for all types of jobs, especially university posts, are awarded, also, it appears, have little ability to change them; those who protest are blackballed and many leave to find academic or architectural work elsewhere because the doors are closed in Italy.

The phoenix rose in Venice, but she rose alone; the case of La Fenice offered hope for the most egregious cases, but that the lawsuit was initiated by a German firm is a reminder that an Italian who bucks the system risks being permanently excluded. Competitions have often been contested in Italy, but earlier in the twentieth century the debates usually concerned differences over approaches to inserting new buildings into historically dense urban tissues, the appropriateness of a particular style in a specific setting or of one style versus another. Emblematic was the uproar over the competition for the new rail station in Florence in 1933. Critics of the winning, Rationalist design bitterly opposed placing what they considered a stridently modern structure effectively in the face of the distinguished fifteenth-century church of Santa Maria Novella, with its facade designed in part by Leon Battista Alberti, author of the first Renaissance treatise on architecture.[17] While time has vindicated the jury's decision in this case, it should not obscure the equally corrupt system that guaranteed the Rationalist victory.[18]

Earlier in the century, an acrimonious battle erupted over the plans of the Fascist Party to erect a new national headquarters building on part of the Fori Imperiali in Rome, between Trajan's market, the forum of Augustus and the Vittoriano.[19] If anything, this site was even more hallowed than that of Santa Maria Novella and most importantly, archaeologists swung into action to oppose the project. Rationalist architects – and subsequent historians – decried the decision to award the competition to a design described as only modestly modern, rather than to a flagship steel-and-glass structure such as the one submitted by a group headed by Giuseppe Terragni. In the end, the polemics led to a change in site not once but twice, until a pedestrian version of the building was erected on the northern perimeter of the city. In retrospect, revoking the decision to build on the Forum was a wise choice, for none of the prominent designs, regardless of style, could have compensated for the loss to the nation's cultural patrimony. Debates, in short, concerned genuine conflicts over how new structures should be inserted into urban fabrics, even if in many cases the personal power of figures such as Marcello Piacentini and Alberto Calza-Bini decided the competitions' outcomes.

From the 1950s through the 1980s, many of the architectural debates constituted ideological conflicts between right, left, and centre political positions, usually reflecting the interests of the country's many political parties, with each endowing its own architect-friends with projects. The ideological arguments that accompanied Corviale, La Martella and most public housing projects are cases in point. The dismal condition of many of these projects testifies as much to the designers' absorption in ideological clashes as it does to the lamentably poor construction that resulted from the state-mandated reliance on low-bid competitions.

A mirror image of this situation is an organization created in the late 1990s known as AIDA (Agenzia Italiana d'Architettura), a business lobby. This organization brings together a combine of architects, magazines (*Area*, *Materia*), construction, and materials and interiors companies, who then act as a body to promote one another. The companies advertise their products in the magazines, using designs produced by the offices that are part of AIDA, and in turn the magazines publish buildings by the architects, who recommend that their clients use the products of member firms.[20] I need hardly add that no whiff of criticism or critical inquiry rustles the highly polished pages of their publications – certainly not any criticism of the work or products of their members – nor do those outside of the consortium easily find a venue for their projects therein. The only restraint on AIDA is the existence of older, looser but arguably better-connected groups.

Individual critics in newspapers, books and magazines routinely denounce such manipulations of power and influence, but have often singled out architects as the cause of the problems rather than seeing architects as the last link in a long chain of abuses, visible emblems of a deeply compromised system that extends from the halls of parliament to the built environment, football and the world of criticism itself. Anyone who has participated in an architectural conference or written for an Italian publication knows that conflicting parties draw battle lines, and accepting the invitation of a representative from one side could be a declaration of war against the competing forces. Earlier in the twentieth century, at a time when both architects and critics came from the ranks of the prosperous urban bourgeoisie, this practice was somewhat attenuated. During the Fascist period, the different groups were not aligned with political parties – there was after all but one; instead they jostled to provide the ideal modern architectural image for the new state. Edoardo Persico and Giuseppe Pagano in *Casabella*, Marcello Piacentini in *L'architettura* and Gio Ponti in *Domus* published the work of architects representing different points of view, to be sure, with varied degrees of tolerance. Least tolerant were the most radical Rationalists (Pagano) and traditionalists (Ugo Ojetti). In the second half of the century, when political parties dominated public life again, this openness tended to diminish. Nonetheless, throughout the 1950s and 1960s, publications such as *Casabella*, *Domus* and *L'architettura* maintained lively debates over the fate of architecture and cities in the rapidly modernizing country.

Respected critics with weekly columns in news magazines, such as Bruno Zevi, played a large role in bringing architecture and matters associated with it to a wider public audience, but they were also deeply partisan agitators whose position on any competition or issue was almost always

Franco Minissi,
Museo Archeologico,
Agrigento, with
Telamon to the
right, 1960–62,
and a detail of
interior revetment.

a foregone conclusion. Criticism in general is understood less as critical analysis, even if impassioned, than as part of the system of patronage and partisanship, for which the only available critical mode is that of frontal assault, attacking and destroying work that falls outside one's own circle – without impinging on the bankrupt system that sustains it. For matters of style this approach is especially pointless, since so much depends upon taste. Arguments of substance, however, such as those involving environmental, social, political, ethical or even functional issues, are a different matter. Nonetheless, it is worth noting that by contrast with most Italian architectural magazines today, Zevi published opposing viewpoints in the pages of his monthly magazine, *L'architettura: Cronaca e storia*.

Not incidentally, serving as a public critic is often also a mechanism for enormous self-enrichment and self-aggrandizement. Once a critic gains a foothold in a weekly publication, his power (for they are in fact all men)

210

grows exponentially. Such has been the case with the art and architecture critic Vittorio Sgarbi, who published *Un paese sfigurato* ['A Disfigured Country'] in 2003.[21] Much as in his other publications, he took aim and fired at only the most visible of targets – the architects – while ignoring the system of political favours and corruption of which architects are but one of the components and for which he, as a former member of the Chamber of Deputies, bore a far greater responsibility. (He had already staked out his turf many years earlier when, as a television commentator during the eruption of the Mount Etna volcano in Sicily in the early 1990s that threatened homes along the flanks of the mountain, he applauded the prospect that houses he deemed ugly would be destroyed by the lava flow.) It was easy for Sgarbi to choose buildings to disparage and with which to castigate the architectural profession in *Un paese sfigurato*, although to be sure he could not explain what was wrong with them other than that they did not satisfy his taste. Or, as in the case of Meier's building for the Ara Pacis, even if Sgarbi's opposition to the project was appropriate, his decision to extend an invitation to students to bomb it was not.[22] Refusing to acknowledge a system that rewards those who are often the least rather than most talented, and that resolves architectural competitions the way it does football matches – on the basis of money, connections and reciprocal favours rather than skill and ability – renders criticism easy, and harmless. Relatively few critics are prepared to denounce this system because in the majority of cases, like Sgarbi's, they themselves benefit handsomely from it.

Sgarbi also launched a campaign against Franco Minissi's Museo Arceologico in Agrigento.[23] Home to ceramics, jewellery, statuary and other artefacts unearthed in the area of the Valley of the Temples, the museum sits in a complicated and layered site. The remnants of Greek colonial structures, including a semicircular theatre, as well as the cloister of the ancient abbey of S. Nicola, made site planning extremely difficult. Minissi chose to wrap the entrance route around most of the ruins, to leave the cloister largely intact and gut the deconsecrated church to carve out exhibition space. Minissi's modern museum wings, though nearly half a century old, do not reveal their age: they could have been erected yesterday. The museum's simple elegance and its generous spaciousness make for a delightful visit, while the double-height central space accommodates the breathtaking, towering figure of one of the telamons unearthed on the site. Even though the architect avoided precious, high-maintenance materials, he crafted details with care, introducing textures, colours and variations with seamless integrity. This unexpectedly rich architectural jewel merits support rather than such an assault.[24]

Post-war Debates, Discourse and Debacles

In such a thickly incestuous system, perhaps the first casualty is the possibility of open and challenging debate and discourse on architecture. Such has certainly been the case in Italy. Earlier I discussed the interwar debates and post-war interpretations of them; the debates were no less vexing in the post-Second World War years. In chapter Four I noted the arguments advanced by Ernesto Nathan Rogers in the pages of *Casabella-Continuità* from 1953 until his death in 1969. In soberly challenging the hegemony of empty formalist exercises during the entire two-decade run of the Fascist regime, he also echoed a criticism levelled at the time by another astute observer, Edoardo Persico. With the then-young group of architects that included Aldo Rossi, Gae Aulenti, Vittorio Gregotti and others, Rogers argued for an architectural practice that focused more on problems to be solved than formal exercises; he also encouraged the study of history not as a repertoire of forms but as a rich repository of challenges addressed and traditions modified to engage contemporary needs, all confronted with a 'free and ranging critical mind'.[25]

This culture of openness enjoyed only a brief season and only within the group associated with *Casabella*. By 1959, when Rogers presented the BBPR design for the Torre Velasca at the Congrès International d'Architecture Moderne (CIAM) conference in Belgium, the vicious reaction of Peter Smithson to the design illustrated the growing dogmatism and rigidity of the supporters of a peculiar view of modern architecture.[26] Lashing out at the expressionism of the stanchions and struts girding the projecting residential floors, Smithson also charged that the design represented a closed society and was therefore immoral. Jacob Bakema further asserted that the building represented a retreat from modern life. That same year, Reyner Banham lamented what he viewed as a retreat from modernism, precisely embodied in the work and theory of Rogers, a style he labelled Neo-liberty.[27] Celebrating the promise of modern architecture to shed the dated clothes of yesterday, Banham disparaged the eclecticism found in the work of Paolo Portoghesi, Roberto Gabetti and Aimaro d'Isola, and Rogers, among others. Such critiques continued to be directed against these and other Italian architects who strayed from a rigidly modernist line through the late 1980s, usually on the same nebulous grounds.

The approach Ernesto Rogers delineated for architecture and urbanism depended upon principles far from the emphasis on style that characterized the most adamant post-war modernists. The support of a variety of architects for similar views culminated in what was called *la Tendenza*, or the Tendency, in the XV edition of the Milan Triennale in 1973, curated by Aldo Rossi. Rossi's *Architecture of the City* (1966) elaborated ideas along the lines Rogers suggested in far greater detail precisely for the architect, emphasizing the need for architecture to spring from a city's specific history, from its citizens' collective memories, values and experiences, with all of the specificity and uniqueness so characteristic of Italian cities. In this sense, for *la Tendenza* as proposed by Rossi, architecture should be rational precisely in the clarity of its complex relationships with history, the city and the collectivity, not to mention its own history. Where the modern movement banished history, for Aldo Rossi and *la Tendenza* it was necessarily the starting point for the choices that underlay any valid architecture. The early decisions of BBPR for the Torre Velasca in Milan and of Quaroni for the INA Casa Tiburtino quarter exemplified this rejection of anti-historical and anti-urban modernism, precisely the reasons for which they received such strident criticism from virtually all professional quarters. The same ideas did not animate all of the architects included in the XV Triennale, and indeed, the moment of presumed unity under the banner of *la Tendenza* turned out to be just that, an ephemeral moment that dissolved rapidly into a range of conflicting ideas.

The sterile debate about form – in which its supporters claimed moral stature for 'correct' modernist form – held sway for most of the subsequent decades. The years of political and social turmoil surrounding 1968 bred a profound disenchantment in a younger generation of architects with the empty formalism and debates of their seniors and with what they viewed as the alarming co-option of modernist architecture by the capitalist machine. As Umberto Eco was developing his ideas on semiology based upon his readings of Ferdinand de Saussure and Roland Barthes, he explored architecture as one of the fields in which such concepts could be explored. With Eco's arrival as professor in the department of architecture at the University of Florence in 1966, faculty and students alike pursued with growing interest the idea of architecture as sign, as part of a system of visual codes.[28] Initially this gave rise to a series of demonstrations organized by the UFO (Unidentified Flying Object) group, but some of the ideas spread to other avant-garde groups in Florence and elsewhere.[29]

In part as a reaction to the dogmatism and formalism, in 1971 the group Superstudio formed in Florence.[30] In general adopting a stance best described as a challenge to architecture not dissimilar to that of the contemporary group in Britain, Archigram, the members of Superstudio often refused to produce sections, elevations or three-dimensional views. Among the more conventional of their projects were those the Yale School of Architecture journal *Perspecta* published in 1971, such as the accretion of a cultural and exhibition centre figured as a 'machine' grafted onto the decaying fortress erected by Lorenzo de' Medici at Poggibonsi, Siena, but left incomplete at his death.[31] Presented in Emilio Ambasz's 1972 exhibition

Paolo Portoghesi,
Mosque, Rome,
1975–91, general
view and colonnade
detail.

at MOMA in New York as an example of Italian radical architecture, Superstudio, along with Archizoom and others, occupied a space designated for
'counter-design', a notion apparent in many of their polemical projects.[32]
One attempt to carve out a space independent of commercial capitalist
and consumerist architecture by Superstudio, for example, consisted of a
2,000-ton ceiling descending menacingly on a complacently efficient architectural 'machine'.[33] They also emphasized the immense social transformations of the post-war era – a shift from factory production, linear and
clear, to an architecture of networks, which they dubbed 'technomorphic',
a remarkably prescient vision of what we know as the internet. Widely
published in Italy and elsewhere, groups such as Superstudio aimed to
disrupt 'business as usual' in the architectural profession and to awaken
a greater critical sensibility in architects as well as the public.

The critic and historian Manfredo Tafuri acknowledged the depth and
sincerity of this and other radical groups' challenges to an architectural
culture complicit with the forces of capitalism and consumerism, but
nonetheless dismissed such groups as miserable failures, incapable of slow-
ing the capitalist juggernaut. In his critiques not only of radical architecture
but also of the sleek formalism of resurgent modernists and the newly
'speaking architecture' promoted by Paolo Portoghesi and others in Italy,
Tafuri pessimistically outlined the emptiness of architecture's fate in a
world of capitalist economics.[34] Certainly this critique resonated among
many of the architects, radical and otherwise, discussed above, but the
choices they made as a consequence differed remarkably. While for some,

Tafuri's gloomy analysis could only produce paralysis, others elected to shift to matters over which the designer could operate. Although the political dimension of these critiques largely disappeared during the 1990s, other considerations replaced it. Adolfo Natalini of Superstudio, for example, focused upon site, material and craftsmanship in his later career, an attention to structure and tectonics that became increasingly common from the 1980s onwards. Portoghesi continued to argue for a non-neutral architecture that 'spoke', culling elements from historical architectures as readily as from a specific programme, such as in his Mosque of Rome (1975–91), an aesthetic that came to be known as postmodernist. As president of the Venice Biennale, Portoghesi mounted the 1980 exhibition, entitled The Presence of the Past but popularly known as the Postmodern Biennale, precisely to give space to alternate visions. Portoghesi lined the nave of the Arsenale – the former factory renamed La Strada Novissima (The Very New Street) for the occasion – with twenty facades designed by top international designers, postmodern and not, and fabricated of temporary materials as though a stage set.[35] The mere fact of reducing the architecture on display to narrow facades aligned on both sides of the ancient factory for many was a postmodern gesture to reject the sterile sameness of modernist design. But the project by Rossi for the Teatro del Mondo (Theatre of the World, 1979, originally assembled for the Carnival of Venice of that year) stole the show and far outlived any of the other exhibits. The wooden structure, with its blue trim and simple cupola, floated in the Venetian lagoon with an exhibit of Rossi's architecture inside throughout the Biennale, then travelled to the Dalmatian coast and later the Port of Genoa. In its utter and disarming simplicity, like many of Rossi's designs it effortlessly embodied an iconic and somehow timeless vision of architecture as precisely what Rossi understood it to be: the backdrop against which the events of life can unfold.

Portoghesi's significant accomplishment here was to gather the growing reaction against a bland, often vapid modern architecture and give shape to it in the form of a transgressive exhibition that opened the way to a fresh perspective on architecture's diverse history, materials and colours. The prohibition against referring to history, already subject to Robert Venturi's challenge in his *Complexity and Contradiction in Architecture* (1966), came under relentless attack in the exhibit, which instead celebrated inventiveness and non-dogmatic openness in the facades by architects as diverse as Riccardo Bofill and Rem Koolhaas, Frank Gehry and Christian de Portzamparc. Although critics decried the exhibit for lacking a theoretical and conceptual grounding, the success of the show then and the development of postmodern architecture in subsequent decades suggest that at least in some respects, they erred. The underlying theoretical impulse, rooted in a post-Enlightenment vision of history as a repertory of the human past and human memory, was a vision they believed could and should be revealed not only in historical objects themselves but by architects giving shape to temporal sensibility through the adaptation of the signs and symbols of that past in contemporary projects. Instead of rejecting history, many of the architects embraced it, not just as a capricious foray into the past but as the evidence of human interactions with nature and with others across time. Not all of them did so, however; the rejection of a bland, corporate modernism took many forms, which is exactly what Tafuri lamented in a review of the exhibition. He questioned an exhibit that presented as a single group the works of architects that contained so many diverse points of view.[36] Critics lamented many of the same things about the xv Triennale, the *Tendenza* exhibit seven years earlier. In effect, Tafuri challenged the absence of a coherent school – the otherwise astute critic having completely missed the point.

It is some irony that the architecture of the modernists – that of Le Corbusier, even Frank Lloyd Wright, and later iterations of modernism in the 1970s and 1980s in the work of Renzo Piano and Richard Rogers (in the Centre Pompidou), Skidmore, Owings & Merrill (the Air Force Academy in Colorado) and Peter Eisenman, among many others – has most tellingly evinced the ravages of time and the need for massive expenditures to restore buildings in most cases not yet 35 years old. The rapid decay of such iconic modernist projects unfortunately reflects the corrosion of less celebrated works, such as Corviale and many of the buildings at EUR. To be sure, the poor quality of the materials shares responsibility for some of the decay along with inadequate maintenance, but a modernist design – and most recent avant-garde styles – depends upon pristine perfection if it is to appear anything other than slapdash, and that in turn demands costly maintenance, something often lacking.

Not surprisingly, some architects embraced a particularly vacuous version of postmodernism, exploiting connections to a resurgent Socialist Party under the leadership of the corrupt and charismatic prime minister Bettino Craxi to obtain commissions and building permits.[37] Such was the case for the glazed skyscrapers of the Professional Centre erected by Rolando Gantes and Roberto Morisi (1987–90), fortunately situated on the relatively remote periphery of Milan, which succeeds masterfully in being at once garish and monotonous. But the apex of Italy's bankrupt modernist design emerged in a setting weighted down by the best of intentions and impossibly miserable results: the reconstruction of Gibellina, a Sicilian town 80 kilometres from Palermo destroyed by an earthquake in 1968. The old city of Gibellina, cascading down from the slopes of Monte Roccatonda with steep stairs for its main street, dated to the Middle Ages but flourished

Rolando Gantes and
Roberto Morisi,
Professional Centre,
Milan, 1987–90.

especially during the seventeenth century. In the 1960s its 6,000 residents still mainly worked on the land and lived in houses many of which lacked running water – not an uncommon condition at the time.[38] The quake that struck on 15 January 1968 left not a single structure intact, and the surviving residents soon settled into temporary prefabs; the authorities buried old Gibellina under tons of concrete. Some of the finest minds of architecture and urban planning – or at least, some of the most prominent ones – were summoned to construct a replacement community for the remaining displaced residents, on a site 20 kilometres away from the original settlement. Franco Purini, Laura Thermes, Ludovico Quaroni, Oswald Mathias Ungers, Vittorio Gregotti, Giuseppe Samonà, Roberto Masiero and Francesco Venezia, among others, worked on devising various aspects of the new town, into which a dismayingly large number of discredited planning and architectural ideas inherited from the modern movement found a home.

Even for such a modestly sized community, the architects seized eagerly on an organizing concept based upon zoning and the amorphous American suburb, with curving streets sometimes terminating in cul-de-sacs and often lined with the features long known to have killed street life in U.S. cities: private garages and parking spaces lining the streets. To inoculate against a promiscuous mixing of activities, they placed the social centre and botanical gardens at one end, the town hall and municipal buildings in the centre, the museums along one perimeter and sporting facilities at another, and the cathedral on a small rise more or less between the town hall and the museums – and this for a town of 4,600 people! But the residents can rejoice over five windswept, empty *piazze* and a host of outdoor sculptures erected by artists as prominent as Pietro Consagra, Arnoldo Pomodoro, Fausto Melotti and Alessandro Mendini (also responsible for the campanile). No doubt for festive occasions and holidays residents do populate these places and spaces, but a casual workday tour of Gibellina finds a visitor greeted by vacant piazzas, empty (but wide and hospitable to cars . . .) streets – a sense of emptiness and desolation present elsewhere in Italy only in some of the ancient and long-abandoned

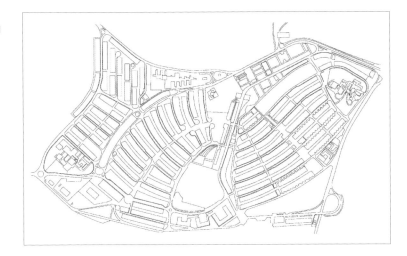

villages of provincial Lazio or other mountain zones, but which at least have the grace to be picturesque.

To add insult to injury, the roof of the cathedral (Chiesa Madre, Mother Church) designed by Quaroni and built slowly in the years after 1985, collapsed on one of the Virgin Mary's major feast days, the Assumption, on 15 August 1994, and rebuilding remains incomplete at this time.[39] Another building sits rotting, unfinished, on a hill on the town's periphery. The theatre designed by Consagra is also incomplete, and residents complain about the second-storey pub rendered impossible to use except during the winter by the extensive glazing and resultant stratospheric heat gain. In 2002 the city council decided to repair the church, finish the theatre and restore Venezia's elegant but crumbling Palazzo di Lorenzo.

All things considered, perhaps tons of cement ought to be dumped on this incarnation of Gibellina, just as they were on the old town. How could the architects and planners get it so wrong? Blinded by the dogmas of the modern movement and their own formal and linguistic exercises, they simply ignored the people who would be living there. On a sunny day in early spring, as I surveyed the verdant and beautifully tended fields of the Belice plain and contrasted them with the barren, inhospitable streets, neglected buildings and piazzas of Gibellina, the often disparaged new towns created during the Fascist era came to mind. Those lively centres outlived the political intentions of the state that commissioned them and the architects and planners who designed them; they hug the Mediterranean coast of southern Lazio and fairly throb with life and energy. Economically successful, they also sport a range of variations on themes of modern architecture. The frequently belittled effort of fascist officials and

Vittorio Gregotti,
Alberto and Giuseppe
Samonà, Town Hall,
Gibellina, 1979.

architects to straddle tradition and modernity turns out to have been a far better strategy for making liveable cities than the tenets of an orthodox and much celebrated, but profoundly flawed, modern movement.

It is some testimony to Italy's deeply politicized architectural discourse that apart from an initial flurry, little if any criticism of Gibellina has surfaced in architectural publications.[40] Even political enemies largely ignored this massive failure, possibly due to a consensus that serious criticism is anathema to all concerned. If anything, the articles that magazines do publish celebrate efforts to restore and preserve the projects by Quaroni, Consagra and Venezia.

Suburban-style
housing, Gibellina.

Francesco Venezia,
Palazzo di Lorenzo,
Gibellina, 1981.

chapter seven

Landscape and Environment

The issues and the buildings considered in the previous six chapters resurfaced in the late twentieth century and through the beginning of the twenty-first. The twin problems of housing and urban sprawl continue to vex citizens, architects, planners and politicians, without any of the constituents ever managing to assemble coherent responses to an increasingly alarming situation. To this add a growing awareness of the problems associated with poor building practices, overbuilding, loss of agricultural land, illegal construction, environmentally unsound construction, and climate change as a result of a wide range of human activities throughout the world. Awareness does not lead automatically to action in Italy any more than it does elsewhere, and indeed, Italian politicians and government employees at almost every level have tended either to ignore a problem until it has become a disaster, or to respond with paralysis or by grasping for quick fixes, often compounding the original problem with even more severe doses of collateral damage. No book about contemporary architecture and design can ignore environmental matters; this chapter examines the country's tradition of illegal building and also constitutes an indictment of Italy's failed environmental policies.

In Italy, the practice of illegal building is known as *abusivismo*. Born in part of the desperate need for housing in an urbanizing and modernizing nation, in part of the promise of huge profits for *palazzinari* (apartment builders, or developers), *abusivismo* destroyed the integrity of the many master plans carefully produced in city offices and approved after contentious political debates. The proliferation of illegal building rendered useless virtually every vision for controlled expansion in Italian cities. The phenomenon would not be so pervasive if it were not so successful: of the millions of tons of cement illegally fashioned into buildings, especially since 1945, only a handful have actually been halted, and all too often, the stop has only been a pause in an otherwise relentless and ongoing pattern of illegality. The prizes for unlawful building go to four southern regions: Campania, Sicily, Puglia and Calabria, where by some estimates one in four houses lacks a building permit. In these areas, the power of organized crime (Cosa Nostra, or the Sicilian Mafia; the 'Ndrangheta

Illegal housing, Agrigento, 2010.

syndicate in Calabria; the Camorra in Campania) and its links with poli-ticians and building enterprises have rendered public controls difficult if not impossible to maintain. Officials in Campania seeking to abolish illegal villas in protected woodland on the coast received anonymous let-ters containing bullets; local businesses refused to bid for the demolition contracts and in the end, the army undertook the job.

Illegal building is nonetheless a national, not just a southern, phenom-enon. In 2008 the Agenzia del Territorio (Territorial Agency) announced the results of an aerial survey of the peninsula conducted by photograph-ing cities and villages one by one, and comparing those images with the maps developed by the landed property offices of individual cities (*cata-stri*).[1] After documenting approximately half of the country's towns, the agency identified more than 1.2 million unregistered, or 'phantom', build-ings with, not surprisingly, the greatest number in the south, such as the Campania region (208,409), followed by Lazio (155,410), Puglia (135,954) and Sicily (102,611). Not far behind, however, are central regions such as Lazio (155,410), Tuscany (88,607), and those of the north, such as Emilia-Romagna (100,117) and Lombardy (93,748).

The Mediterranean, Adriatic and Sardinian coasts underwent an assault of illegal building of astonishing proportions over the last 50 years, laying waste to miles of pristine coastline and precious pine forests and claiming public property for private use. Sometimes cities issued building permits, but for entirely different uses and scales. In March 2006, the forestry serv-ice halted the nearly completed compound of 285 villas and apartments at Villaggio del Parco, along the coast near Sabaudia. As approved, the prop-osal anticipated the construction of a retirement community on a slice of land between open fields and the beach but, with the apparent collusion of city employees, the contractors were instead erecting an expensive hol-iday retreat.[2] The 1970 construction campaign in Palermo overseen by Vito Ciancimino mentioned in chapter Five, although putatively legal because the city issued permits, instead constituted yet another form of *abusivismo*, since the city's parks and green spaces – protected by regional and national laws – were among the sites opened up to speculation. Also in Sicily, the panorama of the southern section of Agrigento, viewed from the terrace adjacent to the Valley of the Temples, consists entirely of speculative apart-ment blocks erected with full confidence that subsequent government actions would legalize them.

In a rare success against *abusivismo*, between 1998 and 2000, bulldozers levelled 400 illegal villas in the pine forest along the Mediterranean coast near Eboli, an unusual victory against such developments. The forest was itself a recent insertion into the landscape, a device to help guard against erosion of the dunes and to combat the effects of the massive reclamation projects that took place in the area in the first part of the twentieth century. With the national government largely absent in the years following the Second World War, individual families simply erected their own small villas in the pine forest, without permits, without owning property and without opposition. Although some of the houses belonged to figures in organized crime, Gerardo Rosanìa, communist mayor of Eboli, spent the first four years of his elected mandate fighting to destroy the houses, removing them from the 8-kilometre-long stretch of forest.[3] To do so he had to overcome the refusal of businesses to compete for the demolition contract, and he needed the support of a prefect willing to summon the military to undertake the job. Rosanìa also ignored subtle – and not so subtle – threats (such as the bullet in the mail) and the open animosity of many citizens; on the other hand, a far larger but generally low-key majority tacitly supported his efforts.

Not far up the coast, about 20 kilometres north of Naples in Castel Volturno, the Società Immobiliare Fontana Blu, owned by the Coppola brothers, began construction in 1960 of a huge building complex, Villaggio Coppola. The developers claimed that they were providing spectacular seaside apartments to families assigned to the NATO base in Naples. Within a few years, the NATO officers were gone and the site's slide into degradation picked up speed. Dozens of former luxury units gradually fell into the hands of illegal immigrants, drug dealers and, inevitably, organized crime syndicates. In the end, the village consisted of a series of enormous apartment blocks, including eight residential towers planted directly on the beach, over a total of 1.5 million cubic metres. Operating unimpeded by any official intervention, the brothers dropped 30,000 square metres of cement on 5 kilometres of protected dunes and pine forest – without building permits and primarily on public lands belonging both to the state and the city. Despite the outrageous flouting of the law in building luxury complexes on the seaside, because the builder was a prosperous family with sufficiently powerful connections, the deeds went unpunished. Subsequent investigations suggested links between the Coppolas and the Camorra, which may be why it took until 2001 to bring down the first of the eight towers. Rumour has it that the new plan for the area consists of a fashionable new port and luxury resorts, also under the control of the Coppolas. The same family also constructed illegal buildings on the eastern periphery of Rome, near the Casilina district. In one case, the *comitato di quartiere* (neighbourhood committee, or action group) at Borgata Finocchio fought the unpermitted building until they managed to have the eco-monster demolished. They then oversaw the transformation of the land into a park, Collina della Pace.[4] Such victories are hard-fought and rarely won; many of the builders who are connected to organized crime have ways of persuading opponents to desist, while politicians simply refuse to inter-vene for a variety of reasons, not least of which is that they too often profit personally from averting their eyes. The small victories south of Salerno and north of Naples were indeed amazing events, even if time has shown them to be marginal; nonetheless, that these victories were accomplished in the south, where the national government's presence has been at best limited, is even more remarkable.

Part of the difficulty lies in official connivance with organized crime, those often responsible for massive illegal and speculative developments.[5] During the spring 2010 election campaign, a leading figure and minister in Berlusconi's Popolo della Libertà (PdL) cabinet, former showgirl Mara Carfagna, announced to the voters in Campania that if the PdL won, the government would block the mass destruction of unpermitted and spec-ulative apartment blocks in the region. True to her word, the government soon presented a law to parliament blocking the judicially ordered dem-olitions until June 2011 – granting enough time to legalize them through a new *condono*, or amnesty, to be enacted by the government. Unfortunately for the government, when the matter came up for a vote most of the majority party politicians could not be found, even though they received ample notice, and the law did not pass. At the time of writing the matter remains unresolved, as the parliamentary majority argues to nullify the vote – an unheard-of violation of the Chamber of Deputies's practices.[6] The immediate effect of the law's failure is that the magistrates have a green light to continue demolitions.

Illegal building first emerged in the shanty towns erected by rural emi-grants at once drawn to the city by the prospect of jobs and pushed from their homes by the steady decline of agricultural income. Most of these people whose families had worked the land often for generations failed to gain title to it, therefore the allure of the independence to be gained by working in urban areas often proved difficult to ignore.[7] They arrived in increasing numbers in the country's largest cities from the late nineteenth century and throughout the twentieth, setting up squatter camps on urban peripheries that gradually transformed into more permanent houses, all without permits and often, for long periods of time, without minimal services such as electricity and water supplies, sewerage systems, not to mention shops, cultural facilities and public transport. Local officials looked the other way (or received cash to do so) and the unplanned and disorgan-ized building proliferated, in part aided by periodic *condoni*, the mass regularization of illegal building announced well in advance so that people who planned to erect structures without permits could finish before the *condono* expired.[8] Often these *condoni* were mechanisms for replenishing the empty coffers of the state, as was the amnesty announced in 2003 under

Self-built suburb, Torre Maura, Rome, 2010.

the Berlusconi administration (having proclaimed another one in his previous government in 1994), when people paid modest fines to regularize their buildings. Idroscalo, a self-built community at the mouth of the Tiber river, has flourished for over 30 years. Rome city officials are attempting to demolish it on safety grounds, reasons that evidently do not apply to what palazzinari are proposing for a luxury complex on the site. Typical of the current state of such illegal suburbs of the 1950s and '60s are the houses in Torre Maura, near the Casilina in Rome. Erected in effect one room at a time, the houses reflect the owners' varying imperatives and the differences between those with and without resources to remodel and refine their homes over time. Even today, makeshift and potentially dangerous wiring and sewers, although declared legal, continue to pose risks.

That legalizing such structures did not make them any safer emerges in the steady sequence of disasters that followed: the collapse of unauthorized stairs and a terrace on a cliff-side house on the Amalfi Coast killed one person and injured several more in August 2007, while nearly an entire family perished in a landslide caused by construction on a denuded hillside on the island of Ischia in May 2006.[9] The area where the latter tragedy occurred had long been identified on official maps as at high risk for just such eventualities, but nonetheless illegal houses peppered it – and most of the owners were just at that time seeking a *condono* for their houses. Indeed, despite the extreme danger of the location, the mayor categorically stated that 'the house of the Buono family was certainly legalizable.'[10] The list of similar incidents is not short. Not counting the costs of homes and property lost, in 1997 a landslide in Pozzano, at Castellamare di Stabia, saw four people lose their lives and dozens of others injured; the next year four communes in the provinces of Salerno and Avellino suffered landslides, killing 137; two years later, four people died in a slide in Val Caudina, and in Nocera in 2005 another three people died. In every case, when warnings went unheeded, illegal land clearance and subsequent building contributed to the disasters.

Although all Italian cities went through at least two, and often several, master plans over the course of the twentieth century, unplanned suburbs, which spread like oil patches around their peripheries, soon rendered them irrelevant. In Rome, such illegitimate housing enclaves by the 1960s had already spread well outside the city's ring road, and their numbers only increased over time. The film mentioned in the Introduction, *Il ladro di bambini*, eloquently chronicles the consequences of this practice along the degraded coastlines of southern Italy and the squalid, overbuilt periphery of Milan, but equally sordid peripheries surround Naples, Bari and Rome.

Throughout the twentieth century, some architects celebrated the vernacular architecture of the country's coastlines, hills and mountains as an antidote to a deeply politicized and compromised modern architecture.[11] Architects such as Giuseppe Pagano found the simple stone or brick structures, and especially the white, flat-roofed houses of Italy's coastal cities, to be linked to the lean, austere lines of Rationalist designs, and in one book he argued for greater attention to be paid to such humble structures. The rhetorical dimensions of such positions should not be overlooked, because much of the criticism levelled against Rationalist designs emphasized their international associations, with 'international' being a code word for 'communist' – precisely the political theory which fascist ideology opposed. In the post-war period, support for vernacular architecture was equally rhetorical in that it was linked to an often belated opposition to the Fascist regime and the two most common architectural styles of the regime: neoclassicism and Rationalism. In any case, neither group of architects supported the version of the vernacular found in the shanty suburbs and self-built accommodations erected on the periphery of Italian cities during the twentieth century: neither picturesque nor orderly, this particular type of vernacular housing regularly prompts widespread condemnation from the architectural community.

When discussing *abusivismo*, most historians and critics focus on the low-cost, self-built informal suburbs, implicitly identifying *abusivismo* as a largely lower-class phenomenon. The facts speak otherwise. The panoramic view of Rome from the Janiculum hill reveals a cityscape of illegal rooftop constructions, sometimes two to three storeys piled atop what were three-to-four storey medieval and Renaissance buildings. These are not cheap, low-cost units designed to address the needs of the working class; on the contrary, they even have names (*attico / superattico*) and they consist of apartments sold or rented at high prices. During the 1950s, politicians and entertainers erected palatial residences along the entire via Appia, a storied road of enormous architectural and archaeological significance laid out in ancient Rome. Much of the new building occurred without permits, or with authorization for much more modest enterprises, precisely because of the abundance of artefacts on and beneath the soil. The

Panorama, Rome, 2006.

property owners simply erected their homes, collected the antiquities they unearthed and displayed them in their living rooms.[12] None of this could have been done without the explicit or tacit connivance of city and other government officials at all levels. Even if caught, owners typically paid a trivial fine, while their villas remained intact – just as the builders of illegal apartment blocks historically have been assured that eventually the buildings will be regularized by government fiat.

In these cases, individuals of all social classes built or added to their own homes. The larger problem lies elsewhere. By far the greatest quantity of illegal building came from speculators and *palazzinari* who claimed land on the outskirts of cities but also on the nation's coastlines; their activities dominated the illegal housing market from the late 1960s onwards. Until the onset of the so-called 'economic miracle' in the late 1950s, extraordinary poverty, massive rural migration into cities and efforts to replace the large quantity of housing destroyed by bombs marked the years immediately following the Second World War. Unlawful construction allowed individuals to respond to immediate and pressing needs for shelter.

Pier Paolo Pasolini documented in literature and film the self-constructed shelters erected in this fashion, above all in his novels *Ragazzi di vita* (1956) and *Una vita violenta* (1959), set in the *borgata* on via dei Monti di Pietralata, in the northeast quadrant of Rome, where

> the road leading to Montesacro, with the asphalt reduced to a few fragments on the crumbling dirt scattered with filth and garbage, led behind the Aniene [river]. The river ran below stinking slopes, especially at the mouth of the Polyclinic's sewer.[13]

Tommasino, the young protagonist, lives in one of the *baracche*:

> The mother was there, in the other room: other room so to speak, because it was all one shanty, separated only by a stained grey curtain and by a piece of cardboard badly nailed to an armature of unmatched pieces of wood. Tommasino knelt down and fumbled around under a chest that, with a small credenza that was falling to pieces, the single burner and two chairs, was all that there was in the little room, and at that it barely fit . . .[14]

Filthy, muddy streets, piles of rubbish and refuse everywhere, and barely enough to eat: the youngsters in Pasolini's stories battle over crumbs in a city that seems to have forgotten them. The urban texture of the original shanty towns remains even where the houses have been remodelled and updated: narrow streets, dead ends, absent pavements, inconvenient commercial organization and limited access to public transportation, not to mention the absence of green areas, characterize most unplanned suburbs.

Illegal building also appeared in films, such as Vittorio De Sica's *Il tetto* (1956), in which a young couple organizes to build a single room with a roof, because once the roof was in place, tacit agreements meant that the police would not force them to move; other rooms could follow over time. The quality of this rapidly constructed housing was certainly not high, but then neither were the standards of most housing: even in industrializing Milan, 42 per cent of all living units lacked bathrooms in 1960.[15]

Post-war Italy still suffered population pressure, in part from migrants from southern Italy and in part from residents pushed out of city centres by the decline in available housing because of the influx of banks, insurance companies and other institutions. In this phase, speculators propelled illegal building, cynically exploiting the housing shortage for profit while leaving it up to the city to address essential infrastructure such as roads, schools and sewerage systems. Construction was rapid and not always to code, particularly during the 1950s and 1960s. By some estimates, builders employed inadequate materials in up to 64 per cent of this housing, whether erected with or without building permits.[16] On one cold Rome night in December 1998, when an entire 1950s-era apartment building in via Vigna Jacobini collapsed, 27 people died in their beds. Subsequent investigations pointed to the poor quality of concrete compounded by the vibrations from a large printing press in the building's basement. The earthquake in the Abruzzo region in April 2009 exposed yet more flaws in construction, when even centuries-old structures fared better than newer ones, and the loss of life exposed the rotten underside of the country's construction industry. A hospital only a few years old virtually collapsed, as did a student dormitory connected to the university, with considerable loss of life.[17] One of the oddities of this story is that by 2001, the populations of Italy's thirteen largest cities was in decline: Milan, Florence, Genoa and Naples all had the same population numbers in 2001 as in 1951, and Rome's as it was in 1971. Nonetheless, in cities such as Naples, new construction more than doubled the size of the city's urban fabric. Nearby villages filled up with former urbanites returning to their jobs in the city from their new duplexes erected on former agricultural land. The earthquake in L'Aquila exposed the poor construction to the eyes of the world; would that it were the only such example . . . The hospital erected in Cona, on land purchased from a relative by the mayor on behalf of the city of Ferrara, twenty years and millions of euros in the making, turns out to have been built on marshland without, of course, the appropriate footings and foundations.

Not all illegally built suburbs were of poor quality; in the Milanese suburbs, *coree* sprang up to the north and south of the city throughout the 1950s and 1960s to house immigrants to the Lombard capital, chewing up thousands of acres of fertile agricultural land in the process. So named because the self-built housing resembled the images published in newspapers and, after 1954, on RAI, the state television network, of the housing seen in Korea during the Korean War, the houses were actually more substantial and of higher quality than many contemporary observers acknowledged.[18] Most of the male inhabitants usually worked in factories or in the Lombard building industry, but even those who were not builders were often skilled carpenters and masons who emigrated from the Veneto, from the Polesine in the Po Delta after the disastrous floods of 1951, or from southern Italy. Beginning usually with just two rooms, kitchen and bathroom, the houses underwent expansion over time and owner-occupiers typically gave way to absentee-owners renting to more recent immigrants. Overcrowding became more common when tenants squeezed into smaller apartments carved out of the earlier structures. Those who constructed their homes in the *coree* brought with them the traditions and habits of rural life by erecting small, single-family houses with kitchen gardens, terraces and courtyards, in an implicit rejection of urban living: they might have to work in the city, but they could still live in rural villages.[19] For decades, the only institutional presence in the *coree* was the Catholic Church, which became a social, cultural and educational centre for the communities. As in other low-income suburbs, such as Primavalle in Rome, the churches provided nursery and elementary schools as well as after-school football and other sports for boys, and screened films for the entire community. In both Idroscalo and Corviale in Rome, two priests erected chapels and work with the community, including participating in their struggles with authorities.

Outside the major cities, illicit building created different problems. Tons of cement poured on sensitive slopes and valleys profoundly alter an area's hydrology: specifically, they eliminate the land's capacity to absorb rain.[20] When major storms dump large quantities of water on denuded hills, they collapse and rivers flood their concrete banks, as happened in Piedmont in 1994 and 2000, and in the Val d'Aosta in 2000. A river of mud submerged large parts of the town of Sarno in the province of Campania in 1998, with lives and houses lost. In July 2006 in Vibo Valencia in Calabria, much of a deforested hill with illegal housing clustered around its flanks ceded, with a river of mud destroying houses and lives, and when it flowed into the sea, the pollution it carried in its wake then slaughtered thousands of fish. On the other hand, the monsoon-type rains of November 2010 filled rivers in the flatlands of the Veneto. In an area draped abundantly in cement and highways, and in the absence of adequate drainage, 2–4 metres of water spilled into the historic centres of Verona, Vicenza and adjacent communities. Citizens now pay the price for the unwillingness of city councils to deny a building permit, but neither citizens nor politicians paid any attention to the cumulative effect of endless construction.

Critics from organizations such as Italia Nostra (Our Italy) and Legambiente (Environmental League) rose to protest these and other abuses, in the name of preserving both the landscape and the country's architectural patrimony, with varying degrees of success, often depending upon the political composition of the regional or national government. This situation is hardly unique to Italy, however; city officials in Los Angeles and Houston, Texas, discovered how earlier efforts to channel rivers and bayous to permit the construction of buildings and suburbs on the surrounding lands have ended up becoming dangerous, fast-moving rivers that also overflow their banks, sometimes disastrously. Unfortunately, as is the case in many countries, Italy's cities fund their public coffers by taxing residences, thereby offering incentives to avoid such taxes by building illegally, and by setting high fees for building permits, therefore encouraging cities to approve as many new building projects as possible.[21] Shopping centres, prefabricated industrial complexes and apartment blocks require permits, and those permits, combined with annual property tax bills, account for between 25 and 35 per cent of many city budgets, with the highest percentages collected in the central and northern regions and the lowest in the south, with the significant exception of Milan.[22] In 2008 the Berlusconi government eliminated the unpopular tax on first residences and as a consequence diminished local revenues; it is of some comfort to know that many cities and towns are making up the difference by enforcing traffic and parking laws more vigorously. Public policies as well as lack of enforcement, in other words, equally encourage illegal building and what Italians term *la cimentificazione* ('the paving over') of the countryside. So badly planned are many of these industrial complexes that when the original tenants go bankrupt, new owners do not appear, so the countryside is also dotted with empty, rusting hulks, even while new complexes and industrial sheds spring up nearby.

The public perception of illegal building usually centres on the hastily constructed houses erected by individual occupants to replace shanties. This is far from the reality. The overwhelming majority of unauthorized building is due to builders and *palazzinari*, usually with political connections that allowed them to operate freely. The entire southern flank of the Sicilian town of Agrigento, seen from a terrace near the entrance to the Valle dei Templi, rose in this fashion. While informal (and illegal) suburbs in the immediate post-war period consisted of small, single-family homes, multi-storey apartment blocks dominated the second phase of unlawful subdivisions. Silvio Berlusconi, the richest man in the country and three-time prime minister, repeatedly hauled into court for a variety

Landslide, Sarno, 1998.

Silvio Berlusconi,
Milano 2, 2006.

of white-collar crimes as well as for encouraging under-age prostitution, orchestrated his meteoric rise through close associations with members of the Mafia, with Bettino Craxi and with the Socialist Party, but also as a *palazzinaro* in Milan, especially at the mega-residential quarters Milano 2 and Milano 3.[23] How he developed his first large housing complex is typical of the way *palazzinari* practise illegal building. Having received permission in 1964 to erect five-storey housing blocks in Brugherio, a town near Milan, Berlusconi nearly doubled their size, making them eight storeys high; when challenged by the city administration, he paid a fine, the buildings remained and his profits accelerated accordingly. The city official who approved the variation then joined Berlusconi's company.[24] It comes as no surprise that decreeing an amnesty for unlawful buildings was a priority the first two times he became prime minister, in 1994 and 2001. A 41 per cent increase in illegal building preceded the second amnesty in 2003.[25]

No one is shocked to learn that Berlusconi chose not to live in the quarters he developed, having allegedly connived with his lawyer Cesare Previti to wrest the historic family estate from an orphan at Arcore, where Berlusconi still regularly holds court.[26] He also built a vast compound on the coast of Sardinia, at Porto Rotondo, large sections of which apparently lacked building permits – including a 500-seat outdoor theatre, a football field and an artificial lake – all in violation of the region's rigid environmental codes in a profoundly delicate area. Challenged by magistrates who suspected that he did much of the work without permits, he passed a decree in September 2004 declaring the entire enterprise a state secret.[27] When the country's leaders violate building laws with impunity, it is no surprise that ordinary people view such laws with comparable contempt.

The backdrop of legal construction against which many illegal building activities took place in post-Second World War Italy was often no less unattractive. Millions of lire and more recently, euros, cascaded particularly (but not only) into southern Italy for public works projects that, despite the enormous expenditures, often remained incomplete. The national capital of incomplete public works is the city of Giarre in Catania, Sicily, a small town of about 20,000 people that boasts a theatre, public swimming pool, multifunctional centre, multi-storey car park, flower market, senior citizens' home, palace of justice and, best of all, polo fields – all funded with public monies and all incomplete and unusable.[28] Highways to nowhere (or others constructed to facilitate the travel of a specific politician or prime minister to his home) and hulking, empty factory buildings pepper the countryside in numbers depressingly high. With such colossal – and official – indifference to the landscape, why should individuals care about the possible impact of their own, private illegal buildings?

Anyone who travels outside of Italy's fabled tourist centres will have encountered an abundance of rotting carcasses of buildings, industrial parks and *capannone* (industrial sheds). Even though builders constructed many with permits, albeit often ill-advised ones resulting from bribes to city officials, the failures of the businesses that once inhabited them has left many vacant. To capitalize on the permit fees, cities continue to grant permits to new *capannone*, so there is little incentive for buying the old ones, which were often poorly constructed in the first place. On the southeast perimeter of Ferrara, an enormous complex known as the Palazzo di Vetro (Glass Palace) quietly rusts away. Magistrates confiscated the property because of the original owner-developer's alleged involvement with organized crime, and there it has sat for more than two decades, home to illegal immigrants, drug dealers and the homeless. At the same time, new and massive complexes such as Darsena City Village rise but a few hundred metres away.

Unfortunately, the recession that hit the country in 2008 and 2009 triggered yet another alarmingly inadequate response from the centre-right government. To reignite the building industry, the government proposed allowing individuals to enlarge their houses or apartments with additions that would otherwise be unlawful. That a government formed

Palazzo di Vetro, Ferrara, 2009.

of many who made their fortunes via cement and illegal building, or through close associations with others who did, proposed such a solution is no surprise; that the opposition should voice so few and feeble criticisms is also unsurprising, since their storehouse of ideas for addressing the crisis was no richer. Whatever scars illegal building in all of its forms has inflicted on Italy's landscape, legal buildings have equalled if not exceeded them, regardless of which political party is in power.

Painful as it is to admit, illegal building in Italy cannot be disconnected from unauthorized refuse dumping and environmental pollution, and neither phenomenon is a purely southern problem. On the contrary, the entire country is involved. The playgrounds of medieval and Renaissance urban centres quickly give way to the toxic waste and environmental catastrophes of the peripheries of major cities and damaged agricultural land across the country.

Environmental Disasters

The world watched, appalled but morbidly fascinated, as mountains of plastic-swathed rubbish choked the streets of Naples and its suburbs during the winter and spring of 2008, and again in late 2010. International news reports on the increasingly tense situation alluded to the fact that the city's refuse industry lies in the hands of organized crime, with the current disaster stemming in part from internecine feuds among various branches of these crime families, as well as struggles between the Camorra and regional and city governments over where and how to treat refuse. Who but those involved knew that garbage companies (controlled by the Camorra) shipped Neapolitan waste to Germany to be piled in immense dumps, with traces of radioactivity reportedly found in some of that sent to Hamburg? In exchange, rumour has it, contaminated refuse from Germany and northern Italy lies buried in a toxic no-man's-land encircling the southern city's perimeter. In early 2012, police officials discovered a huge illegal waste deposit with thousands of tons of asbestos and other toxic materials in the province of Caserta, with much of the material leaking into the adjacent Aniene River. As part of a stand-off between the government and organized crime, the latter simply ceased collecting the rubbish, hence the massive piles of putrid waste lining Naples's streets. Exasperated local residents responded by setting fire to the piles and, according to alarmed experts, released highly toxic dioxins into the atmosphere in the process and ultimately, back into the food chain. Crime families profit enormously from trade in waste disposal and have conspired to block the construction of new refuse treatment facilities, in part, it appears, with the help of corrupt politicians.[29]

Another aspect of the problem in Campania can be found at one of the city's chief refuse sites, Pianuro, where frustrated residents conducted a blockade on the grounds that mismanagement led to the release of toxic matter into the atmosphere and as a consequence, a precipitous rise in cases of cancer in adjacent communities, particularly of the liver, stomach and kidneys, as well as birth defects – a charge confirmed in scientific analyses of the region. Scientists identify the 'triangle of death' in Naples's eastern segment as a site of an unusually high incidence of cancer, with the blame falling directly on the Pianuro treatment facility. Among the failed strategies for dealing with refuse in the region are the so-called 'eco-balls' stored at the Calvano facility. Liquid and solid waste are supposed to be sorted and formed into balls, which are then piled up and burned – except that those at Calvano cannot be incinerated because the sorting never took place. As the unburned mounds of eco-balls decompose, toxic fluids seep into the underground water system – contaminating water and therefore the food chain. Needless to say, the city and region have also failed to implement programmes whereby residents sort waste prior to refuse collection with a view to encouraging recycling and potentially putting a brake on the problem at the outset.

The apparently intractable problems stem from a number of sources, chiefly the decades-old, intimate interface between organized crime and politicians. Although the situation in Naples drew international scrutiny, it is but one of a multitude of similar problems besetting the peninsula. In

Garbage at Casal di Príncipe near Naples, 2008.

the province of Chieti, the Camorra openly deposited tons of toxic waste from northern Italy and elsewhere in Europe in 10-metre-deep holes, close to the underground aquifer – contaminating topsoil, the earth beneath it as well as the aquifer, not to mention the region's streams and rivers – resulting in a precipitous increase of birth defects and tumours. Health officials and politicians either ignored, or received bribes to ignore, the entire process, and a first effort at a clean-up, due for completion in 2006, was halted for reasons still obscure.[30]

Northern Italians, egged on by the divisive political party, the Lega Nord, like to blame southerners for the environmental damage, relying on traditional stereotypes and prejudices about southern irresponsibility and criminality; in reality, factories and businesses located in prosperous regions of the industrial north are equally if not more at fault, for evading regulations designed to control the disposal of toxic substances. Much of the refuse stored in illegal landfills in the Campania region arrived in Camorra-controlled trucks from factories and businesses in northern Italy to be dumped unceremoniously together with ordinary household rubbish. This often highly toxic mix landed initially in enormous abandoned quarries, but in recent years has spread to previously fertile farmland. Roberto Saviano documented this lucrative enterprise in his explosive best-seller, *Gomorrah* (2006), and in the subsequent film of the same name (2008). The typical tactics of the Camorra – threats and intimidation – succeed in driving farmers off their land to free it up for illegal dumping. Elsewhere, they simply show up to greet otherwise honest owners of agricultural land and agritourism complexes with the statement that they plan to bury waste on their properties. Owners know that they have few choices: certainly Italian institutions will provide them with no protection, least of all the state, whose political parties (with but one exception) are, to one degree or another, in bed with organized crime, and the property owners obviously cannot protect themselves. In the end, they are forced to concede, allowing the Camorra to inter waste, which in many cases must be toxic, on their properties.

In the face of these highly visible actions, the national governments of both left and right have been either complicit or paralysed – in either case, they have abdicated responsibility. The efforts of Italy's judicial system and of Legambiente, the leading environmental organization, to combat the illegal dumping have met with fierce, often lethal resistance from the Camorra and virtually no assistance from the government. Witnesses prepared to testify against the Camorra, such as Michele Orsi, former head of one of the waste management companies beholden to the Camorra, left unprotected by the government despite the evident danger, are killed. And Orsi was not alone. Clearly such intimidation tactics work: increasing numbers of farmers, fearing assassination, are frightened into being driven off of their land. Fines and admonitions from the EU fall on deaf ears, as key Italian politicians at best stand silently by, at worst line their pockets with ill-gotten gains distributed by the Camorra. Most of the public companies designated to treat refuse and waste are intimately connected with local politicians: they sit on their administrative councils and determine to which companies contracts are issued and what controls will be maintained (if any).[31] Not surprisingly, given the interconnected boards and the political control over waste disposal, little or nothing has been done to develop recycling projects or differentiated refuse collection in many parts of the country, because such enterprises would reduce the profits of companies operating the incinerators. This, then, is the new Italian landscape, one of pollution and death: no beautiful buildings, restored historic palaces or elegant new highways can conceal the rot within.

In the Italian nation's first century, progress was indexed by factors

Italy was one of the last members of the original European Economic Community (EEC) nations to adopt lead-free gasoline for automobiles, and it has one of the worst records for curbing pollution – in fact, by even the most optimistic measures, pollution has increased rather than decreased in the last decade. Politicians at local and national levels failed to enact serious legislation to control or minimize waste and where legislation exists, it often goes unenforced. Reliance on expensive foreign sources of energy has boomed as well, with Italy also lagging behind other European countries in efforts to construct sustainable buildings and to convert existing ones into more energy-efficient structures. In its failure to encourage a healthier use of resources Italy shares much, unfortunately, with the policies of the EEC.

In the Italian nation's first century, progress was indexed by factors such as the extent to which the government was able to provide the infrastructure for modernization, including dams, highways and other important public works, as well as schools and up-to-date health care facilities – units of measure also common to other industrializing nations. The noxious consequences of internal combustion engines were not readily apparent at the time, but they have been abundantly clear at least since the late 1950s. Although Italy, along with many nations around the world, signed accords in Kyoto in 1997 promising to reduce greenhouse gas emissions to help protect the ozone layer, the country has earned the unique status of being the only signatory whose emissions have increased rather than decreased since signing the treaty. The country's major buildings and monuments undergo regular and expensive cleaning, such as the decade-long project of the Catholic Church to clean its churches in Rome prior to the Jubilee year in 2000 – but within a few years most were as dirty as they had been before, with the emissions from internal combustion engines the primary

Garbage, Trapani,
2008.

Garbage on the Po
near Occhiobello,
2009.

culprit. Italy is certainly not the only modern nation to suffer from the effects of the automobile, but it was uniquely tardy in responding to this evident problem. In fact, the country lagged in applying many of the strategies that have made a dent in greenhouse gas emissions elsewhere, such as the construction of effective mass transit in its major cities (including Rome, Turin, Naples and Palermo), in ceasing to distribute lead-based gasoline, and in curbing the incentive to drive into cities by eliminating free parking. Instead, the government funded more and more highways and widened secondary roads to service exponentially increasing car and truck traffic.

If Naples is a stinking mess of refuse, the Po Valley, one of the premier agricultural areas in the world, suffers more subtle damage. The valley includes parts of the regions of Piedmont, Emilia-Romagna, Lombardy and the Veneto, extending from the Adriatic to the westernmost Alps. By contrast with the Italian south, these are prosperous and apparently well-governed regions; but beneath a veneer of modern infrastructure and expansive new post-industrial districts, such as the Bicocca, Fiera Milano quarter and former Pirelli complexes in Milan and parts of the Spina Centrale in Turin, lie other environmental problems in the making, even without considering the many often poorly planned infrastructural facilities scattered across the peninsula.[32] Dams erected to provide hydroelectricity for northern homes and factories have reduced the river Po to a sliver of its former self, forcing communities to extract ever more water from underground aquifers, relentlessly shrinking the water table. Farmers drain yet more water from the Po for irrigation in a desperate struggle to combat the effects of climate change, as annual rainfall shrinks and concentrates in a few days of torrential downpours, and the pollution from fertilizers and rubbish inevitably makes its way into the ocean. Northerners often point their fingers at the organized crime groups buying up legitimate businesses in the north, as if by contrast, virtuous northerners duly avoid contributing to environmental pollution. The case of the Teksid corporation, based in Carmagnola in the Piedmont, underscores the national dimensions of the problem. Producers of cast iron and aluminium, Teksid found it inconvenient and expensive to dispose properly of the asbestos used in its manufacturing processes, so for decades, according to the testimony of workers, supervisors ordered employees to dump the residue into the Po. The spread of lung disease caused by asbestos in the region can probably be blamed both on this practice and on the actual manufacturing processes themselves: the ovens used in the production of aluminium, for example, were asbestos lined.[33] The case that made the international news in 2012 concerned the Eternit factory in Casal Monferrato, where despite knowing the dangers of asbestos and the care with which it must be worked, the owners not only failed to ensure proper precautionary practices but minimized and concealed evidence of the causes of illness and deaths, not only of workers but of their families and neighbours. In February 2012 a historic sentence in Turin successfully prosecuted the owners for criminal misconduct in addition to civil penalties.

Smog over Turin, 2009.

Having drawn water to irrigate their produce from this same Po river, farmers struggling against climate change often find that their struggles

are for naught. Under the presumably unquestionable mantra of free trade, trucks traverse the Continent, guzzling fossil fuels, spewing toxic particles and transporting produce, livestock and other goods from old Eastern bloc countries to the toe of Italy, and from the most remote parts of southwest Portugal to the tip of Scandinavia. Just as the EC's regulations since the 1950s promoted the dubious policy of industrialized agriculture (maintaining lower prices at the expense of quality and diversity), so policymakers enthusiastically embraced the idea of importing out-of-season foods from around the world. Tankers criss-cross the Atlantic Ocean transporting cherries and strawberries from Chile in December, beef from Argentina, tomatoes from China, sugar from the Antilles, and other perishable foodstuffs to countries in the EU where such goods formerly abounded, albeit seasonally and with prices designed to support a working family, in places such as the Italian countryside. Closer to home, Italian hills, mountains and countryside bear the scars from generations of excavating marble, granite and travertine to embellish the fireplaces, counters and floors of prosperous individuals internationally – and these denuded mountains are more than eyesores. The quarrying triggers erosion, landslides and other complex environmental problems.

Recent and repeated scandals highlight the dangers of foods produced in countries where environmental controls are non-existent, but as we have seen, these locales may be little worse than the profoundly damaged countryside of Italy, where spot checks in 2008 revealed toxic substances in the buffalo mozzarella produced in Caserta, a well-known Camorra stronghold where even the police are often reluctant to intervene. In the global economy, growing produce in economically backward countries and shipping it to wealthier nations only makes good business sense because governments do not hold companies responsible for the real costs of conducting business – so-called externalities, the largely negative repercussions that extend well beyond the borders from whence the goods are shipped. Thus the immediate costs of fossil fuels consumed in transporting these goods by truck or tanker elevate the price to consumers, while the long-term costs, even only of the CO_2 that they spew into the air, are not borne by the businesses selling or transporting them but rather are distributed unevenly throughout the rest of society, in the socialized costs of accelerating climate change and increased instances of

Abandoned Teksid factory, Carmagnola, 2010.

Quarries near
Verbania, 2008.

environmentally related diseases, among others. And these are the consequences of but one of the pollutants released into the environment. Scientists
estimate that up to two-thirds to three-quarters of cancers owe their origins
to toxic elements in our environment, and the instances are higher where
toxins are concentrated, such as in the section of the Veneto region known
as the Alto Polesine and in the northern region of Emilia-Romagna adjacent to it, also known as the triangle of death.[34] Beyond these sobering
concerns are the long-term consequences to the landscapes and the communities that inhabit them, or formerly inhabited them. Residents abandon
entire villages when it is no longer possible to work the land and support
a family. They require a living wage but end up unable to compete with Asian
factories fuelled by cheap, often child labour, non-existent environmental
controls and equally corrupt politicians. Such families still migrate to already
burgeoning cities in search of work and housing, leaving their land in
the hands of corporations that practise even more destructive industrial
agricultural methods.

Unscrupulous corporations in Italy have quickly realized that the country's energy industry could be a cash cow, since the government provides
subsidies, tax credits and the like without bothering to look closely at
the context and the larger implications of so-called eco-strategies. In the
case of the communities in the province of Rovigo, there is insufficient

agricultural waste to feed the incinerators already approved, much less those under consideration by other nearby communities. In fact, *all* of the agricultural production, not just the byproducts, of this part of the province of Rovigo, and then some, would be needed to fuel these biomass plants. In effect, farmers would produce to feed the plants, not people. Furthermore, leaving the byproducts behind on the land helps nourish the soil. Fortunately for investors, and to the dismay of residents, under Italian law, if insufficient agricultural byproducts are available after five years, the plants can then legally burn household and other waste – exactly what nearby residents fear, because of the long history of inadequate supervision by the government and the intervention of organized crime in the refuse industry. Alternatively, incinerator companies can import material to burn from elsewhere as the Marzotto group does for its Portogruaro incinerators, allegedly bringing wood from the Black Sea – with the consequent increase in greenhouse gas emissions, waste of fossil fuels, damage to roads, and so forth. A good example of ruptured accords about the quantities of particulates emitted by an incinerator is that of the nearby city of Ferrara, where even incontrovertible evidence of pollution has yet to halt the burning. In an area already contaminated by plastics factories, agricultural fertilizers, incinerators and other pollutants, and where the incidence of cancers matches that of Campania, the plan to erect yet more incinerators and generate yet more pollution ought to sound alarm bells. It does for some but not, apparently, for local, regional and national politicians or administrators, and only they enjoy the power to enact any changes. As is also the case in the United States, environmental controls are less rigid in rural areas; exactly what unscrupulous entrepreneurs count upon. Add these waste-burning facilities, which, if the experience elsewhere in Italy holds, will include illegal toxic materials, to the endless miles of abandoned industrial sheds and the new ones being erected, and you have a province in dire straits indeed.

In this unremittingly grim scenario, communities and certainly politicians seem to ignore the most readily available and cheapest source of energy: solar. Here, as in other fields, Italy lags in the shift of energy supply from fossil fuels to solar and other sustainable sources – despite the fact that one of the early prophets of solar energy was Giacomo Ciamician, chemistry professor at the University of Bologna, who argued on behalf of directing research to the development of solar energy already at the turn of the century. He was followed by another pioneer, Giovanni Francia. To be sure, the EC and the Italian ministry of public works supplied funds for experiments in solar design, including a solar design at Orbassano (1982–4) near Turin by Roberto Gabetti and Isola, but these isolated examples simply reaffirm a persistent unwillingness to confront energy issues until a crisis explodes.[35] In the summer of 2008, at the height of an energy crisis, under the third administration of Silvio Berlusconi, the Italian government revived the idea of nuclear reactors as solutions to the energy problem – a choice experts decried as utterly inappropriate. The world's resources in enriched uranium will be exhausted in 40 years, by some estimates, and the direct costs of constructing nuclear reactors far exceed those of capturing solar energy – not to mention all of the indirect costs associated with the construction and maintenance of such plants, and the perennial problem of nuclear waste disposal, still unresolved today. On the other hand, construction companies will get rich, and politicians from the highest to lowest levels will have their pockets lined, so the appeal of such a project is all too evident. Given the experience of Campania in the business of refuse dumping, one can only tremble in anticipation of mountains of radioactive waste from the nuclear reactors and the galloping corruption of the freewheeling branches of organized crime – the Camorra, the 'ndrangheta and the Mafia.[36] Burning fossil fuels is also not a sustainable strategy – apart from the toxic particles released, it helps destroy the ozone layer, while solar energy is effectively free *and* sustainable. There are also many other strategies for erecting healthy, sustainable and energy efficient buildings, but the Italian government offers high rewards for one of the most problematic means of energy production – burning agricultural byproducts and other materials in costly incinerators.

As in many schools of architecture around the globe, in Italy the faculties set aside only a limited number of studios, or laboratories, to address issues of ecologically sound, sustainable design. Although some offer specialized degrees in the field, the unacknowledged assumption – and not only in Italy – is that sustainability is an add-on, an appendage, to formal design, rather than the *first* order of business to consider in any architectural project. The serious work of rethinking construction and design strategies rather than continuing mindless copying of canonical buildings and so-called architectural masterpieces have not become a stable component of the curriculum. Schools have yet to assume a leadership role in what is arguably the most important issue to be addressed in any building and landscape projects in the twenty-first century. The same criticism applies to most architectural schools in Europe and the United States, to be sure; the notable exceptions are universities in the Scandinavian countries. Future architects still prisoners to the old, twentieth-century modernist, 'hero ethos' embodied in the personae and designs of too many international architectural stars will be incapable of meeting the dramatic challenges confronting the planet in the twenty-first century. Indeed, individual property owners have arguably been more eager to turn to solar systems than have architects.

One example stands for many. In 1994, Renzo Piano won the competition to build concert facilities of various dimensions for the city of Rome.[37] The structure, inaugurated in 2002 but completed in 2003, consists of three separate structures shaped like lutes, according to Piano – but because of their beetle-like forms, promptly baptized 'cockroaches' (*bagarozzi*) by Romans – able to accommodate between about 600 and 2,500 people. After noting his commitment to the sustainable city, Piano celebrated the way his structures appealed to the architectural history of Rome, and particularly, the use of lead cladding for the huge roof shells.[38] While it is true that domes designed in Renaissance Rome (and later) sometimes employed lead cladding, the toxic properties of lead have long been known – not only for people, but the damage it inflicts on soil, aquifers and rivers – in this case, the nearby Tiber. Even if city officials approved such a polluting material, Piano as an architect cannot claim ignorance. The Parco della Musica complex may merit high marks for acoustics, but nothing can compensate for the choice of material.

Landscape of Ruins, Tourist Paradise

Despite the abuses chronicled here, Italy remains an attractive tourist destination for global travellers. Why this is so derives from several factors, chief among them the plethora of historic buildings and artworks, the cuisine, and the landscapes of ruins evocative of the past. Visitors to Italy as early as the eighteenth century waxed poetic about the abundant crumbling buildings in its cities and villages. In Marie-Henri Beyle Stendhal's *Promenades dans Rome* ('Walks in Rome', 1829), he wrote of the silence of the Roman Colosseum, a silence that 'aids the imagination to take flight into the past'. One must be alone in the Colosseum, Stendahl urged, 'It is the most beautiful of the ruins; there one breathes all of the majesty of ancient Rome.'[39] Long before labourers abandoned their farms and fields, Stendhal wrote of his journey through the Roman countryside one August when it was 'deserted, [with] that immense solitude that surrounds Rome', that 'Most viewpoints are dominated by the ruins of an aqueduct or a tomb in ruins, which gives the Roman countryside a grandeur that cannot be approached elsewhere.'[40] While the panoramas in Switzerland are boring, he continued, those of Italy are not, because one is caught up in reflections on the people who once produced the great culture that flourished, and then decayed despite the grandeur of the structures they erected.

At the dawn of the twentieth century, Alois Riegl also noted the importance of ruins as indicators of the passage of time and triggers of historical memory. Outdated and damaged buildings should be allowed to decay at their own pace, Riegl argued; as reminders of our own destinies in a far from stable universe of constant transformations, as narratives of the inevitable processes of change and decay, they are fundamental features of the cultural landscape, he believed, of which the visible signs of time and its effects on materials constituted an essential element.[41] He needed look no further than Italy to find innumerable structures from republican Rome onwards, undergoing the ravages of time and human despoliation.

The appreciation of ruins as artefacts in themselves had already been evident in the works of the eighteenth-century architect and printmaker Giovanni Battista Piranesi, who recorded the vestiges of ancient Rome and elsewhere, particularly the newly discovered Greek and later Roman town Paestum, south of Salerno, in multiple series of prints. While Piranesi also produced fanciful reconstructions of what Rome's town plan might have been in his *Il Campo Marzio dell'antica Roma* ('The Campus Martius of Ancient Rome', 1762), in general he documented structures such as aqueducts, temples and mausoleums as they were lived in his own time, festooned with laundry and surrounded by water buffalos, cattle, women, men and children. As archives of human memory, such ruins testified to the grandeur of ancient Rome as much as they did to the process of transformation, which appeared to mirror the evolution of the lives of individuals as well as cultures. In his account of his journey to Paestum published in 1837, Mercurio Ferrara described the site and its surroundings, having fallen from an early era of flourishing success, as follows:

Column, *c.* 500 BCE, Paestum, 2010.

But today all that is offered to the gaze is a squalid and solitary countryside, covered with stagnant waters, ruins, and brush, where the only grandeur is found in those valued [Greek temples] that summon visits and admiration on the part of all travellers.[42]

Giambattista Vico's conception of history as a cyclical sequence of crises, of ascent followed by destruction and decline, positioned ruins as the most visible expression of that pattern in eighteenth-century Italy, and the nearly contemporaneous discovery of the buried cities of Herculaneum in 1739 and Pompeii in 1748 explicitly certified ruins as vivid testimony to the fate that any culture and its artefacts faced.[43] Ruins fulfilled many imperatives in the eighteenth and nineteenth centuries. Their romantic appeal is unavoidable, but during the Risorgimento ruins also stood as reminders of the glories of the Italian past, just as they also testified to the triumph of time over human ingenuity.

With the burst of industrialization in the late nineteenth century and its sequel after the Second World War, the crumbling monuments of the past sat between competing vectors of preservation and elimination. As noted earlier, intellectuals and politicians acknowledged the appeal of such ruins to tourists, but they also recognized the claims of proponents of clearance to make way for modern amenities such as wider roads, highways, service and train stations, airports and other trappings of modern life. However many battles to preserve important relics failed, those on behalf of Roman antiquity and remainders of medieval and Renaissance structures could lay claim to validity because of what Riegl had defined as their art value and their historical value.

But what of the villages and houses of the regions of Lazio, Tuscany, Emilia-Romagna, the Veneto and Lombardy, depopulated over the course of the century as rural residents moved to cities and towns in search of work? Empty houses, barns, stalls and *barchesse* (buildings adjacent or attached to patrician farmhouses or rural villas for the storage of agricultural equipment, stalls and courtyard animals) still dot the embankments of the Po river, abandoned after the great floods of 1951; others are scattered through the farmlands of northern and central Italy, abandoned not because of natural disasters but because of the introduction of industrialized farming methods at the encouragement of the European Economic Community.[44] Without the need for sharecroppers to work the land, the farm buildings they formerly occupied inevitably fell into decay.

The pre-unification rural landscapes of Italy held little value other than as sites for agricultural production, which normally included varied types of crops and products, from pasta and wine to olive oil, cheeses and sausages, and as a consequence, diverse structures to accommodate their production.

Abandoned rural
farmstead, Trecenta,
18th century, 2010.

Once industrialized methods took over, the landscape's value lay strictly
in its usefulness for a type of farming that did not include such variety or,
at most, segregated each crop in separate plots. The imperatives of this
type of monoculture farming left in its wake a landscape often stripped of
trees and dotted with ruins apparently lacking economic and artistic value,
a condition by the 1960s that formed the characteristic appearance of the
regions of northern and eastern Lazio, southern Lombardy and Piedmont,
and huge swathes of the land on both sides of the Po in Emilia Romagna
and the Veneto. For most small towns, the answer to these empty landscapes lay in inducing industries of various types to move in, as they did
in the countryside around Verona, Vicenza and Padua in the north, and
around the Tuscan city of Prato, to name but a few. The EEC also sponsored
attempts to enhance monocultivation by fundamentally altering the
terrain, bulldozing terraced hills and dynamiting others.

By contrast, city dwellers and especially northern Europeans travelled
through these desolate landscapes and saw not abandoned houses but

picturesque barns and farmsteads in need of restoration and available for purchase at ridiculously low prices. Lacking running water, electricity, modern sanitation and drainage systems, these houses certainly presented little romantic appeal to the former inhabitants, who had laboured on the land but did not own it. Quite the contrary obtained for foreign tourists. Such ruins appealed not only because of their picturesque qualities but because they summoned references to what was *not* there. That liminal space between the ruin and the allusion to its history is precisely where fantasy steps in to fabricate a past, if only an imagined one, in which the artefact's propinquity allows the observer to share. Abandoned dwellings and service structures lend themselves to such fanciful reconstructions perhaps more than the massive baths and temples of ancient Rome, precisely because they evoke the viewer's quotidian life. Purchasing and renovating such buildings allowed that dream, that imagined past, to become real, however fantastic the reality turned out to be. The cumulative visions of countless foreigners and Italian urbanites seeking a different life in a transformed setting over the course of the past half-century fundamentally altered the landscapes of numerous districts in Italy. North of Turin in the

Abandoned Benedictine monastery, Gaiba, c. 14th century, photo taken 2010.

small town of Mathi, in 2011 MARC architects (Michele Bonino and Subhash Mukerjee) revamped a crumbling structure used for making cheese into an elegant addition to the nearby house, in particular providing an indoor pool and recreation rooms. The success of this structure encouraged the owners to restore other structures, ending up with a small bed and breakfast inn.

The Chianti region so appealed to British expatriates that it became widely known as Chiantishire. As the enterprise of wine production gained steam in the region, EEC policies regarding the licensing and control of locally produced agricultural products, including wine, helped this valley and other parts of rural Tuscany to undergo economic expansion at a rapid pace and, as a consequence, a repopulation of its countryside. No longer sharecroppers, or even Italians, these new residents reconfigured their lands to farm specific crops, and many also took advantage of EEC incentives to convert old rural holdings into sites of agricultural tourism, or *agriturismo*.[45] To be sure, these enterprises were not without their own contradictions. Instead of terracing hills for their vineyards, owners still made use of industrial methods by planting the grapes on the rolling hills for ease of access to tractors and other modern equipment. When torrential rains come – as they increasingly do – these hills quickly cede, leading to erosion and landslides.

Latecomers who no longer found cheap abandoned farms to buy could now at least spend a few days in a remodelled farm house, stables, barn or dovecote, eating 'authentic' Italian cooking consisting of ingredients produced on the farm itself and employed in 'traditional' recipes: sausage, cheese, marmalade, bread, limoncello, olive oil, wine and vegetables. By the late 1980s, agritourism hotels and restaurants proliferated throughout the Italian countryside. For the tourist, these transformed landscapes marketed as 'traditional' represented an imagined rural Italy of small farms and independent landowners, producing specialized foods according to time-honoured methods – a fictional image that had little to do with the actual history from which these buildings emerged. The feudal landscape of lord and serf, king and peasant, of backbreaking labour by entire families to feed the taste for luxury of an absentee owner – none of this surfaces in the literature about, nor indeed the reality of, these new settings.

Rural repopulation in this new guise extends from southern Piedmont's Langhe wine-producing region to Campania's mozzarella manufacture, especially in the area of the Sele river valley, adjacent to ancient Paestum. Of these regions, the most successful in crafting a new rural landscape was Tuscany, which enacted strict laws to outlaw new buildings, control restoration of old ones and to require land and structures be sold as one. Global shifts in consumer taste and a growing reaction against the highly fertilized,

Bartolino Ploti da Novara, Rocca Estense, San Felice sul Panaro, 1406, view after earthquakes in May 2012.

often flavourless foods produced by industrial agriculture favoured this process enormously.[46] Beginning in the 1970s, Italian cooking and its ingredients became increasingly popular in other countries, to the point that extra virgin olive oil, Parmigiano (Parmesan) cheese and pasta became staples in many American kitchens, not to mention the enormous success of Italian coffee (espresso, cappuccino, caffè latte, to name only a few) and pizza. Italian peasant fare such as bruschetta (toasted bread rubbed with garlic and topped with olive oil) and panzanella (a slice of dry bread soaked in water and mixed with tomatoes and olive oil) made its way onto the menus of exclusive restaurants in the United States, and thence to the kitchen tables of Middle Americans, in multiple variations.

The newly exported version of Italian cuisine erased the image of spaghetti and meatballs as the standard fare of Italy, as American and other tourists became educated in the nuances of northern and southern Italian cooking and the varieties of pastas and sauces that abound, just waiting to be discovered by inquisitive visitors. Italy's inert politicians have yet to figure out that Italian ingenuity in cuisine and niche marketing of local products has played a leading role in the transformation of tastes and culinary practices globally, and as a result the government fails to offer adequate incentives to push quality agricultural practices, with all of its varied territorial repercussions, to a higher level. The same ignorant politicians, lacking the imagination to translate the commercial accomplishments into systematic political successes, also fail to recognize the economic benefits of the nation's cultural patrimony, from architecture to paintings, and therefore in 2010 and 2011 during the economic crisis, the government slashed funds for culture (and education) more than any others.[47] The consequences of such short-sighted policies became abundantly clear when an earthquake, possibly triggered by the practice of 'fracking' in the search for shale oil, struck in Emilia Romagna and the Veneto on 20 and 29 May 2012. The past two decades of neglect led to the loss or severe damage of many extraordinary ancient buildings, such as the Este Castle (Rocca Estense) in San Felice sul Panaro, a town close to the epicentre.

A significant marker of the triumph of Italian cooking is the growth of the Slow Food movement, initiated by Carlo Petrini in 1986 and described in his book, *Slow Food Nation*. Slow food proposes to counter the proliferation of American-style fast food, with all of its attendant health and ecological problems, by returning to a more 'authentic' type of food production and, as a consequence, consumption. This movement converged with the EEC's increasing acknowledgement of a quite different model of agriculture, independent of industrialized production but based upon niche marketing and local production of high-quality foods, and of the parallel growth of the organic food industry. Not only has this winning combination transformed dining habits in Italy and beyond, it has helped change some of the empty landscapes of the 1960s into vibrant new ones. Although only thinly, if at all, related to the types of cultivation extant prior to the Second World War, these landscapes are now tourist attractions in their own right, appealing additions to the country's huge catalogue of museums, churches, aristocratic palaces and medieval hill towns. Nonetheless, abandoned rural structures and villages still exist, along with terraced vineyards such as those in the Canavese area of northern Piedmont and in the Val d'Aosta, where neglected stone walls that once buttressed local wine production (Barolo is one of the most famous varieties produced there) are slowly crumbling away. These too become appealing examples of ruins for native and foreign tourists to contemplate, along with the sections of ancient Roman roads that occasionally emerge into the countryside and the innumerable abandoned oratories and shrines that also comprise this often ravaged, complex landscape.

chapter eight

Entering the Twenty-first Century

The struggle over the legacy of the modern movement heated up in Italy in the three decades following the end of the Second World War, complicated, as we have seen, by the perceived links between fascism and Rationalist architecture. Critics and theorists through the 1980s sought ways of minimizing the connections between the regime and Rationalism. These concerns receded during the first decade and virtually disappeared in the second; architects and scholars drew distinctions between a 'good' modernism (hence not Fascist) and a 'bad' (Fascist) classicism, manipulating the histories to make the model fit their tastes. Unfortunately for this argument, many of the 'good' modernists were committed fascists, from Giuseppe Terragni to Giuseppe Pagano. With that tired approach exhausted, the focus shifted to other equally obfuscating distinctions – between material and metaphysical, for example, meaning a distinction between architects who simply sought to build and address social concerns, and others who focused on the 'spiritual' values of the regime.[1] Just how one might measure such values is an open question. At the same time, a persistent concern to find a specifically Italian version of modernism remained alive, something neither resolutely modernist nor totally classicizing. Surprisingly enough, this state of uncertainty and restless searching issued in some remarkable and enduringly interesting architecture.

Among the most iconic and unique monuments to post-war ambivalence towards modernism is the unusual Torre Velasca office building in Milan (1957–60, BBPR: Lodovico Barbiano di Belgioioso, Enrico Peressutti and Ernesto Nathan Rogers). Unlike the bland Sarom skyscraper in Milan (1956–9) by Melchiorre Bega, the Torre Velasca's design as a modern high-rise tower alludes to, without mimicking, Milan's medieval traditions. BBPR accomplished this feat in the city centre's first skyscraper (in an area levelled by Allied bombs in 1943) with an eighteen-floor base of offices and shops, topped by residential apartments thrusting out above the shaft. For a mid-twentieth-century reinforced concrete skyscraper, the tower's projecting upper offers an unusual profile, its struts at once suggestive of the city's medieval towers and continuing down all four elevations as slender piers, a subtle reference to engaged columns. The profile

Mario Botta, MART, Rovereto, 2002.

itself, though apparently distinctly medieval in inspiration, in fact also resulted from careful calculations of the city's building code requirements for spaces designated office or residential – hence the larger footprint of the upper section of the tower. The added benefits of placing the apartments atop the office tower include providing spectacular views of the city and rising above the worst smog – one of Milan's most pressing problems. To these functional considerations we must add the architects' willingness to tolerate criticism for being 'nostalgic' and 'historicist', then and later. The vexation of contemporaries and historians in attempting to attach a name to the building's style – calling it everything from Neoliberty to Brutalist to postmodern – only reinforces the evocative power of designs that elude precisely such facile labelling, something that unites many of Italy's most memorable structures of the post-war decades. In fact, the Torre Velasca has become a beloved landmark of the Milan skyline.

Critics levelled similar charges of 'nostalgic', 'old-fashioned' and unmodern against some prominent post-war Italian film-makers, including

Pupi Avati and Ermanno Olmi. After completing clever films such as the smart horror film *La casa con le finestre che ridono* ('The House with the Laughing Windows', 1976), Avati also generated period pieces that celebrated a unique and wonderful past, in films such as *Gita scolastica* ('School Trip', 1983), and *Storie di ragazzi e ragazze* ('Stories of Boys and Girls', 1989). Despite their heady nostalgia these films were far from the typically banal Cinecittà productions of the time. In *Storie*, for example, Avati traced the awkward encounter of two families in the context of the prospective marriage of a young couple from different classes and different regional cultures. Ermanno Olmi's profound Catholicism and his deeply regional films also provoked mixed reactions from critics. Unlike most other directors of the post-war era, Olmi was neither a son of the prosperous bourgeoisie nor of the decadent aristocracy, but of Lombard peasants; as a young man he worked as a clerk. Both a persistent regionalism and a deep affinity for workers surface repeatedly in films such as *Il posto* ('The Job', 1961) and *I fidanzati* ('The Engagement', 1962). In particular, Olmi depicted the post-war urban worker struggling to survive yet caught between the conflicting imperatives of keeping his job and retaining his dignity. In *L'albero degli zoccoli* ('The Tree of Wooden Clogs', 1978), Olmi chronicled tenant farmers who still lived according to millennial rhythms of nature in late nineteenth-century Lombardy, while in *Il mestiere degli armi* ('The Profession of Arms', 2001) he recounted the life of Giovanni de' Medici dalle Bande Nere, the warrior who died while valiantly battling Charles v's *lanzichenecchi* and holding them north of the Po river. His death allowed Charles v to proceed to the sack of the holy city in 1527.

Olmi's *Cento chiodi* ('One Hundred Nails', 2007), set in the Po Valley, triggered criticism because of the deeply religious, Christian character of the film and its romanticized depiction of nature. One hundred ancient volumes nailed to the library floor point to the apparent culprit, a young philosophy professor who has vanished and is believed dead. In fact he has fled to take up residence in the ruins of a house along the banks of the Po, where the community slowly adopts him as a reincarnated Christ-figure. Living a simple life in proximity with nature and free of the twentieth-century obsession with the acquisition of things, Olmi's hero instead constitutes a model for a way of life configured of close personal relationships, with all of their limitations – a life sensitive to the world and all of its inhabitants: flora, fauna, landscapes and people. Rather than being nostalgic or tradition-bound, Olmi offered a vision to counter the mindless exploitation omnipresent in Italian television, particularly on the channels and in the films (not to mention books and newspapers) owned by Mediaset, the Berlusconi empire. Remember that once he managed to acquire the right to broadcast his television stations alongside those of

Ignazio Gardella,
Padiglione d'Arte
Contemporea, Milan,
1949–53.

the state, Berlusconi made his mark with the sexploitation game show *Colpo grosso*, the chief feature of which was strutting, bare-breasted young women – and his channels only went downhill from there. If this represents modernism in the Italian media, then the appeal of the films of Olmi and Avati is comprehensible. In any case, in architecture as well as in cinema, the dogmatic insistence on a particular interpretation of modernism in which all links to past values, traditions, images and styles are summarily banished with Faustian abandon is indeed strange. 'Nostalgia' in architectural circles today is a dirty word, so professors and critics denigrate any design that hints of it. One wonders who makes such rules, and why others piously obey them. Not only is this foolish, such a totalitarian approach to culture is at odds with the putatively democratic aspirations of many of modernism's avatars.

Among other remarkable post-war projects in which the architects refused to pay obeisance to an unreflective modernist aesthetic are Ignazio Gardella's Padiglione d'Arte Contemporanea (Pavilion of Contemporary Art, 1949–53) in Milan's Villa Reale park, and his Casa alle Zattere (Casa Cicogna) on the Giudecca Canal in Venice (1953–8). The interiors of the pavilion are high, sunny spaces for displays of sculpture, with a more sheltered section raised one floor up for paintings, while on the exterior, sliding metal panels are elegantly wedged between the slender piers of the facade. Like Luigi Moretti's Palazzina del Girasole (see chapter Five) and BBPR's Torre Velasca, Gardella's pavilion and the Casa are truly beyond style – unique and unrepeatable examples of formal and typological analysis and inventiveness based in no small measure on a profound grasp of history. Along similar lines is another unusual public building by Adalberto Libera (with Sergio Musmeci), a building likewise designed outside the terms of contemporary formal debates: the regional government building in Trento. Obstinately persistent in pursuing his own path, Libera designed this complex as a replacement for a branch of the Banca d'Italia levelled by bombs during the waning years of the Second World War. He eschewed an aesthetic derived from the Italian Rationalist tradition of the 1930s in favour of explorations of mass, form and structure on a site adjacent to a park and the city's railway station. The body of the structure facing the piazza rests on two massive, curved ground-floor piers, with extruding external stairs and an iconic circular pod for council meetings. For all its boldness, structural exuberance and the compelling detailing typical of Libera's architecture, the ensemble nonetheless remains a curious element on the periphery of the ancient city;

fortunately, it is not entirely glazed and not high enough to constitute a blot on the skyline.

On the Adriatic coast at Riccione, between 1961 and 1963 Giancarlo Di Carlo erected a summer colony for dependants of one of the nation's major utilities, Società Idroelettrica Piemontese (SIP). Located along the coastline with several other summer resorts for children of various organizations and institutions, Di Carlo exploited the proximity to the shoreline (far closer to it than are any of its neighbours) by configuring the large

Giancarlo Di Carlo,
SIP seaside resort,
Riccione, 1961–3.

open court so that it faced the sea. Di Carlo here developed one of the themes he explored over the next decades: that of the building conceived as a small city. Interpenetrating spaces in section and elevation, its low scale and elegant details make the colony stand out among its nondescript neighbours. Despite the design's quality and the procedure under way at the Ministry of Culture to designate it a historic monument, new owners abandoned it to deliberate and inevitable decay by 2003, as they then sought and received permission to raze it and replace it with a far higher (eight-storey) luxury tourist hotel. The many colonies erected on both Italian

260

coasts from the 1930s through the 1960s responded to a need for holidays for poor urban children whose families were otherwise unable to afford such luxuries. Time and greater wealth has obviated those needs, but surely such buildings could be fruitfully modified for different uses. The local architecture school at the University of Bologna (in Cesena) dedicated exhibitions and thesis projects to the prospect of modifying some of the more interesting resorts for different uses, but to no avail. Speculators would not enjoy abundant profits with such a strategy; unsurprisingly, speculation once again trumps adaptive reuse.

Italy's Post-war Cemeteries

It is not without irony that two of the most significant and most famous post-Second World War architectural projects in Italy are cemeteries. In 1969, Carlo Scarpa began assembling a monumental tomb for the Brion family at San Vito d'Altivole (near Asolo, completed 1978). Themes evident in the architect's earlier work emerge here, particularly the deeply personal expressiveness of his handling of concrete in the cemetery's sprawling pathways through water channels, and verdant garden. It is rich with symbols from antiquity: the propylaeum of cypresses marking the monumental entrance passage, the *arcosolium* (small arch) over the crypts, intersecting circles representing the proximity in death of two who had loved in life. The family tomb sits on communal property, hence Scarpa designed a chapel not only for the family but for the entire community; the private feature is a small pavilion on a pool of water, inaccessible to visitors. Employing the simplest materials – concrete, glass, water, grass, cypresses, steel, mosaics – with a conceptual richness and rigour in which the concrete is scored, carved, moulded, framed and cut away, Scarpa realized a project that engages all of the senses, as even alighting on paving stones sounds musical tones in counterpoint to the cascading water of the pool. Scarpa even provided for his own entombment, almost as though a member of the family, in the Tomba Brion. Because his was a private client, Scarpa was able to control the quality of construction which, despite the extensive use of rough, unfinished concrete, weathered beautifully over the intervening decades. One of his last projects, the Brion Tomb represents the mature culmination of a lifetime dedicated to the exploration of form and material, symbol and personal expression, integrated into a harmonious whole. Indeed, in less sure hands the symphony of form and material realized so compellingly here could well have sunk into cacophony – as many other projects have. Droves of architectural tourists and students troop to this remote site in the Veneto region to admire this sprawling testimony to a highly personal vision of modernism, usually

left: Carlo Scarpa,
Tomba Brion, San
Vito d'Altivole,
1969–78.

Aldo Rossi, San
Cataldo cemetery
with Gallaratese
housing complex and
Teatro del Mondo,
drawing.

Aldo Rossi, San
Cataldo cemetery,
Modena, 1971–,
ossuary interior.

between stops at monumental rural villas by the sixteenth-century Vicentine architect, Andrea Palladio.

Just a couple of years later, Aldo Rossi entered and won a competition to enlarge the existing Cimitero di San Cataldo in Modena (1971). In certain respects his design took its cues from some of the key elements of the existing complex and translated them into a modern architectural language, but he added significant new features, including a giant and brightly hued cubic ossuary, double-height corridors lined with tombs on both sides, and individual smaller structures for family crypts. The blue, metal roofs, the raking light streaming in at regular intervals from the stairwells and the hauntingly beautiful succession of wings of tombs drew international attention to a work Rossi conceived as a city for the dead, analogous to the city of the living. Even before construction began, the design had been published across the world, in part because of the evocative and powerful drawings with which Rossi presented his competition entry. By contrast with Scarpa's Brion Tomb, Rossi's San Cataldo Cemetery is among Rossi's earliest projects, the work of a young man investigating hallowed themes while negotiating his own response to an oppressively dominant modern movement. As with many of his later works, Rossi returned repeatedly to the cemetery in subsequent drawings, recasting the deep Pompeian red-orange cube within the foursquare blocks as a leitmotif that surfaced in ever shifting form over the next 30 years.

Unlike Scarpa, Rossi had no control over the execution of this publicly financed structure. The quality of design far outstripped the quality of construction; like most public projects in Italy, the city awarded the building contract on the basis of bids, with the lowest bidder winning the job. At the time, the head of a firm that tendered a bid told me that the complex could not be built well at the cost projected by the lowest bidder, and he was right. Within ten years the poor quality of the concrete and sloppy detailing were already robbing the cemetery of some of its appeal, and time has only worsened matters. Neither carelessness in design nor inattentiveness to detail created this problem, but rather a public works building process that rewards slipshod performance and treats a work of art like a sewer construction project.

Surveys of architecture continue to publish these two cemeteries. How did two cemeteries come to acquire an iconic hold on architectural imaginations, and how did these two in particular achieve their enduring status? Perhaps the functional purity of a cemetery – a monument to the end of life of individuals, communities and families, a complex wherein the living honour the dead, which must only serve as an inspiring backdrop for one of the two essential and irreversible moments of life – facilitates a treatment of equal formal purity. And yet Italy has many cemeteries and

Massimiliano Fuksas,
cemetery, Orvieto,
1984–92.

many cemetery additions which neither aspire to nor achieve such status: think of Prima Porta in Rome. Ultimately it was the extraordinary response of the two observant designers who, confronted with one of life's most essential moments, approached the challenge with modesty, empathy and poetic clarity, that has garnered such fame for the two designs. Scarpa drew upon his palette of tried and true materials, techniques, symbols and forms to produce his enigmatic tomb, the product of a lifetime of studying, drawing and building that had already attracted wide attention. Rossi challenged the nude white purity of the modern movement ethos by rendering the roofs blue and the ossuary a red-orange cube – at the time stunningly bold gestures – as well as by adopting double-height columns, pitched roofs and an industrial staircase within the ossuary. Without adding ornament or depending upon highly crafted artisanship he produced poetry, simply by manipulating forms and masses in rhythmic sequences and by choreographing light and shadow to work their magic.

New cemeteries, and additions to existing ones, continue to engage the offices of established architects as well as those of a younger generation, resulting in surprisingly different interpretations of a building type found in even the smallest villages. In 1992, Massimiliano Fuksas completed a small cemetery addition for the town of Orvieto. Shielding the cemetery from curious eyes behind a wall has long been a common strategy in Italian cemeteries, but Fuksas's ramparts modifies the tradition, by drawing close parallels with the ancient walled city, as does the interior ossuary, formed of a segmented ellipse that from below faintly recalls the city's famed spiral well.

Massimiliano Fuksas,
cemetery, Orvieto,
and a view though
the ossuary.

Vittorio Fava, AIG
Architects, cemetery
addition in Alonte,
1996–2010.

An even smaller cemetery addition by Vittorio Fava under construction at Alonte, in the province of Vicenza, illustrates how to endow even a modest project with dignity and restraint at a challenging site below street level, slightly sunken and framed by woods and rocky escarpments. The new wing links to the existing, nondescript, early twentieth-century one by means of a slender, steel-framed, glazed loggia, which also houses back-to-back burial niches. To the north of the site, a wall abuts a shallow cliff, while the new chapel terminates the main east–west axis. The cemetery's small scale called for a modestly sized chapel, here rendered in glass and wood, the latter chosen to expose the effects of time and weathering in a setting designed to serve as a site of remembrance. Both the Fuksas and Fava projects share the sensibility particularly of Rossi's San Cataldo Cemetery – that is, engaging traditional cemetery types without imitating their architectural language or refusing to accommodate new practices.

International Recognition

Whatever the problems Italian architects confronted in attempting to establish their practices and acquire commissions, they often found recognition and success far more rapidly outside Italy. Throughout the twentieth century, many of the country's most prominent architects travelled elsewhere, to Europe, the United States, the Middle and Far East, designing major buildings and urban complexes. Many simply emigrated, making new homes and building respectable if unspectacular careers elsewhere, such as Raimondo D'Aronco, who pursued his career further in Thailand; and Pietro Belluschi and Ciro Contini, who both established important studios in the U.S. after settling on the west coast during the 1920s and 1930s respectively. Belluschi became the premier architect of the city of Portland, Oregon, producing the first true curtain wall skyscraper in Portland (1948), long before those of Mies van der Rohe in Chicago.[2] Contini practised and taught in southern California after fleeing Italy's racial laws during the Fascist era. Another compatriot who fled to the new world, Rino Levi, an Italian architect who was born in Brazil but studied in Italy, authored the country's first manifesto of modern architecture and where he was an early leader in the country's modern architecture movement.[3] More recently, when Fuksas realized that it would be next to impossible to develop the type of practice he sought in Italy, in the 1970s he decamped to France and a successful career there, opening an office in his native Rome only decades later.

Other architects travelled to other countries for specific projects. Luigi Piccinato translated his experiences with the fascist new towns south of Rome into producing a master plan and low-cost housing projects for Istanbul during the immediate post-war years. Of particular note is Piccinato's design for Emlak bank's Ataköy social housing development along the west coast of Istanbul, in collaboration with the Turkish architect Haluk Alatan (1956–9). The very success of the early low-cost housing scheme quickly robbed it of its low cost, as most of the original residents soon sold their apartments for much higher prices. In another instance of international cooperation, Ernesto Rogers travelled to Argentina in 1948 and consulted on the master plan for Buenos Aires with Clorindo Testa, an Argentinean architect born in Italy.

Sometimes the reverse occurred, and success at home led to commissions abroad. Such was the case with Francesco Minissi who, on the heels of the striking success of his museum projects in Italy, completed the museum of mosaics at Sousse in Tunisia (1964); the Museum of the Ships of Cheops in Cairo (1963); the restoration of the monumental complex of the Ribat, Damano and Zikkaka Mosques in Sousse, Tunisia (1964–9); and the restoration and conservation of the grand frescos in the Mayan temple at Bonampak, Mexico (1962), among many others. The thoughtfulness and originality Minissi demonstrated on his Italian commissions caught the attention of museum experts internationally, who then sought his expertise in their own countries.

For others, the rise to prominence came after having attracted attention through smaller projects completed in Italy, but broad recognition only followed success in building internationally, which in turn led the architects to receive more commissions at home. Both Rossi and Renzo Piano

designed many projects that became international icons for the celebration of Italian design, and Rossi in particular produced buildings
throughout the world, from the u.s. and Japan to Germany and France,
before finally receiving more than the occasional commission in Italy.[4]
Among his most stunning projects completed outside of Italy is the Scholastic Building located in New York City's Cast Iron district (1997), one of
the last buildings he designed (completed after his death by partner Morris
Adjmi). Sandwiched between structures dating to the end of the nineteenth
century and early twentieth, Scholastic summarizes Rossi's practice of
observing, transcribing, translating and intervening in cities. The two facades
– a formal public face on Broadway, a more industrial and functional one
on Mercer Street – respond to the main expressive features of their neighbours (heavy masonry with cast-iron window details on one side, a more
delicate cast-iron foliate tracery set within ornate terracotta panels on the
other) but render them in his distinct language. On Broadway, this consists of robust white columns, rust-red steel lintels with hefty pop rivets,
green mullions, stacked lintels for a cornice and a recessed, glazed curtain

wall; on Mercer Street it takes the form of stacked layers of webbed, rust-red steel flanges, recessed glazing and green mullions to convey a rougher, more industrial sensibility on what is chiefly an alley for delivery trucks. Rossi's final two projects – the Scholastic Building and the project for the reconstruction of La Fenice in Venice – could hardly differ more, and yet he designed them contemporaneously.

An earlier Rossi project, also in the Veneto, provided a town hall for the community of Borgoricco. A rural settlement with no institutional or public centre, Borgoricco needed a town hall to serve as the focal point for future development for the rest of the town's core. When erected, the town hall sat in a field of weeds, but over time additional buildings, such as the theatre (Aldo Rossi and Arassociati, 2004), rounded out the municipal complex. Rossi drew directly from the sixteenth-century villa typology developed by Andrea Palladio for the working villas of the Venetian nobility. Lateral wings frame an open courtyard while the barrel-vaulted communal meeting room is wood-lined inside and revetted in copper without, with the copper gaining a rich patina over the decades since construction ended. In many of its details the design drew from local building traditions, in others from Rossi's own palette, but they flow together in a seamless web to produce an elegant, grand municipal building and public library. Equally importantly, Rossi was responsible for the master plan that gave the town a centre and its coordinated growth scheme over the past 25 years.

Aldo Rossi, Town Hall, Borgoricco, 1985.

Renzo Piano, *New York Times* building, New York, 2007.

No contemporary Italian architect has received as many major international commissions as Piano, even if critics have not reviewed all of his designs favourably. The Centre Pompidou in Paris (Richard Rogers and Renzo Piano, 1972–7), is a scar on the ancient city produced during a moment of techno-euphoria at the tail end of the modern movement for which, to be sure, Piano alone is not to blame, although he seems to take pride in calling the design a parody of the technological imagery of the era.[5] Following the Centre's second closure for cleaning and restoration (the first, in 1997, cost €135m, the second concluded in 2012) a scandal erupted in France over the sums Piano received for consulting on the project – many times greater than the original cost of the building's construction. Two of Piano's most recent projects, an expansion and renovation of the Los Angeles County Museum of Art (LACMA, 2008) and the *New York Times* Building in New York (2007), whatever their functional merits, reveal a sensibility more indebted to engineering than to architecture, and a persistent interest in foregrounding white steel trusses, typically suspended over crisp and starkly nude spaces illuminated with varying degrees of intensity. Elegant is perhaps the most descriptive term for many of Piano's post-Pompidou projects; the 52-storey *New York Times* tower has double-pane glazing with a grid either of thin ceramic tubes or of metal-and-glass louvres floating in front of it, intended to convey lightness and transparency. Given the downright gaudy and hyper-corporate consumerism of just about everything else in the Times Square area, including

Renzo Piano,
church of San Pio
di Pietrelcina, San
Giovanni Rotondo,
2003.

an audacious if not very interesting adjacent tower by Arquitectonica, perhaps here one can be grateful for Piano's evident restraint. For the Menil Collection museum in Houston, Texas, another quintessentially under-stated and elegant project (1987), Piano kept direct lighting away from most of the interiors to protect the artwork by deploying what he called 'concrete leaves' – curving concrete elements as shading devices for the entire structure. For the headquarters of the Italian newspaper *Il Sole 24 Ore* (Milan, 2004) Piano remodelled a former factory complex. Although touted as energy efficient and sustainable, it is difficult to see how this could be so when the building is entirely sheathed in glass. Web Office Controls (WOC) allow employees to control the climate and lighting of their own offices by logging into an ordinary web browser on their com-puters: the entire system involves the integration of heating, ventilation,

Renzo Piano, *Il Sole 24 Ore* building, Milan, 2004.

Renzo Piano,
Il Volcano Buono
shopping centre,
Nola, 2007.

lighting and sun blinds. Apart from being dirty, however, the extensive glazing admits light deep into the interior – and the public areas, atrium and café are already by June uncomfortably hot. Whatever the advantages for individual offices, the task of cooling the interiors during the hot, humid summers and warming them in Milan's cold, overcast winters remains problematic.

For the church dedicated to the venerated Franciscan monk (now sainted) Padre Pio, in the town of San Giovanni Rotondo in Puglia (2003), Piano chose a local stone for the structural elements, a series of stone arches of decreasing spans (the longest is 50 metres) that spiral inwards. They in turn hold aloft a revetted, shallow copper dome, while the facade consists of simple glazing. The church, reached by a stone-framed series of ramps for the pilgrims who regularly crowd into the plaza, responds to the mountainous setting and sweeping vistas from the square in front of the church, swinging low to embrace both setting and view. Nonetheless, the church is placeless: it could sit indifferently anywhere in the world, and perhaps better anywhere other than this ancient mountain town. By contrast, Piano designed the Paul Klee museum in Bern, Switzerland, with its sweeping, shallow curves, to fit modestly and precisely into the landscape, perhaps echoing the peaks and valleys of the surrounding Alps.

Although a bit late, Piano finally joined the ranks of architects prepared to confront environmental issues with, among other things, an earthen-sheathed, full-service shopping centre situated adjacent to the motorway between Nola and Naples. Its name, Il Volcano Buono (The Good Volcano, 2007), is apparently meant to summon references to the

274

nearby and far more famously menacing volcano, Vesuvius. Beneath the green shell Piano inserted a hotel, a supermarket, multi-screen cinema and some 180 shops. Unfortunately, the earthen coating envelopes an exceedingly mundane shopping centre, so one cheers the advent of a fledgling environmental consciousness while nonetheless lamenting the banality of the rest of the structure.

A third Italian architect to receive significant international recognition over the last 30 years is Gae Aulenti, one of the participants in the competition for the reconstruction of La Fenice. Aulenti had enjoyed a long career both in connection with architectural magazines such as *Casabella-Continuità* in the 1950s and '60s (as art director) and with her own office before she won the commission to transform the nineteenth-century Paris train station, Gare d'Orsay, on the banks of the river Seine, into a museum. In a country where no other woman architect even came close to achieving comparable prominence, Aulenti has stood out as an important interlocutor and professional over 50 years, completing projects in Italy, Europe and the United States. Notably, until 2000 she had not designed an independent building other than individual houses; whatever the strength of her reputation, the very clients who awarded her large renovation projects failed to commission major new buildings from her for years, even while they delivered big jobs to male architects, such as Giovanni Agnelli's many commissions to Renzo Piano. Despite these obvious

Gae Aulenti, Musée
d'Orsay, Paris,
1980–87.

limitations, Aulenti strongly rejects any notion that she has received less favourable treatment because she is a woman.[6]

Prior to the Musée d'Orsay, Aulenti had already renovated a venerable late eighteenth-century Venetian palace on the Grand Canal, Palazzo Grassi, for the automobile magnate Agnelli, in 1983–4, with a colourfully historicizing adaptation of the crumbling palace from its original incarnation into an all-purpose exhibition space (subsequently remodelled for a new owner into a museum for modern and contemporary art by the Japanese architect Tadao Ando).[7] Here she established a reputation for historicizing preservation – in effect, for reconfiguring interiors – one that she developed more fully at the Gare d'Orsay.

The train station, a beloved Beaux-Arts landmark adjacent to the Seine river (Victor Laloux, 1900) erected in time for the famous Exposition Universelle, had become redundant by 1980, so as with many other obsolete buildings, the French government decided to transform it into a museum, in this case for nineteenth-century art. Aulenti received the commission in 1980 and completed the project in 1987. Like other nineteenth-century stations, the Gare d'Orsay consisted of a long, glazed and barrel-vaulted central hall – in itself an inhospitable space within which to display paintings. Aulenti disposed sculpture in this central space and carved out lateral, stone-framed galleries for paintings. Much criticized at the time on the typically tedious grounds of not being sufficiently modernist and for putatively echoing elements of Italian Fascist architecture of the 1930s, the museum instead proved to be a largely comfortable, even intriguing home for the diverse artworks it displays, although some problems relating to glare were not fully resolved. Much as Aldo Rossi did, Aulenti appropriately spurns the attempts to fix a label to her designs (critics derided the Gare d'Orsay for being postmodern) precisely because she tries to respond to structures themselves, their histories, surroundings and new destinations, and not to fleeting contemporary dogmas on style.

Aulenti's subsequent projects in Italy include remodelling the long-abandoned former papal stables in Rome on the Quirinal Hill into yet another museum (Le Scuderie al Quirinale, 1998–9), and the transformation of the Savoy duchy's massive hunting estate, the seventeenth-century Venaria Reale, into a museum, conservation centre and congress hall (1997–ongoing). In the first case, Aulenti managed to transform a formerly utilitarian space with only modest architectural definition into a remarkably successful museum, and while the Venaria modification is still under way, the completed parts are magnificent settings for many types of art, a high achievement in a complex site. The re-remodelling and reorganization of Piazzale Cadorna in Milan (2000) included the construction

Gae Aulenti, Venaria Reale museum, Turin, 1997–.

276

of the metro terminal and facilities for transportation to Malpensa airport. In homage to nineteenth-century transportation hubs of iron and glass (such as the Gare d'Orsay), Aulenti here designed a series of covered walkways of glass and steel to frame the busy piazza. Their chromatic exuberance (deep blue-green and red) contrasts markedly with the surroundings but certainly renders the site memorable. As a final, whimsical touch, the roof beams double as water channels that pour waterfalls into shallow pools. Unfortunately, the chromatic variety fails to give discernible order to a major transit point that remains extremely confusing for the visitor.

In her niche as an architect primarily of interiors and urban infrastructure, Aulenti made a significant mark without needing to develop a signature design – perhaps one of her greatest accomplishments. Nonetheless, the fact that clients were long reluctant to award her a large, freestanding new building testifies to the status that even women architects of remarkable accomplishment still hold in Italy: that is, far inferior to many markedly less gifted but perhaps better politically connected males.

With buildings, designs, renovations and exhibitions across the globe, from Georgia to Japan, Massimiliano Fuksas established himself as a consummate professional capable of bringing poetry and technology together in original and unusual ways without the rhetorical formal bombast of so many globetrotting architectural stars of today. Two emblematic examples are the Armani Tower (Tokyo, 2007) and Palatino Centre (Turin, 2005). The first, situated in Tokyo's Ginza district, is a twelve-storey, 7,370-square-metre glass tower of stunningly understated elegance. Fuksas distinguished the glazed exterior with cascades of luminous leaves that vary subtly in response to external nocturnal and diurnal alterations in light. The interior reflects features of the fashion house itself, with delicate explorations of texture, light, transparency, opacity and chromatic variety. The Palatino Centre, on the other hand, replaced a heterogeneous mix of market stalls with a single covered structure. Two levels below ground accommodate parking and infrastructure, while the three floors of commercial space for shops, bars and the like are enclosed within a steel frame and layers of pale-green glazing, ingeniously gliding smoothly from airy and transparent to increasingly dense towards the lower levels. Within, the shops frame an open core criss-crossed by ramps and escalators. A wonderfully tactile and original treatment of surfaces unites these and many of Fuksas's other projects, including the new trade fair and convention centre complex at Rho-Pero, Milan, completed in 2005. And it was Fuksas who claimed the prize of the new airport in Beijing, completed in 2008.

Rather less agreeable is Fuksas's project for a skyscraper in Turin for the new Piedmont Region headquarters, a glass block of subtle qualities. The funds for the project initially sank into the swamp of the 2006 Olympics

but it seems now to be revived, having also been moved to the site of Lingotto. Along with Renzo Piano's new Intesa San Paolo tower for the bank's headquarters, the plan is to insert massive skyscrapers into the city fabric and transform its skyline into a 'modern' one. The reference to 'modern' comes from the Turin's former mayor, Sergio Chiarampico, who accused opponents of the Piano project of being 'anti-modern'. Such a belligerent use of 'modern' aims to silence opponents with epithets rather than to evaluate the project, which is precisely what happened here. By mounting a major exhibit and publishing a glossy catalogue with public funds celebrating Piano's project, the Turin Polytechnic lent its prestige to the enterprise. Far from being modern, as Guido Montanari of the same university has noted, such skyscrapers are associated with the past, in particular with flawed historical assumptions of unconstrained economic growth and unlimited resources to waste.[8] Arguably, it is far more 'modern' to work within a comprehension of limited resources and the vibrancy of the local.

Turin already had one skyscraper inserted directly into its dense urban core, the Torre Littorio by Armando Melis de Vila and Giovanni Bernocco (1933–5), whose height, 100 metres, had been fixed by Mussolini himself. Although a profound intrusion into the historic centre, the tower at least had the distinction of being one of the two earliest steel constructions in Italy. No such claims can be made for either the Fuksas or for the Piano projects. Certainly both are fully aware of the inappropriateness of their projects,[9] but the lure of building and more fame seem to trump good sense here as elsewhere – and only steady economic decline might halt the production of such structures.

By contrast, certainly one of the most intriguing and successful expatriate Italian architects is Benedetta Tagliabue, who formed a partnership with Enrique Miralles (EMBT) in Barcelona in the 1990s. Even after Miralles's unexpected death in 2000, Tagliabue managed to guide the firm in the completion of projects already under way and in the design of new ones, both in Spain and internationally. The most stunning and complex of these is the Scottish Parliament building in Edinburgh, Scotland (1998–2004). Having wrested control over its own governance away from England after hundreds of years of domination, the new government wanted a building that would celebrate that hard-won independence and look to the future with boldness and energy – which is precisely what EMBT gave it. The buildings fanning out on the Holyrood site so burst with ideas that it seems impossible to imagine that they could be fused into some unified whole – yet Tagliabue did precisely that with masterful rigour. A similar explosion of joyful energy radiates from her remodelling of an abandoned Barcelona convent, Santa Caterina (2005), with the happy confluence of old convent

EMBT, Santa Caterina Market, Barcelona, 2005.

EMBT, Scottish Parliament, Edinburgh, 1998–2004.

walls and colourful, curving roof sheltering a market and new housing inserted to the rear of the market. To these two remarkable completed projects should be added the delightful design for the Spanish pavilion for Expo 2010 Shanghai, where Tagliabue emphasized the temporary nature of the structure by draping it in wonderful sweeping wicker curves, and the new plaza for the town of Lleida, Spain.

Notably, and unusually, under Tagliabue the EMBT office has also aggressively pursued a 'green' agenda, with energy saving and sustainability a major emphasis in all of the firm's work. It is worth emphasizing the differences between the EMBT projects and those of Piano and Fuksas noted above. However different the Scottish Parliament building is from the staid architecture of Edinburgh, it sits apart from the city centre and does not ignore height limitations. Parliamentarians wanted a distinct building that would emphasize their new-found independence, and the studio managed to do this with grace, elegance and, especially, originality. The Fuksas and Piano projects, by contrast, indifferently sited and indistinct from thousands of other skyscrapers, offer nothing new, and certainly nothing needed, in downtown Turin.

Other contemporary architects whose offices have established a presence in other countries include Vittorio Gregotti, whose large and highly professional studio has accomplished elegant and grand projects such as the Centro Cultural de Belém in Portugal (with Manuel Salgado, 1992); the much-praised Olympic stadium in Barcelona (1992); apartments for the IBA (an international building exhibit), in the south Tiergarten, Berlin; and many large commissions in Italy, including the massive urban project for the ex-Pirelli factory complex in Milan, a project that has received highly negative reviews. Burdened by the need to remodel existing factory structures for other uses, unfortunately many of these former industrial areas – including the Bicocca – respond more to the failed urban logic of the modern movement and less to the ways people use and inhabit large cities; for this reason people still crowd into the old city centre and abandon these urban deserts in the evenings and on weekends. What sets Gregotti apart

Santiago Calatrava,
Bridge of the
Constitution
(previously of Peace),
Venice, 1997–2009.

both from many of his generation, and younger generations of designers, is his apparently endless capacity for reflecting upon architectural practice, theory and history; no practising architects writes more consistently, and so consistently challengingly, about the discipline and the profession today.[10]

If Italian design and designers found ready clients all over the world, foreign architects also received commissions in Italy over the past three decades. Historically, non-native architects found it difficult to bring projects to fruition in Italy: Mussolini spurned Le Corbusier's attempt to design a new town during the Fascist era, Frank Lloyd Wright had no greater success with a project for a hostel in Venice, nor did Corbusier manage to construct the hospital he designed for Cannaregio in Venice. In fact, the only contemporary architect to add to Venice's historic centre is

Spanish architect Santiago Calatrava, who erected a fourth bridge across the Grand Canal, whom the city is now suing for the enormous cost overruns (from €3.8 to 11.2 million). Money is not the only issue; the bridge – unfortunately named Il Ponte della Pace, The Bridge of Peace – has suffered enormous problems, because the Spanish architect allegedly did not account for the structural requirements of the site: aesthetics trumped engineering. The expert summoned by the city of Venice to assess the bridge's problems, the engineer Massimo Majowiecki, reported in 2012 that the arch is too low (a curve of 5.2 per cent as opposed to the standard 12–33 per cent), therefore the foundations receive too much thrust, creating horizontal displacement, rotation and pressure on the joints, thus the two banks are slowly moving. In 2001, consulting engineer Giuseppe Creazza identified the potential (now actual) problem, and proposed a micro-tunnel between the two foundations. When Calatrava ignored this proposal, according to Majowiecki, Creazza resigned. In summing up his analysis, Majowiecki reported that the bridge would require 'heroic treatment' in terms of continuous testing and maintenance and that it presented a burdensome legacy of expensive upkeep unmatched by any other bridge in Venice.[11]

Good sense prevailed, at times, over megalomania, sparing other Italian cities from the economic disaster Venice now faces. After an invitation from the city of Bologna to prepare a master plan for an area on the city's perimeter, Kenzo Tange came up with a plan for an enormous city for millions – a plan the city quietly rejected in 1967 but that lived on in a half-life at the Bologna Fiera district to the north of the city. Recently, foreign architects managed successfully to push several of their projects through construction, with the overall results a decidedly mixed bag. Richard Meier completed a church for the Jubilee year of 2000 (completed only in 2004) at Tor Tre Teste in Rome. But however irresponsible the design in terms of materials and climate control, parishioners at Meier's church on the eastern fringe of Rome express pride in their mini version of the Sydney Opera House and the attention it draws to a neglected part of the city. The provincial city of Modena, on the other hand, narrowly escaped Venice's grim fate when Frank Gehry's gateway project expired from lack of funding.[12] Another oddity of the recent past from a foreign architect is the reconstruction of Le Corbusier's L'Esprit Nouveau pavilion in Bologna (1977). In its original incarnation the pavilion was but one of several at the International Exposition of Modern Industrial and Decorative Arts in Paris (1925) and was never destined to last beyond the end of the exhibition.[13] Lovingly reassembled and erected in its Bologna incarnation at the urging of Giuliano and Glauco Grisleri, with far greater structural integrity than the original, the two-storey Esprit Nouveau graces the city's

Tadao Ando, Punto della Dogana, Venice, 2008–09.

Fiera district. Its rebuilding is a stark reminder both that modernism is alive and well on the peninsula and that the ghost of Le Corbusier still exerts an arguably unwarranted grip on architectural imagination.

The Teatro della Scala (often referred to simply as La Scala) in Milan is one of the world's most famous opera houses. Although La Scala as an institution dates back to the eighteenth century, the building we see today, just blocks away from the Duomo, rose phoenix-like from the ashes of the original, destroyed by Allied bombs towards the end of the Second World War. When the Swiss architect Mario Botta received the commission to enlarge La Scala and add facilities to it (2002–4), his task called only for respect for the setting, a requirement he met with modest understatement – except for the lights that sparkle cheerfully like those on a Christmas tree at dusk. The new Museo di Arte Moderna e Contemporanea di Trento e Rovetto (MART, 2002) instead entailed designing a spacious and elegant museum and archive for twentieth-century architecture and design. Situated in the tidy town of Rovereto near the northeast shores of Lake Garda, Botta set the building back on a secondary street nestled against the hill, thereby minimizing disruption to the streetscape. The small side street terminates at a signature Botta 40-metre cylindrical atrium, a form also found as the main formal element at the San Francisco Museum of Modern Art (1994). Based upon the dimensions of the Pantheon in Rome (and with an opening in the centre of the dome), MART is also meant to hold 1,200 people, but instead of the striking coffered dome of the Pantheon, Botta here fashioned a 25-metre cupola of steel and glass for

the entrance. When winter snows pile on it, light enters only through the oculus, and the melting snow slowly alters the quality of light within this vast, glazed vestibule. Again, the contrast with the Fuksas and Piano sky-scrapers for Turin could not be greater: here is a quite stunning and effi-cient structure tucked into a rear lot without subtracting anything from the historic centre. *This* is architecture.

Carefully detailed and clad in a pale yellow Vicentine stone, MART follows the same strategy as that found in the Japanese architect Tadao Ando's design for Fabrica ('workshop'), for the Benetton Foundation near Treviso – that is, proposing a structure with a modest profile by sinking one or more floors below street level (2000). Ando's project also revamps a seventeenth-century rural villa, adding a shallow reflecting pool and colonnade leading to the new, concrete and largely underground bunker. He also turned his hand to the difficult setting of Venice, at the Punto della Dogana (2009), the old customs house for materials arriving from the sea. Known for his remarkable subtlety and sensitivity, Ando's mandate required leaving the historic exterior intact while remodeling the interior to accommodate François Pinault's contemporary art collection. Previous restorations concealed the beautiful heavy beams of the trusses and the brick walls, but Ando opened them up, adding but a few new architectural features, in particular a concrete cube in the centre of the triangular structure.

An overview of recent and major commissions in Italy highlights the frequency with which government and quasi-state agencies call upon a handful of international star architects to undertake major projects, such as Foster & Partners, winners of an international competition for the new Florence train station as well as another for the schools and libraries of law and political science for the University of Turin. In defiance of every Italian tradition, the buildings for the university develop in Watergate-esque curves around a circular plaza and, in a typically mindless repetition of questionable modernist planning ideas, set them in otherwise undefined, unarticulated green fields with randomly scattered trees – at least at the time of this writing. Also in Turin, for the 2006 Winter Olympics the city summoned Arata Isozaki of Tokyo to design several venues, including the swimming stadium, the Olympic palace and the Palasport Olimpico stadium. Isozaki too claimed victory in a competition for a railway station, this one in Bologna. Since the city only managed to add passenger elevators to the station in 2010, there is some chance that this tradition of bureaucratic delays, along with the Italian economic crisis, will slow, perhaps permanently, the new station. One can only hope that here, as with several projects proposed for other Italian cities, the snail-like, Byzantine Italian bureaucratic system will finally grind them to a halt in the face of the implacable inertia that anyone who has encountered it will recognize. While it is disagreeable to celebrate that system, it can sometimes be an advantage, as in this case.

Zaha Hadid captured another win for the Naples train station. Hadid also emerged victorious from an international competition for a coveted commission in Rome: a centre housing the archives of major Italian artists and architects, MAXXI, a project under construction since 2002 (though inaugurated in December 2009, it promptly closed again to be completed later in 2010). This new contemporary arts centre is situated at the abandoned military barracks, Caserma Montello, in the Flaminio district along the northern border of the historic centre. Hadid's loosely L-shaped configuration of mostly glazed and criss-crossing elongated spaces flows out over the old urban grid – with, I hardly need add, supreme indifference to its surroundings. Inside, movable panels and extensive natural light modify the spaces for specific types of exhibits – even though abundant light will be problematic for precious documents, especially of the nineteenth and twentieth centuries. Although construction began in 2002 and was to terminate in 2006, the extraordinary complexity of the design led to repeated delays (and cost overruns), to which must be added slow and inadequate government funding. To be fair, it would be difficult to overestimate the difficulty of financing a project that more than tripled the original estimated cost. Years spent in construction did little to aid its quality; some features were shabby even before the first exhibits opened. The gridded metal stairs open over plastic slabs and reveal dirt stubbornly accumulating in corners and along edges, with little thought having been dedicated to how to clean such highly visible details. Dirt insinuates itself into unlikely places throughout the building – as it does everywhere in our world, but at the

Zaha Hadid, MAXXI, Rome, 2010, exterior view of piazza.

MAXXI it does so in particular in and around the various translucent or opaque stairs and passageways, and cleaners will have little luck with this structure. Like other pristine, even pretentiously nude contemporary buildings, the success of the MAXXI depends in part upon keeping those elegant surfaces immaculate, which is why all those dirty corners and treads are so jarring. The failure to maintain that pristine purity risks turning such structures into the typical stained and shabby modern building. It will take a massive overhaul to clean this structure, not because of over-use but because the designers gave no thought to ordinary, day-to-day maintenance and cleaning.

One of the most positive features of the MAXXI is the abundance of diverse types of galleries, from interstitial passageways to huge, double-height spaces, some entirely artificially lit and others bathed in natural light. Curators can mount a wide range and size of exhibitions within spaces that are at times intriguing, at times puzzling, but never dull. There is even a spectacular panorama of Rome visible from a promontory at one of the MAXXI's highest points, a counterpoint to the art on display within. In other respects the building is well constructed and relatively well detailed, though the decision to extend an overhead ramp over a large chunk of the entrance plaza, only to eliminate it in the area directly before the entrance, is at best puzzling, at worst irritating. A bookshop and café finally opened opposite the building and has brought some life to the otherwise barren plaza, at least when it is open. The millions spent on the MAXXI are nonetheless a high price to pay for a few hours of moderate liveliness in a semi-public square. That the museum's expenditures are excessive became clear when the Fine Arts Ministry decided to invoke its special powers and take direct control of the MAXXI in April 2012. A new director, the secretary-general of the Fine Arts Ministry, Antonio Recchia, took over operation of the museum a month later, and the museum's top administrators resigned. With a deficit of €11 million on the books, the maintenance costs of at least €1 million (steadily rising) are certainly one of the primary problems.[14]

Far more successful in many respects is Odile Decq's adaptive reuse of the old Birra Peroni factory in Rome (1908, see chapter One) as a centre for contemporary art, the Museo d'Arte Contemporanea di Roma, (MACRO, 2010). Without the artifice and pretension of the MAXXI, the MACRO offers its own version of spatial variety and networks of walkways, and it too accommodates a wide variety of artefacts and exhibition types. In the interstices of the medievalizing factory, Decq deftly inserted the new facilities, including a closed interior courtyard uniting two blocks of the old structure. For the exquisitely detailed interiors she utilized grey and white paint and added a glazed arcade to modernize the internal exterior elevations, while elsewhere the bright white paint of the old sections of the factory stands in counterpoint to the new, darker entrance and transit spaces. From outside the building is unchanged except for the entrance, glazed the full height of the structure to make the recent interventions visible. Like Hadid, Decq provided sweeping cover over the entrance piazza – except for the zone just before the doorway. Both architects clearly intend to diminish the import of a historically cherished feature – the entrance – but that this demanded no overhang at all is not at all apparent, and is vastly inconvenient.

Under construction since 2006 in Brescia are two unappealing twisted glass towers by Daniel Libeskind for Editoria Bresciana, while the Austrian firm of Coop Himmelb(l)au (Wolfgang Prix, Helmut Swiczinsky, Michael Holzer) is completing yet another largely glass convention centre on the shores of Lake Garda. City officials in Rome engaged Rem Koolhaas in 2005 to transform the old general markets (Mercati Generali) on the via Ostiense into a multi-use shopping and entertainment centre over the next few years. One of the largest of the new building complexes replete with designs by non-Italian architects is that for the Milan Expo 2015 fair, for which Hadid, Libeskind, Isozaki and Pier Paolo Maggiora won an international competition. Like so many of the other designs by foreign architects, the plans here call for funny-shaped glazed skyscrapers, either twisted (Hadid), curved (Libeskind) or corrugated (Isozaki), complemented by a round structure vaguely recalling Frank Lloyd Wright's Guggenheim

Odile Decq, MACRO,
Rome, 2010. Below is
a formerly open area
remodelled; modern
gallery on left, old
factory chamber
to right.

museum in New York. What explains the predilection for these designs? Institutional patrons seek spectacle, and these architects deliver, although they tend to package the same formal solutions more or less interchangeably from venue to venue, which cannot help but diminish their prestige. If institutional clients are eager to attract high-rent tenants, one wonders whether these buildings will do so in the long term.

Why city and national government officials have been so eager to invite international stars to design new buildings is no mystery, although many would agree that Italian cities need add nothing to the country's rich patrimony of architecture, art, restaurants and urban texture to attract tourists: they come, and in abundance, for the history, architecture, food and picturesque rural landscapes, all of which exert an apparently inexhaustible appeal. With the exception of architects and architecture students, the chance to see new, ultra-modern buildings drafted by international architectural stars who are big only in a small firmament is most certainly not the primary draw for visitors. The rationale of public officials and the architectural community lies not in capturing fickle tourists, but in being – and appearing – modern. If architects and politicians in the nation's first decades sought to answer the question of what an Italian and national architecture should be, at the end of the second millennium and the beginning of the third, the new imperative is not to ask questions but to align Italian architecture and cities with the international (and too often self-appointed) architectural elite by means of 'signature' buildings. Emphatically rejected in these settings are efforts to engage in a dialogue with Italian traditions, or sites, let alone environmental issues; rather they go for globe-trotting styles that can be found unchanged from Berlin to Beijing, Mumbai to Montreal. Public officials and architects alike decry the country's failure to join the modern world by outfitting the peninsula's cities with spanking new spectacle buildings – stadiums, office towers and the like. As we have seen, officials did just that for the 1961 anniversary of Italian unification in Turin, for the 1990 World Cup held throughout the country, for the 2006 Winter Olympics in Turin, and so on, leaving a legacy of empty, useless, decaying structures rendered possible by ruthless invasions into the landscape – not to mention a staggering deficit attributable precisely to the expenditures on the Olympics. In pressing this imperative upon the rest of the country, they pre-empt the vision of what it means to be modern, just as dogmatic supporters of mid-century modernism did for several decades. The jury is coming in on the appropriateness of this ambition today, and the verdict is not favourable to the international archi-pretentious designs. Certainly the all too frequent decision to rely on non-Italian superstars also conveys little faith in native talent and little appreciation for Italy's existing treasures.

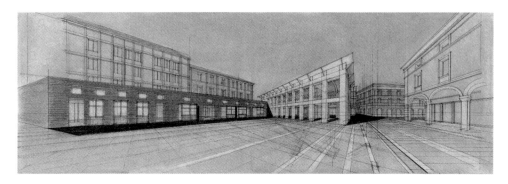

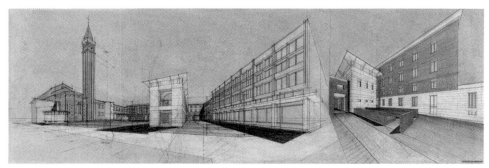

Gino Malacarne,
Piazza della Libertà,
Cesena, 2003.

Prospects for the Future

For younger generations of architects, the future holds ambiguous promise. In the panorama of corruption and favouritism in the world of competitions, it is something of a miracle that promising work appears and that
young architects still enter competitions. Sometimes unknowns win, although
they mostly win the so-called idea competitions, where the likelihood of
a building being constructed is faint but prize money and recognition are
sufficient to attract a large pool of competitors. In 2005, the team of Studio
Bertolotto e Vacchelli Associati and Chiara Visentin (BVV) won a Rotary
Club competition for a Palazzo della Musica at the site of the ex-PalaFenice
theatre in Venice, and two years earlier, Gino Malacarne and his team won
another to redesign Piazza della Libertà in Cesena. As part of another team,
Visentin took top honours in a competition for ideas for a gate for Belgrade.
In each case, the winning designs illustrate the exceptional talents of mid-
career architects who nonetheless but rarely achieve recognition. Victories
in such competitions can nevertheless be springboards for acquiring commissions directly.

Arassociati, formerly the office of Aldo Rossi, scored a major accomplishment with the completion of a headquarters building for the internet

BVV, Palazzo della Musica, Venice, 2005.

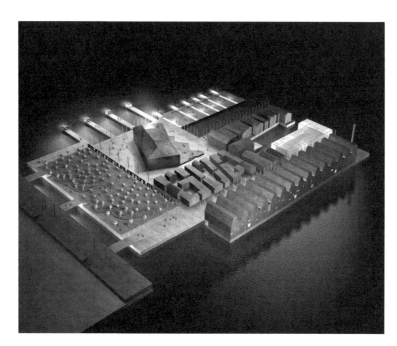

Arassociati, Tiscali headquarters, Sardinia, 2003..

Elena Manferdini, museum in Appignano, 2008–.

Arassociati, Museo d'Arte Moderna, former tobacco factory, Bologna, interior of galleries, 2000–07.

company Tiscali in Cagliari, Sardinia (2003), a handsome and understated essay in modernist design for Renato Soru, the company head who later became governor of the island. Given Arassociati's years of experience in his practice, it is something of a surprise that the design bears but few echoes of Rossi. They also masterfully completed Rossi's design for the rebuilding of La Fenice, and the firm also converted a disused tobacco factory in Bologna's fairgrounds district. The most intriguing feature of the renovation project is the Museum of Contemporary Art inside the former bakery. With its vast, bright spaces the museum became the third most visited in Italy only three years after completion in 2009. Unusually, rather than being permanently hobbled by the shadow of a talented architect, as were so many of the followers of Le Corbusier and Frank Lloyd Wright, Arassociati's designs depart from the model established by the man with whom some of the partners worked for over twenty years. The work of Arassociati exemplifies not only their talent, but Rossi's supple and non-dogmatic leadership; unfortunately, not all of his students and co-workers have been able to forge comparably independent paths.

After completing her degree in architectural engineering in Bologna, Elena Manferdini went to the United States to acquire a Master's degree in architecture at the University of California, Los Angeles. Knowing how difficult it would be to establish a career in Italy, she worked for firms in the Los Angeles area for a few years until she opened her own office, initially collecting small but prestigious jobs designing objects for Alessi, Guzzini and other companies, as well as window displays for the fashion designer Valentino's many stores and the West Coast pavilion at the architecture biennale in Beijing in 2006. In 2006 she also began work on two major projects, one in Italy and one in China. The former is a master planned area adjacent to the historic centre of the small town of Appignano, Macerata. Once home to industrial sheds, the lot had been vacant for over half a century; the new museum and theatre (under construction as of 2008) will be the centrepieces of a larger complex of 80 apartments Manferdini is also designing. Reinforced concrete and glass are the primary materials of the ground-hugging museum, but the sensuously sleek trusses and extruding lacy panels are of stainless steel, also doubling as shading devices over the glazing. And in Guiyang, Guizhou Province, Manferdini draped stainless-steel filigreed sheets down a 15,000-square-metre multi-functional tower set on a verdant hill, where cascading waterfalls add sounds to the site's beauty. Here she transforms the traditional notion of the facade as skin into an unexpected and sinuously delicate revetment that doubles as a sun shield. In both cases, the architect's ongoing exploration of fabrics, textures and metals serves as a vehicle for taking a fresh look at what is by now a well-established building type; they set her apart not only from architects of her generation but of older, more experienced practitioners as well. Although the projects have become protagonists in the currently fashionable dialogue on digital projects, as with the work of many of her most celebrated peers, Manferdini's designs exhibit but little interest in environmental and sustainability issues.

As was the case for the 1960 Summer Olympics in Rome, the 2006 Winter Olympics in Turin led to a frenzy of building. Although international stars such as Isozaki captured the big commissions, local talents also received important projects, such as those for the residential districts for athletes and journalists that became student housing at the conclusion of the games. Among these, Cristina Bevilacqua's block of four apartments,

Cristina Bevilacqua, university housing complex, Turin, 2002–5.

Michele Bonino and
Subhash Mukerjee
(MARC), Giulio Pagani
boathouse, 2007.

Residenza Universitaria Lungodora (2002–5), stands out for its simple elegance and attention to energy conservation. Situated near the snaking curves of the future political science and law faculties designed by Foster & Partners, Bevilacqua's design spurns Foster's obsession with extensive glazing in favour of far greater attention to energy use, in part controlling the temperature through passive solar devices such as reticulated panels and building orientation, to altogether handsome effect.

Needless to say, focus on environmental concerns has not predominated in the work of younger Italian architects any more than it has in that

ZPZ Associates (Tullio Zini, Michele Zini and Claudia Zoboli), Loris Malaguzzi Center, Reggio Emilia, 2009, atrium.

of the older generation. When such matters do take centre stage, however, recognizing the accomplishment might encourage others to follow suit.[15]

Perched along the shore of Lake Como in the town of Torno is a boat-house by MARC architects (Michele Bonino and Subhash Mukerjee) for a sports club specializing in rowing with a facility to store boats and provide bathrooms and changing rooms for the athletes.[16] On an extremely limited budget, the architects relied on club members for much of the labour of construction, and together with the members sought to leave as modest a footprint in the pristine setting as possible. Designed to have the demountable boat lockers adjust to the shifting levels of the lake and even to be removed when necessary, the complex nestles the other facilities, fabricated of concrete, into a shallow cove adjacent to one of the town's most popular public spaces. Although low-key and modest, the base sparkles on the lakeside in the evening.

On the other side of the country in the Emilia-Romagna region, some of the schools completed in recent years synthesize adaptive reuse with sustainability and pre-school education. By contrast with many comparable examples, the national competition in 2000 for ideas on how to address early childhood education, won by a firm based in Modena, ZPZ Associates (Tullio Zini, Michele Zini, Claudia Zoboli), in collaboration with Gabriele Lottici and Andrea Branzi, actually led to a commission, the International Center Loris Malaguzzi, which was completed at the end of 2009 inside Locatelli, a warehouse built in 1926 for Parmesan cheese. Because of the sensitive activity of aging cheeses, the original builders had provided double masonry exterior walls with an air chamber between them, and

a sophisticated ventilation system to maintain a constant comfortable temperature even during the area's hot, humid summers. The ZPZ team retained these features as well as the organization of the wings along a spine, but added connecting links to lateral points. An auditorium and a restaurant lead off the atrium and, along with an atelier, are available to the community for evening events. Throughout design development, the team recognized the high quality of construction and the unusual sensitivity to climate and ventilation in the original building, so they retained virtually everything of the old structure, including the old heating system. Quite clearly, the governing principles here encouraged the architects to allow broad concerns for function to drive the renovation, and in so doing they produced an elegant and engaging design. Such wonderfully adaptable early twentieth-century warehouses are not in abundant supply, so the challenge is to take the lessons so patently successful in the Malaguzzi school and apply them to other renovations and to new structures as well. Building double-shell masonry walls is not the cheapest way to go in the short term, but it may well be so on a long-term basis.

Casa Ditta, by Maurizio Oddo and Alessandro Barracco (2009), offers another approach to addressing climate and ventilation issues. Set on a long, narrow lot on the edge of the seaside town of Erice, Sicily, the house takes its cues from a long history of coastal residential construction on the shores of the Mediterranean, with its cubic forms, flat roof and double-height central space. Oddo turned to an Arab tradition deeply rooted in Sicily to devise the air channel, also known as a *scirocco* chamber, with a true wind tower to circulate fresh, cool air throughout the interior. A rooftop garden

Casa Ditta, detail
of garden elevation.

and brise-soleil on the exterior recall some of the best features of early
twentieth-century modernism, while the colourful ceramic tiles at the
garden entrance pay homage to millennial Sicilian and Arab practices. As
Casa Ditta demonstrates, it is possible to design environmentally sophisticated structures at once elegant and modern; beauty need not be sacrificed
to fulfil this important function.

On the international scene, Italian architects are also proposing environmentally and economically sound projects, such as the centre for female
health in Ouagadougou, Burkina Faso, designed by FARE architects
(Riccardo Vannucci and Giuseppina Forte) and funded by the Democratic
Party of Italy and the EU (2007). A leading figure in a long-term struggle
against female genital mutilation, the clinic supports a range of programmes for women in the region. Beneath two flat roofs of recyclable PVC,
the design team organized a group of colourful mud-brick building units,
raised off the ground. Appropriate ventilation, heating and cooling, low
cost and the use of available regional and native skills and technologies were

Maurizio Oddo,
Alessandro Barracco,
Casa Ditta, Erice,
2009.

FARE studio, centre for female health, Burkina Faso, 2007.

the basic principles that guided this project, and local residents helped erect the structures. The complex sits lightly on its site, mimicking neither high-style Western design nor humble self-build structures, and like the schools in Emilia-Romagna, its understated elegance testifies to an approach to design light years away from the brash architecture of the world's archi-stars.

What the future holds for architects producing the high-quality buildings described above remains to be seen. Already compromised by the corrupt practices detailed earlier, the global crisis following the economic meltdown of 2008 presents yet further challenges to architects. Investors are reluctant to commit to grand new projects (other than the deeply compromised TAV, the highspeed rail line designed to pass through Piedmont's Susa Valley, a completely useless project that duplicates an existing rail line). This massive construction project appeals to organized crime because of the enormous sums involved and the consequent ease of money laundering, skimming and bribery; it is no accident that the concrete and construction industries are largely in the hands of organized crime. Other than this disaster, perhaps by sheer force of circumstance designers and small investors will begin to think small, both in terms of new constructions and rehabilitation of old ones. It may be wishful thinking, but if this proves to be the case, if Italy and Europe choose to confront the enormous fiscal crisis facing them with tools different from those traditionally proposed by bankers and financiers, then the singular creative talent of so many of Italy's designers might just end up emerging again.

References

chapter one: **Building a New Nation**

1 Martha Pollak, *Turin, 1564–1680: Urban Design, Military Culture, and the Creation of the Absolutist Capital* (Chicago, 1991). For an overview of Italian history, particularly from the nineteenth century onwards, see Christopher Duggan, *A Concise History of Italy* (Cambridge, 1994).

2 Simona Colarizzi provides an overview of the early years of the new Italian state in *Storia del Novecento italiano: Cent'anni di entusiasmo, di paure, di speranza* (Milan, 2000). For the plans to transform Florence see Vincenzo Fontana, *Profilo di architettura italiana del Novecento* (Venice, 1999). On Vernon Lee and the efforts of expatriates to halt the destruction in Florence, see D. Medina Lasansky, *The Renaissance Perfected: Architecture, Spectacle, and Tourism in Fascist Italy* (University Park, PA, 2004); see also the unpublished paper by Daniela Lamberini, '"The Divine Country": Vernon Lee in difesa di Firenze antica', presented at the conference Dalla Stanza Accanto: Vernon Lee e Firenze Settant'anni Dopo (Florence, 26–8 May 2005). For architecture in Rome, see Roberto Nicolini, *Roma capitale, 1870–1911: Architettura e urbanistica uso e trasformazione della città storica* (Venice, 1984); Valter Vannelli, *Economia dell'architettura in Roma liberale* (Rome, 1979). For a general history of the second half of the twentieth century, see Paul Ginsborg, *A History of Contemporary Italy: Society and Politics, 1943–1988* (New York, 2003).

3 Edward J. Poynter, 'Ancient Florence and Modern London', *The Times* (4 February 1899), p. 4.

4 Peter Burke, *The Historical Anthropology of Early Modern Italy: Essays on Perception and Communication* (Cambridge, 1987); Richard Goldthwaite, *Wealth and the Demand for Art in Italy, 1300–1600* (Baltimore, MD, 1993); Alice Jarrard, *Architecture as Performance in Seventeenth-Century Europe: Court Ritual in Modena, Rome, and Paris* (Cambridge, 2003).

5 Ouida, 'Cities of Italy', *North American Review*, CXLIII/360 (November 1886), p. 472.

6 Quintino Sella, *Dell'Accademia dei Lincei* (Bologna, 1879), p. 3.

7 Francesco Crispi, 'Capitale del Regno', in *Discorsi parlamentari pubblicati per deliberazione della Camera dei Deputati* (Rome, 1915), vol. II, p. 490.

8 Gian Carlo Jocteau, 'Lotta politica e conflitti sociali nell'Italia liberale', in *La Storia. L'età contemporanea: Dalla Restaurazione alla prima guerra mondiale*, ed. Nicola Tranfaglia and Massimo Firpo (Milan, 2001), pp. 667–71.

9 Pasquale Turiello, *Governo e governati in Italia* (Bologna, 1882).

10 Italy's upper classes behaved much as their peers did elsewhere in Europe in these respects, and indeed the country's own history is rich with examples of dukes, princes, emperors and popes asserting their power through architecture. Modern rulers have more sophisticated tools of display at their disposal.

11 Albert Russell Ascoli and Krystyna Von Henneberg, eds, *Making and Remaking Italy: The Cultivation of National Identity around the Risorgimento* (Oxford, 2001).

12 David Atkinson and Denis Cosgrove, 'Urban rhetoric and Embodied Identities: City, Nation, and Empire at the Vittorio Emanuele II Monument in Rome, 1870–1945',

Annals of the Association of American Geographers, LXXX/1 (March 1998), pp. 28–49 (pp. 33–4).

13 Ibid., p. 32.

14 Camillo Boito, 'Spavento delle grandezze di Roma', *Nuova Antologia*, XXX (1875), pp. 190–97.

15 Denis Mack Smith, *I Savoia re d'Italia* (Milan, 1990).

16 Ouida, 'Cities of Italy', pp. 462–77.

17 Francesco Crispi, *Carteggi politici inediti (1860–1892)*, ed. T. Palamenghi-Crispi (Rome, n.d.), p. 457.

18 Ouida, 'Cities of Italy', p. 467. In his rage against the despoliation of irrecoverable treasures, the author continued: 'The scholar, the poet, the archaeologist are all abhorred in modern Italy; their protests are impatiently derided, there reverence is contemptuously ridiculed, their love of art, of nature, or of history, is regarded as a folly, ill-timed and inconvenient, lunatic and hysterical', p. 468.

19 Duse lived in Asolo, near Treviso, where a major museum display chronicles her life and showcases artefacts associated with her, including furniture from her house.

20 Lewis Corey, 'Marquis De Sade: the Cult of Despotism', *Antioch Review*, XVI/1 (1966), pp. 17–31, esp. 24.

21 Lucia Re, 'Gabriele D'Annunzio's Theater of Memory: Il Vittoriale degli Italiani', *The Journal of Decorative and Propaganda Arts*, 3 (Winter 1987), pp. 6–51; John Woodhouse, *Gabriele D'Annunzio: Defiant Archangel* (London and Oxford, 1998).

22 Andrew Giger, 'Social Control and the Censorship of Giuseppe Verdi', *Cambridge Opera Journal*, XI/3 (November 1999), pp. 233–65; Peter Stamatov, 'Interpretive Activism and the Political Uses of Verdi's Operas', *American Sociological Review*, LXVII/3 (June 2002), pp. 345–66.

23 The name derived from a style forged in the halls of London's Liberty department store; its elaborately decorative surfaces were soon indistinguishable from those of Art Nouveau, a style that originated among French and Belgian architects.

24 Paul Greenhalgh, 'Art Nouveau: Politics and Style', *History Today*, L/4 (April 2000), pp. 4–5 (p. 4). See also Deborah L. Silverman's excellent study, *Art Nouveau in Fin-de-Siècle France* (Berkeley, CA, 1992).

25 Lucio Scardino, *Ciro Contini: Ingegnere e urbanista* (Ferrara, 1987)

26 Ferdinando Reggiori, 'Come si è arrivati alla piazza del Duomo quale oggi essa è?', in *Il Duomo di Milano*, ed. Maria Luisa Gatti Perrer (Milan, 1969), vol. II, pp. 83–118.

27 Augusto Castellani, 'L'arte nell'industria', *Monografia della città di Roma e della Campagna Romana* (Rome, 1881), vol. II, p. 395, cited in Alberto Caracciolo, 'Rome in the Past Hundred Years: Urban Expansion without Industrialization', *Journal of Contemporary History*, IV/3 (July 1969), pp. 27–41 (p. 30).

28 Filippo Tommaso Marinetti, 'Fondazione e manifesto del Futurismo' [1909], reprinted in *Manifesti del Futurismo*, ed. Viviana Birolli (Milan, 2008), p. 9.

29 Written in French and translated into Italian, the book was condemned in court as a public outrage in 1910 in Milan, but nonetheless was a major public triumph for the Futurists. See S. Cigliana, *Futurismo esoterico: Contributi per la storia dell'irrazionalismo italiano tra Otto e Novecento* (Naples, 2002).

30 Antonio Sant'Elia, 'L'architettura Futurista' [1914], reprinted in *Manifesti del Futurismo*, ed. Birolli, pp. 138–42.

31 Ouida, 'Cities of Italy', p. 462.

32 Ibid., p. 463.

1   In 1881 the percentage of the population tied to agriculture was 65.4; in 1900 this had already declined to 58.4 per cent. S. Musso, *Storia del lavoro in Italia dall'Unità a oggi* (Venice, 2002), pp. 15–40.

2   Stefano Fenoaltea, 'Notes on the Rate of Industrial Growth in Italy, 1861–1913', *The Journal of Economic History*, LXIII/3 (September 2003), pp. 695–735.

3   Victoria De Grazia, *The Culture of Consent: Mass Organization of Leisure in Fascist Italy* (Cambridge, 1981), p. 154.

4   Giorgio Mori, 'L'economia italiana dagli anni ottanta alla prima guerra mondiale', in *Storia dell'industria elettrica in Italia*, vol. I: *Le origini, 1882–1914*, ed. G. Mori (Rome and Bari, 1992); see also *Torino, città viva: Da capitale a metropoli (1880–1990)* (Turin, 1980).

5   'The Riots in Italy: Scenes in Milan', *The Times* (12 May 1898), p. 5.

6   Ibid.; 'Italian Strike Riots: Terrorism by a Labour Minority', *The Times* (11 June 1914), p. 7.

7   *Rerum Novarum*, in *Tutte le encicliche e i principali documenti pontifici emanati dal 1740*, vol. IV, ed. Ugo Bellocchi (Vatican City, 1995).

8   'Italy', *The Times* (15 February 1864), p. 10.

9   Paola Barbera, 'Architettura in Sicilia tra le due guerre: Vecchie città e province nuove', in Vittorio Franchetti Pardo, *L'architettura nelle città italiane del xx secolo* (Milan, 2003), pp. 295–305.

10 D. Medina Lasansky, 'Reshaping Attitudes towards the Renaissance: The Fight against "Modern Mania" in Florence at the Turn of the Century', in *The Renaissance in the Nineteenth Century / Le 19e siècle renaissant*, ed. Yannick Portebois and Nicholas Terpstra (Toronto, 2003), pp. 263–96.

11 Edward J. Poynter, 'Ancient Florence and Modern London', *The Times* (4 February 1899), p. 4.

12 Poggi wrote about his plans in *Sui lavori per l'ingrandimento di Firenze* (Florence, 1882).

13 Lee's organization, founded on 15 May 1898, contemporaneously with a series of letters to the London *Times*, drew the attention of the English community to the devastation Florence was destined to undergo. A conference exploring Vernon Lee's efforts to save Florence's architectural heritage was held in Florence, 26–8 May 2005: Dalla Stanza Accanto: Vernon Lee e Firenze Settant'anni Dopo. Of particular interest is the unpublished paper by Daniela Lamberini, '"The Divine Country": Vernon Lee in difesa di Firenze anti-ca'. See also D. Medina Lasansky, *The Renaissance Perfected: Architecture, Spectacle and Tourism in Fascist Italy* (University Park, PA, 2004), pp. 19–55; for a more detailed study of Vernon Lee, see Christa Zorn, *Vernon Lee: Aesthetics, History and the Victorian Female Intellectual* (Athens, OH, 2003).

14 Vernon Lee, 'Letter to the Editor', *The Times* (15 December 1898), p. 8.

15 'Vandalism in Modern Rome', *The Times* (6 April 1888), p. 3.

16 Giuseppe Galasso, *Mezzogiorno medievale e moderno* (Turin, 1965), pp. 400–402.

17 Stuart J. Woolf, *A History of Italy, 1700–1860: The Social Constraints of Political Change* (London, 1979), pp. 214–18.

18 Aurelio Romano-Manebrini, *Documenti sulla Rivoluzione di Napoli, 1860–1862* (Naples, 1864), p. 15.

19 T. Eugene Beattie, 'Observations on Southern Italy', *Agricultural History*, XIX/2 (April 1945), pp. 120–26 (pp. 121–2).

20 Costanza d'Elia, *Bonifiche e stato nel Mezzogiorno, 1815–1869* (Naples, 1995).

21 Piero Bevilacqua, 'Il Mezzogiorno nel mercato internazionale', *Meridiana*, 1 (1987), pp. 17–46.

22 Paolo Macry, 'The Southern Metropolis: Redistributive Circuits in Nineteenth-century Naples', in *The New History of the Italian South*, ed. Robert Lumley and Jonathan Morris (Exeter, 1997), pp. 59–82. For a riveting account of how organized crime and Chinese entrepreneurs have exploited the region's trade and distribution economy, see Roberto Saviano, *Gomorrah: A Personal Journey into the Violent Empire of Naples' Organized*

Crime System (New York, 2007, originally published in Italian as Gomorra [Milan, 2006]), trans. Virginia Jewiss.

23 Michael Pacione, 'Socio-Spatial Development of the South Italian City: The Case of Naples', Transactions of the Institute of British Geographers, n. s. XII/4 (1987), pp. 433–50.

24 Jonathan Morris, 'Challenging Meridionalismo', in The New History, ed. Lumley and Morris, pp. 1–19.

25 Gabriella Gribaudi, 'Images of the South: The Mezzogiorno as seen by Insiders and Outsiders', in The New History, ed. Lumley and Morris, pp. 83–114.

26 Pacione, 'Socio-Spatial Development', pp. 441–2.

27 Ibid., p. 450.

28 Simona Colarizzi, Storia del Novecento Italiano: Cent'anni di entusiasmo, di paure, di speranza (Milan, 2000), pp. 9–10.

29 Fabio Troncarelli, Il segreto del Gattopardo (Rome, 2007), p. 18.

30 G. Zucca, 'Delenda Baracca', Capitolium (January 1931), p. 15.

31 Pacione, 'Socio-Spatial Development', p. 443.

32 Eberhard Schroeter, 'Rome's First National State Architecture: the Palazzo delle Finanze', in Art and Architecture in the Service of Politics, ed. Henry A. Millon and Linda Nochlin (Cambridge, MA, 1978), p. 130.

33 Quintino Sella, 'Approvazione della convenzione di Basilea per il riscatto delle Ferrovie dell'Alta Italia e per altri provvedimenti ferroviari', 27 June 1876, in Discorsi parlamentari, vol. II (Rome, 1888), pp. 278–9.

34 Monte S. Finkelstein, 'The Johnson Act, Mussolini and Fascist Emigration Policy: 1921–1930', Journal of American Ethnic History, VIII/1 (Fall 1988), pp. 38–55 (p. 44). In 1901 the government established a commission to facilitate emigration to North America.

35 Finkelstein, 'The Johnson Act', p. 40. The other group massively penalized by this legislation was the Jews.

36 Ibid., pp. 40–41.

37 Ibid., p. 45.

38 Legge 31 March 1903, n. 254; Regio Decreto 27 February 1908, n. 89. For a thorough history of the organs developed to erect low-cost housing, see Istituto Autonomo per le Case Popolari, Case popolari: Origini dell'Istituto case popolari (Milan, 1972).

39 T. Angotti, Housing in Italy: Urban Development and Political Change (New York, 1977); N. Ginatempo and A. Cammarota, 'Land and Social Conflict in the Cities of Southern Italy: An Analysis of the Housing Question in Messina', in M. Harloe, Captive Cities (Chicester, 1977), pp. 111–22.

40 Ouida, 'Cities of Italy', North American Review, CXLIII/360 (November 1886), p. 466.

41 Rodolfo Lanciani, 'The Sky Scrapers of Rome', North American Review, CLXII/475 (June 1896), pp. 705–15 (p. 709).

chapter three: Architecture and the Fascist State, 1922–1943

1 Araldo di Crollolanza, introduction to Ministero delle Opere Pubbliche, Opere Pubbliche, 1922–1932 (Rome, 1934), p. 3.

2 'Italian Riots: Shops sacked and Food Seized', The Times (7 July 1919), p. 12.

3 'Serious Riots in Italy', The Times (15 October 1920), p. 9.

4 Secretary of Education Martini, rather than Massimo d'Azeglio, appears to have been the first to make this observation shortly after Italian unification. Simonetta Saldoni and Gabriele Tuci, eds, Fare gli italiani: Scuola e cultura nell'Italia contemporanea, vol. I (Bologna, 1993), p. 17.

5 'Greater Rome: Town Planning on the Tiber', The Times (19 February 1931), p. 11.

6 'Highways of Italy: Modern Roads to Rome', The Times (31 July 1931), p. 11.

7 Ministero Lavori Pubblici, Opere Pubbliche, pp. 203–23.

8 Diane Ghirardo, 'Italian Architects and Fascist Politics: An Evaluation of the Rationalist's Role in Regime Building', *Journal of the Society of Architectural Historians*, XXXIX/2
   (May 1980), pp. 109–27.

9 Edoardo Persico, 'Prophecy of Architecture', Part 1, trans. Diane Ghirardo, *Archetype*,
   I/1 (1979), pp. 26–8; Part 2, trans. Ghirardo, *Archetype*, I/2 (1979), pp. 17–19.

10 These views dominated the discussion for over half a century after the First World War;
   see Giulia Veronesi, *Difficoltà politiche dell'architettura in Italia, 1920–1940* (Milan,
   1940); Bruno Zevi, *Storia dell'architettura moderna* (Turin, 1950); Luciano Patetta,
   L'architettura in Italia, 1919–1943: Le polemiche (Milan, 1972); Silvia Danesi and Luciano
   Patetta, *Il razionalismo e l'architettura in Italia durante il fascismo* (Venice, 1976),
   catalogue of the 1976 Venice Biennale.

11 Dennis P. Doordan, 'The Political Content in Italian Architecture during the Fascist Era',
   Art Journal, XLIII/2 (Summer 1983), pp. 121–31 (p. 122). Doordan went to great lengths
   to distinguish between Rationalist architecture and everything else produced under
   fascism, on the one hand arguing that style is not enough to distinguish a fascist design
   from one that is not, and on the other continually resorting to precisely such distinctions
   to separate a fascist from a modern – hence not fascist – design.

12 Ghirardo, 'Italian Architects and Fascist Politics', pp. 109–10; N. Cennamo, ed.,
   *Materiali per l'analasi dell'architettura moderna: La prima Esposizione Italiana di
   Architettura Razionale* (Naples, 1973). This argument, which I first outlined some 30
   years ago, began to be embraced in the 1990s by scholars such as Giorgio Ciucci in his
   book *Gli architetti e il fascismo* (Turin, 1989), and in his introduction to *Giuseppe
   Terragni: Opera completa* (Milan, 1996); the argument has subsequently been developed
   by others, including American scholars who have also proposed quite different and rich
   analyses of diverse elements of architecture and culture under fascism, including Brian
   McLaren, Krystyna von Henneberg, D. Medina Lasansky and Ruth Ben-Ghiat.

13 The regime actively promoted attendance at a wide variety of exhibitions and visits to
   important architectural and historic sites through both sharply discounted train fares
   and the diffusion, particularly during the 1930s, of short documentary films celebrating
   them. See Victoria de Grazia, *The Culture of Consent: Mass Organization of Leisure in
   Fascist Italy* (New York, 1981) for a detailed analysis of these and other regime initiatives designed to stimulate pride in an Italian cultural heritage.

14 Pietro Maria Bardi, *Rapporto sull'architettura per Mussolini* [1931], reprinted in Michele
   Cennamo, *Materiali per l'analasi dell'architettura moderna*, vol. II (Naples, 1976), p. 128.
   Bardi ventured similar comments in his introduction to *Quadrante*, 35–6 (October 1936).

15 Giorgio Ciucci, 'The Classicism of the E42: Between Modernity and Tradition', *Assemblage*,
   8 (February 1989), p. 83.

16 Ibid., p. 84.

17 The typical periodization and attendant valuation consists of an early period (1925–30)
   of stabilization, bureaucratization and centralization; the second phase (1930–36) as
   one of experimentation and pluralism; and the third (1936–43) a period characterized by
   coercive patronage and a greater reliance on Nazi monumentalism as a reference for Italian
   architecture and culture more generally. See for example Marla Stone, *The Patron State:
   Culture and Politics in Fascist Italy* (Princeton, NJ, 1998), pp. 6–7; Giorgio Ciucci outlines
   the same trajectory in *Gli architetti e il fascismo*.

18 Diane Ghirardo, 'Politics of a Masterpiece: The *Vicenda* of the Decoration of the Façade
   of the Casa del Fascio, Como, 1936–39', *Art Bulletin*, LXII/3 (September 1980), pp. 466–78.

19 Giuseppe Terragni, 'La costruzione della Casa del Fascio di Como', *Quadrante*, 35–6
   (1936), pp. 5–6.

20 Giorgio Ciucci, ed., *Giuseppe Terragni: Opera completa* (Milan, 1996), including a full
   bibliography; Attilio Terragni, ed., *Atlante Terragni: Architetture costruite* (Milan, 2004),
   useful primarily for the old and new photographs of the buildings.

21 The bibliography on EUR is extensive; see in particular Commisariato Generale, ed.,
   Esposizione Universale di Roma (Rome, 1939); Virgilio Quilici, ed., *E42-EUR: Un centro*

per la metropoli (Rome, 1996).

22 Lucio Scardino, *Itinerari di Ferrara moderna* (Florence, 1995).

23 *Angiolo Mazzoni (1894–1979): Architetto nell'Italia tra le due guerre*, exh. cat., Galleria d'Arte Moderna (Bologna, 1984).

24 Anna Maria Ruta, 'Un piccolo museo futurista', in *Il Palazzo delle Poste di Palermo*, ed. Maria Antonietta Spadaro and Anna Maria Ruta (Palermo, 1998), pp. 15–23.

25 Angiolo Mazzoni, *Futurism* (14 May 1933), cited in Maria Antonietta Spadaro, 'L'Immagine "forte" dell'architettura del regime', in *Il Palazzo delle Poste*, ed. Spadaro and Ruta, pp. 7–13 (p. 11).

26 The exhibition catalogue contains plans, images of most of the rooms and exhibits, explanations of the Mostra and its component parts: Dino Alfieri and Luigi Freddi, eds, *Mostra della Rivoluzione Fascista: Guida storica* (Rome, 1933).

27 Libero Andreotti, 'The Aesthetics of War: The Exhibition of the Fascist Revolution', *Journal of Architectural Education*, xLV/2 (February 1992), p. 83; Edoardo Persico, 'La Mostra della Rivoluzione Fascista', *La Casa Bella* (November 1932), p. 30, cited in Andreotti, p. 83.

28 Doordan, 'The Political Content', p. 130.

29 José Quetglas, 'The Edge of Words: Prolegomena to Future Work on Terragni', *Assemblage*, 5 (February 1988), pp. 66–89.

30 Among the prominent modern architects and designers to participate in these exhibits were Nizzoli, Sironi, Terragni, Libera, Giuseppe Pagano, the BBPR group (Gianluigi Banfi, Lodovico Belgiojoso, Enrico Peressuti, Ernesto Rogers), Luigi Moretti, Luigi Figini and Gino Pollini.

31 A typical example of such a study was that financed by INEA (Istituto Nazionale di Economia Agraria, or National Institute of Agrarian Economics), *Lo Spopolamento montano in Italia*, vol. II (Rome, 1935), with essays by Prof. Ugo Giusti, 'Le Alpi Lombarde, note riassuntive', p. xLII; and Prof. Giuseppe Medici, 'Varesotto-Comasco-Valle Brembana', pp. 68–70. Subsequent analyses of poverty during the early years of the nation include Rocco Scotellaro, *Contadini del Sud* (Bari, 1954).

32 John Dewey, *Human Nature and Conduct: An Introduction to Social Psychology* [1922] (New York, 2007). After the establishment of the 'Social Palace' in Guise, France, and Saltaire, the town founded by Titus Salt in England, George Pullman, President of the Pullman Palace Car Company, founded Pullman, Illinois, about 10 miles from Chicago, in 1881. It was intended to be a community for the workers in his company as well as those of the Chicago Steelworks, the Pullman Car Wheel Company and others, for a total population at its peak of 12,000. In 1894 it was the site of one of America's epic labour battles. In the wake of a major recession that began in 1893 and Pullman's decision to cut wages without reducing house rents for the captive population, a workers' boycott in Pullman triggered a call for the forces of the United States Army, ordered in by President Grover Cleveland on behalf of the owners, with considerable loss of life and a legacy of bitterness and resentment. The Pullman bibliography is extensive, but for a contemporary celebration see Richard T. Ely, 'Pullman: A Social Study', *Harper's Magazine*, LXX (1885), pp. 452–66. See also Stanley Buder, *Pullman: An Experiment in Industrial Order and Community Planning, 1880–1930* (New York, 1967); and Carl Smith, *Urban Disorder and the Shape of Belief* (Chicago, 1995). Helen Searing, 'With Red Flags Flying: Politics and Architecture in Amsterdam, 1915–1923', in Millon and Nochlin, eds., *Art and Architecture*, pp. 230–69; 'Amsterdam South: Social Democracy's Elusive Housing Ideal', *VIA*, IV (1980), pp. 58–77; Eve Blau, *The Architecture of Red Vienna, 1919–1934* (Cambridge, MA, 1999).

33 Italo Insolera, *Roma moderna: Un secolo di storia urbanistica* (Turin, 1976, and later editions), pp. 65–7.

34 Benito Mussolini, 'Cifre e deduzioni: Sfollare le città', *Il Popolo d'Italia*, 22 (November 1928).

35 The bibliography – and debates – on the process of industrialization in Italy are vast; for recent studies, see Roberto Esposti and Franco Sotte, 'Institutional Structure,

Industrialization and Rural Development: An Evolutionary Interpretation of the Italian Experience', *Growth and Change*, XXXI/1 (2002), pp. 3–41; Carlo Cipolla, 'The Decline of Italy: The Case of a Fully Matured Economy', *Economic History Review*, V (1952); Franklin Hugh Adler, *Italian Industrialists from Liberalism to Fascism* (Cambridge, 1995); and John S. Cohen and Giovanni Federico, *The Growth of the Italian Economy, 1820–1960* (Cambridge, 2001).

36 Ercole Sori, 'Emigrazione all'estero e migrazioni interne in Italia tra le due guerre', *Quaderni Storici*, 29–30 (1975), pp. 579–606; Anna Treves, *Le migrazioni interne nell'Italia fascista* (Turin, 1976).

37 Marcella Delle Donne, 'Rome the Capital: The Impending Suburbs and Strategies of Integration-Decentralization', *Journal of Architectural Education*, XLVI/1 (September 1992), pp. 21–7 (p. 22).

38 Giuseppe Nicolosi, 'Abitazioni provvisorie e abitazioni definitive nelle borgate periferiche', *L'ingegnere* (1936), p. 9.

39 Regio Decreto Legge, 8 March 1923, n. 695; see also Lanfranco Maroi, *Un Ventennio di attività edilizia a Roma, 1909–1929* (Rome, 1929).

40 Rosa Chiumeo, 'Edilizia popolare a Milano tra le due guerre: 1919–1940', in Dario Franchi and Rosa Chiumeo, eds, *Urbanistica a Milano in regime fascista* (Florence, 1972), pp. 135–233.

41 Antonio Munoz, *Roma di Mussolini* (Milan, 1935), p. 373.

42 Ferruccio Trabalzi, 'Primavalle: Urban Reservation in Rome', *Journal of Architectural Education*, XLII/3 (September 1989), pp. 38–46; Trabalzi, 'Low-Cost Housing in Twentieth-Century Rome', in Diane Ghirardo, ed., *Out of Site: A Social Criticism of Architecture* (Seattle, 1991), pp. 129–56

43 Antonio Stefano Cibelli, 'A volte ritornano', *La Gazzetta di Lucera* (14 January 2005), p. 1; the letter from the mayor encouraging Terragni to pursue just such a strategy is cited in Aberto Artioli, 'La Casa del Fascio di Como', (Rome, 1990), p. 20; see also Ada Francesca Marcianò, *Giuseppe Terragni: Opera completa, 1925–1943* (Rome, 1987), p. 306.

44 Marida Talamona, *Casa Malaparte* (New York, 1992).

45 'Another Pontine Town Founded', *The Times* (16 April 1934), p. 13. Virtually every book on the new towns includes the much celebrated aerial photographs snapped on opening day.

46 Although the bibliography for new towns during the fascist era is extensive, among those publications that offer a good background are: Tonino Mirabella and Antonio Parisella, *Architetture dell'Agro Pontino* (Latina, 1988); Brian McLaren, *Architecture and Tourism in Italian Colonial Libya: An Ambivalent Modernism* (Seattle, 2005); Mia Fuller, *Moderns Abroad: Architecture, Cities and Italian Imperialism* (London, 2006); Diane Ghirardo, *Building New Communities: New Deal America and Fascist Italy* (Princeton, NJ, 1989) – a revised version was published in Italian as *Le città nuove nell'Italia fascista* (Latina, 2003).

47 Ghirardo, *Building New Communities*, pp. 28–39.

48 Speech of 18 December 1933, cited in Katia Franchini and Feliciano Ianella, *Sabaudia nella storia* (Rome, 1984), p. 110.

49 Flavia Faccioli and Giancarlo Martinoni, 'Città di fondazione: Tresigallo, un esempio padano', *Atti del Convegno Tresigallo il passato il futuro* (Ferrara, 1990), p. 32.

50 Ibid., p. 27.

51 Ibid., p. 38.

52 The designers for the five towns were: Oriolo Frezzotti (Littoria); Gruppo Urbanisti Romani, headed by Luigi Piccinato (Sabaudia); Alfredo Pappalardo (Pontinia); and Concezio Petrucci, a team of Roman architects consisting of Mario Tufaroli, Emanuele Paolini and Riccardo Silenzi (Aprilia and Pomezia).

53 Antonio Pennacchi, *Canale Mussolini* (Milan 2010). This exceptionally lively and informative novel won the Strega Prize in 2010, and it is well worth the read.

54 Filarete (Antonio Averlino), *Trattato di architettura*, facsimile edn, ed. J. R. Spencer,

Filarete's Treatise on Architecture (New Haven, CT, 1965).

55 Luigi Piccinato, 'The Importance of Sabaudia', in *Sabaudia 1933: Città nuova fascista*, ed. Richard Burdett (London, 1981), p. 15.

56 Giorgio Ciucci, *Gli architetti e il fascismo*, p. 22.

57 In his study of the new towns, Millon identifies differences among the earlier plans of Littoria and Sabaudia, and the later Pontinia, and the architectural forms of Aprilia and Pomezia. In the latter three towns, Millon argues that they embody a shift in attitudes towards architecture both by the government and by architects – a shift, that is, to a more neoclassical, less modern formulation. Henry A. Millon, 'Some New Towns in Italy in the 1930s', in *Art and Architecture in the Service of Politics*, ed. Henry A. Millon and Linda Nochlin (Cambridge, MA, 1978), pp. 326–41.

58 The twelve hamlets are: Borgo Fazio near Trapani (Luigi Epifanio, 1939–42); Borgo Gattuso, Caltanissetta (Edoardo Caracciolo, 1939–42); Borgo Lupo, Catania (Roberto Marino, 1940–41); Borgo Rizza, Siracusa (Pietro Gramignani, 1940–41); Borgo Schirò (G. Manetti Cusa, 1940–41), Borgo Borzellino (Giuseppe Caronia and Giovanni Puleo, 1942–3), Borgo Riena (Ufficio Tecnico ERAS, 1943) and Borgo Manganaro (Ufficio Tecnico ERAS, 1943–5), all near Palermo; Borgo Cascino, Enna (Giuseppe Marietta, 1940–41); Borgo Bonsignore (Donato Mendolia, 1940–43), Borgo Pasquale (Ufficio Tecnico ERAS, 1942–4) and Borgo Tumarrano (Ufficio Tecnico ERAS, 1943–4), all near Agrigento. For illustrations, discussion and up-to-date bibliography, see Maurizio Oddo, *Architettura contemporanea in Sicilia* (Trapani, 2007).

59 Ciucci, 'The Classicism of the E42', p. 80.

60 Cini's comments from 1937 were published in Italo Insolera and Luigi Di Majo, *L'eur e Roma dagli anni trenta al Duemila* (Rome and Bari, 1986), p. 33; they are also cited in Ciucci, 'The Classicism of the E42', p. 82.

61 The description is drawn from Ciucci, 'The Classicism of the E42', p. 85. Ciucci goes on to say, after repeating Rationalist criticism of the time that charged the architects with trying to marry modernism and classicism: 'A few managed to save themselves, not so much by abandoning columns and arches, or by trying to resist the rhetoric of the times, but by keeping alive those premises that had given substance and strength to rational Italian architecture', p. 86.

62 For the entire story of the facade, see Ghirardo, 'Politics of a Masterpiece', pp. 466–78. The letter from Carlo Ferrario is at the Archivio Centrale dello Stato, Roma, Partito Nazionale Fascista, Federazione di Como, Direttorio, b. 168, 29 July 1940.

63 Iain Pears, *The Immaculate Deception* (New York, 2000), p. 15.

64 Vincenzo Gioberti, *Del primato morale e civile degli Italiani* (1843, repr. Turin, 1920–32), and Giuseppe Mazzini, *Scritti editi ed inediti di Giuseppe Mazzini*, ed. Mario Menghini (Imola, 1906–43), both cited in Mark I. Choate, 'The Tunisia Paradox: Italian Aims, French Imperial Rule, and Migration in the Mediterranean Basin', *California Italian Studies Journal*, I/1 (2010), pp. 1–20, available at http://escholarship.org. Among the chief earlier studies of Italian colonialism, see Luigi Einaudi, *Un principe mercante: Studio sulla espansione coloniale italiana* (Turin, 1900); see also Ruth Ben-Ghiat and Mia Fuller, eds, *Italian Colonialism* (New York, 2003).

65 Choate, 'The Tunisia Paradox', p. 3. The literature on Italian colonialism is extensive; two of the most important are Angelo Del Boca's two studies, *Gli italiani in Africa orientale*, 4 vols (Bari, 1975–84), and *Gli italiani in Libia*, 2 vols (Rome and Bari, 1986–8). See also Patrizia Palumbo, ed., *A Place in the Sun: Africa in Italian Colonial Culture from Post-Unification to the Present* (Berkeley, CA, and London, 2003).

66 For a provocative comparison of EUR and the plans for colonial Addis Ababa, see Mia Fuller, 'Wherever You Go, There You Are: Fascist Plans for the Colonial City of Addis Ababa and the colonizing suburb of EUR '42', *Journal of Contemporary History*, XXXI/2 (April 1996), pp. 397–418.

67 Still the best study of colonial architecture in the Dodecanese is Simona Martinoli and Eliana Perotti, *Architettura coloniale italiana nel Dodecaneso* (Turin, 1999).

68 The Gruppo Sette manifestos were translated into English by Ellen Shapiro: 'Architecture' and 'Architecture II: The Foreigners', *Oppositions*, 6 (Fall 1976), pp. 86–102; 'Architecture III: Unpreparedness – Incomprehension – Prejudice', and 'Architecture IV: A New Archaic Era', *Oppositions*, 12 (Spring 1978), pp. 88–104.

69 Few, if any, of the architects with university posts who were not Jewish lost their jobs, and in academia as in politics, no efforts were made to come to terms with adherence to fascism, as if the 1943 switch to the Allied side eliminated the fascist past. Recent studies in other fields demonstrate the persistence of the same university faculties that had sworn allegiance to fascism and who had often participated in the regime's persecution of the Jews; see Giorgio Israel, *Il fascismo e la razza: La scienza italiana e le politiche razziali del regime* (Bologna, 2010).

chapter four: War and its Aftermath

1 As with most of the Fascist period, the bibliography is extensive; nonetheless, the best source for the entire era, including the war years, remains Renzo De Felice's seven-volume series, *Mussolini* (Turin, 1965–97), in particular the volumes on the war years and the fall of fascism, *Mussolini, L'alleato*, vol. I: *L'Italia in Guerra, 1940–1943*, and vol. II, *Crisi e agonia del regime* (Turin, 1990).

2 Simona Colarizi, *Storia del Novecento Italiano* (Milan, 2000), p. 281.

3 Carlo Spartaco Capogreco, 'I campi di internamento fascisti per gli ebrei (1940–1943)', in *Storia Contemporanea*, 4 (August 1991), pp. 664–5; Klaus Voigt, *Il rifugio precario: Eli esuli in Italia dal 1933 al 1945*, 2 vols (Florence, 1993/1996); Klaus Voigt, *Villa Emma: Ragazzi ebrei in fuga 1940–1945* (Florence, 2002).

4 The racial laws prohibited Jews from attending university, teaching, practising medicine, holding jobs in public agencies, and many other noxious provisions.

5 Fabio Corbisiero, *Storia e memoria dell'internamento ebraico in Campania durante la seconda guerra mondiale* (Naples, 1997). I am grateful to Carmine Granito, journalist and historian, for introducing me to Campagna and the story of San Bartolomeo.

6 Voigt, *Il rifugio precario*, vol. I, pp. 18, 58–65.

7 *Il campo di concentramento di Campagna* (Salerno, 2005), with essays by Carmine Granito, Annarita Chiariello and Fabio Corbisiero. The following paragraphs are drawn from this publication. For the story of the police officer Giovanni Palatucci, see Piersandro Vanzan and Mariella Scatena, *Giovanni Palatucci: Il questore 'giusto'* (Rome, 2004); *Giovanni Palatucci: Documenti e cronologia essenziale nel primo centenario della nascita (1909–2009)* (Salerno, 2008). A second internment facility was established in another former convent, that of the Osservanti, at the other end of the city. This facility proved inadequate and was already being dismantled by 1941.

8 Fabio Corbisiero, 'L'internamento ebraico in Campania durante la seconda guerra mondiale', in *Il campo di contentramento di Campagna*, pp. 26–54 (p. 52).

9 Vanzan and Scatena, *Giovanni Palatucci*, p. 38.

10 Personal interview with Costantino Nivola, Rome, April 1977; Paolo Petazzi and Piero Santi, 'La musica italiana fra le due guerre', in B. Bottero, A. Negri et al., eds, *La cultura del 900* (Milan, 1982), pp. 458–60.

11 For more details on such shaming rituals, see Diane Ghirardo, 'The Topography of Prostitution in Renaissance Ferrara', *Journal of the Society of Architectural Historians* (December 2001), pp. 402–31.

12 P. Angeletti, L. Cianciarelli, M. Ricci and G. Vallifuoco, *Case romane: La periferia e le case popolari* (Rome, 1984).

13 Margherita Guccione, Maria Lagunes and Rosalia Vittorini, *Guida ai quartieri romani INA Casa* (Rome, 2002); Francesco Dal Co and Manfredo Tafuri, *Architettura contemporanea* (Venice, 1976); Giorgio Muratori, ed., *Cantieri romani del Novecento: Maestranze, materiali, imprese, architetti, nei primi anni del cemento armato* (Rome, 1995).

14 A broad, if not always critical, evaluation of the programme in 1994 can be found in Paola Di Biagi, ed., *La grande ricostruzione: Il piano Ina-Casa e l'Italia degli anni '50* (Rome, 2001). For an exceptionally clear and detailed account of the programme's origins and the details of the financial package, see the essay by Paolo Nicoloso, 'Geneologie del Piano Fanfani, 1939–1950', in *La grande ricostruzione*, ed. Di Biagi, pp. 33–62.

15 Patrizia Gabellini, 'I manuali: Una strategia normativa', in *La grande ricostruzione*, ed. Di Biagi, pp. 99–111.

16 INCIS stands for the Istituto Nazionale Case Impiegati dello Stato (National Institute for State Employee Housing); IACP for Istituto Autonomo per le Case Popolari (Autonomous Institute for Low-cost Housing).

17 Bruno Zevi, 'L'architettura dell'INA-Casa', in *L'ina-Casa al iv congresso nazionale di urbanistica, Venezia, 1952* (Rome, 1953), cited in *La grande ricostruzione*, ed. Di Biagi, p. 17.

18 Paola Bonifazio, 'Narrating Modernization: Documentary Films in Cold War Italy (1948–1955)', PhD thesis (New York University, 2008). The ECA was the U.S. agency that implemented the Marshall Plan in Italy; commissioning documentary films was but one aspect of this agency's objectives.

19 The story of these films is a fascinating one; Bonifazio's dissertation, ibid., spells out their history in compelling detail.

20 The full team of architects included L. Agati, F. Gorio, P. M. Lugli, L. Quaroni and M. Valori; their project was built from 1951–3. For more details on this and other projects initially set in motion by the UN Relief and Rehabilitation Administration (UNRRA) and its successor, the European Recovery Program (best known as the Marshall Plan), see Marida Talamona, 'Dieci anni di politica dell'UNRRA Casa', in *Costruire la città dell'uomo: Adriano Olivetti e l'urbanistica*, ed. Carlo Olmo (Turin, 2001), pp. 173–204.

21 Manfredo Di Robilant, 'Due quartieri di edilizia pubblica: Il Monte Amiata al Gallaratese di Milano e il Corviale a Roma', in *1970–2000: Episodi e temi di storia*, ed. Francesca B. Filippi, Luca Gibello and Manfredo Di Robilant (Turin, 2006), pp. 27–36; Flaminia Gennari Santori and Bartolomeo Pietromarchi, eds, *Osservatorio Nomade: Immaginare Corviale* (Milan, 2006).

22 Personal observation, visit to Corviale, 5 June 2006.

23 Thomas L. Schumacher, 'Letter to the Editor', *Journal of Architectural Education*, XLV/3 (May 1992), p. 192.

24 Giovanni Carzana, 'L'architettura riparta da Scampia e dallo Zen', *qbr Magazine* (19 April 2009), p. 1.

25 Bruno Zevi, *Storia dell'architettura moderna* (Turin, 1975); Renato Bonelli, 'Quartiere residenziale al Forte Quezzi in Genova', *L'architettura, croniche e storia*, 41 (March 1959), pp. 762–4; the architect's response to Bonelli's criticism soon followed: Luigi Carlo Daneri, 'Luigi Carlo Daneri difende il quartiere ina-Casa di Forte di Quezzi, Genova', *L'architettura, croniche e storia*, 44 (June 1959), pp. 76–112; see also Riccardo Forte, 'Biscione di Quezzi: La promessa non mantenuta', *Il Giornale* (5 July 2006), p. 4.

26 Many of the articles and editorials published over the next few years made such arguments, but perhaps the most effective is the introductory editorial by Ernesto Nathan Rogers, 'Editorial', *Casabella-Continuità*, 199 (December 1953/January 1954), pp. 1–2.

27 Many of Rogers's writings were collected in a volume of essays: Luca Molinari, ed., *Esperienza dell'architettura* (Milan, 1997).

28 In the years following Rossi's death, the working drawings for almost all of his projects were deposited at the Canadian Centre for Architecture in Montreal. They testify to the attention given to the careful elaboration of his projects by trusted collaborators. Shifting this onerous task out of the office has been a common practice throughout the twentieth century, including some of the projects by Frank Gehry. This hardly means that the architects were indifferent to the constructions themselves.

29 Whatever the merits of some of his boutique designs, Le Corbusier's urbanism was a disaster when he first launched it in the 1920s, and has continued to be so ever since.

chapter five: The Economic Miracle

1 For Adriano Olivetti's views on cities and urbanism, see Olivetti, *Città dell'uomo* (Milan, 1960); for more on Olivetti, see Carlo Olmo, ed., *Adriano Olivetti e l'urbanistica* (Turin, 2001).

2 Fulvio Irace, 'La Ville d'Hadrien à Ivrea', in Carlo Olmo, ed., *Costruire la città dell'uomo: Adriano Olivetti e l'urbanistica* (Turin, 2001), pp. 205–32, esp. p. 211.

3 Carlo Olmo, 'Introduzione: Un'urbanistica civile, una società conflittuale', in *Adriano Olivetti*, ed. Olmo, pp. 3–21, esp. pp. 10–11.

4 The apple does not fall far from the tree; in June 2006, Ciancimino's son was arrested for presumed Mafia activities; while declaring an income of less than €50,000 per year, Massimo Ciancimino purchased Ferraris and numerous properties in Sicily. Salvo Palazzolo, 'Arrestato il figlio di Ciancimino', *La Repubblica* (9 June 2006). Massimo subsequently decided to turn informant: he reported on his father's activities to the state police and to magistrates investigating organized crime and the involvement of politicians, describing his father's political contacts in particular.

5 Recent research suggests that the image is at least in part at variance with reality; see Ferdinando Fava, *Lo Zen di Palermo* (Rome and Milan, 2008).

6 Vittorio Gregotti, 'Abbattiamo il quartiere Zen2 e ricostruiamolo come era stato progettato', *Corriere della Sera Magazine* (26 March 2009), p. 13.

7 Alessandro Castagnaro, 'Demolizioni di architettura contemporanea a Napoli', *Presstletter*, 25 (2007), p. 1.

8 Benedetto Gravagnuolo, 'Il naufragio di un'utopia', *Il Mattino* (29 May 2003), p. 10.

9 Quoted in Simona Colarizi, *Storia del Novecento Italiano* (Milan, 2000), p. 331.

10 Silvia Garagna, P. G. Rubini, C. A. Redi et al., 'Recovering Seveso', *Science*, n.s. CCXXXVIII/5406 (26 February 1999), pp. 1268–9.

11 The literature on the post-war immigration is too large to include, but a couple of key recent texts are: Russell King, Gabriella Lazaridis and Charalambos, eds, *Eldorado or Fortress? Migration in Southern Europe* (New York, 2000); Maria Immacolata Macioti and Enrico Pugliese, eds, *L'esperienza migratoria: Immigrati e rifugiati in Italia* (Rome, 2003); Wendy Pojmann, *Immigrant Women and Feminism in Italy* (Aldershot, 2006).

12 Nassera Chohra, *Volevo diventare bianca* (Rome, 1993); Shirin Ramzanali Fazel, *Lontano da Mogadiscio* (Rome, 1999); Pap Khouma, *Io, venditore di elefanti: Una vita per forza tra Dakar, Parigi e Milano* (Milan, 1996); see also Graziella Parati, *Migration Italy: The Art of Talking Back in a Destination Culture* (Toronto, 2005)

13 'Intervista a Vittorio Gregotti: "I nuovi grattacieli? Brutti e fuori contest"', *MilanoMag* (26 July 2009).

14 Andrea Montanari, 'Gregotti: Con la mia Bicocca ho ridato qualità alle periferie', *La Repubblica* (5 June 2005), p. 3.

15 Marcegaglia pays €50,000 per year to rent this huge complex, while a moderately priced apartment in a desirable part of Rome goes for about €2,000 per month.

16 This centenary exhibition saw mountains of publications produced to record the events and exhibits; for more recent analyses of the events, see Sergio Pace, Cristiana Chiorino and Michela Rosso, *Italia '61: Identità e miti nelle celebrazioni per il centenario dell'Unità d'Italia* (Turin, 2005).

chapter six: Old Cities, New Buildings and Architectural Discourse

1 David Atkinson and Dennis Cosgrove, 'Urban Rhetoric and Embodied Identities: City, Nation, and Empire at the Vittorio Emanuele II Monument in Rome, 1870–1945', *Annals of the Association of American Geographers*, LXXXVIII/1 (March 1998), pp. 28–49. See also John Agnew, 'The Impossible Capital: Monumental Rome under Liberal and

Fascist Regimes, 1870–1943', *Geografiska Annaler: Series B, Human Geography*, LXXX/4 (1998), pp. 229–40.

2   D. Medina Lasansky and Brian McLaren, eds, *Architecture and Tourism: Perception, Performance and Place* (Oxford, 2004).

3   In addition to his own publications, on Viollet-le-Duc see John Summerson, *Heavenly Mansions* (New York, 1998); Henry Hope Read, *The Golden City* (New York, 1971).

4   The text in which Ruskin explained his ideas about preservation most fully is *The Seven Lamps of Architecture* (1857, repr. New York, 1989); see also Tim Hilton, *John Ruskin: The Later Years* (New Haven, CT, 2000).

5   Camillo Boito's most complete explanation of his views on architecture and preservation is *Un'architettura per L'Italia Unita* (Padua, 2000).

6   Giovannoni wrote the first and most important impassioned defence of protecting Italy's medieval and Renaissance cities, but he did not disdain contemporary building; his vision embraced change as well as protection; Gustavo Giovannoni, *Vecchie città ed edilizia nuova* (Turin, 1931). A recent study that addresses Italy's early preservation and restoration efforts is D. Medina Lasansky, *The Renaissance Perfected: Architecture, Spectacle, and Tourism in Fascist Italy* (University Park, PA, 2004).

7   For the renovation of Palazzo Costabili, see Serenella Di Palma, 'Dalla casa al museo: Il Palazzo detto di Ludovico il Moro a Ferrara', unpublished laurea thesis (University of Ferrara, 2000).

8   Diane Ghirardo, 'Inventing the Palazzo del Corte in Ferrara', in *Donatello among the Blackshirts: History and Modernity in the Visual Culture of Fascist Italy*, ed. Roger Crum and Claudia Lazzaro (Ithaca, NY, 2005), pp. 97–112.

9   See Medina Lasansky, *The Renaissance Perfected*.

10   Spiro Kostof, *The Third Rome* (Berkeley, CA, 1973).

11   Joe McGinniss, *The Miracle of Castel di Sangro: A Tale of Passion and Folly in the Heart of Italy* (New York, 2000), p. 394.

12   *Il razionalismo e l'architettura in Italia durante il fascismo* (Venice, 1976), catalogue of the 1976 Venice Biennale.

13   Paolo Nicoloso, *Gli architetti di Mussolini: Scuole e sindacato, architetti e massoni, professori e politici negli anni del regime* (Milan, 1999). Nicoloso outlines in painstaking detail how the networks of friendship and mutual obligation governed academic appointments as well as victories in architectural competitions, beginning even prior to the onset of the Fascist regime and continuing into the post-war period.

14   Davide Carlucci, Gianluca Di Feo and Giuliano Foschini, 'La mafia dei baroni', *L'espresso* (25 January 2007), pp. 44–51.

15   The information in the following section on La Fenice derives from interviews and discussions with diverse participants and observers, as well as the following publications: Gianluca Amadori, *Per quattro soldi: Il giallo della Fenice dal rogo alla ricostruzione* (Rome, 2003); Maura Manzelle, *Il Teatro La Fenice a Venecia: Studi per la ricostruzione dov'era ma non necessariamente com'era* (Venice, 1999); *I progetti per la ricostruzione del teatro La Fenice 1997* (Venice, 2000).

16   Its members included jury president Leopoldo Mazzarolli, professor of business administration at the University of Padua; Daniel Commis, professor of acoustics at the Universities of Paris-Belleville and Nancy; Francesco Dal Co, professor of architectural history in the Institute of Architecture, University of Venice; Ernesto Bettanini Fecia di Cossato, professor of building systems at the University of Padua; and Angelo Di Tommaso, Professor of Building Science, University of Bologna.

17   Giuseppe Pagano Pogatschnig, 'La nuova stazione di Firenze', *Casabella* (1933), pp. 3–5; Vittorio Savi, 'Ritorno alla Stazione di Firenze', *Rassegna* (1980), p. 2; Giovannoni, *Vecchie città ed edilizia nuova*.

18   Nicoloso, *Gli architetti di Mussolini*, pp. 153–60. Alberto Calza-Bini, of the Fascist Union of Architects, and Marcello Piacentini served on the overwhelming majority of competition juries, which enhanced their personal power as well as ensured that their

candidates would win. Nicoloso meticulously documented the hold that a few individuals maintained over the public building process during the years of the regime, a hold that extended to academic posts.

19   The various competitions for the Palazzo del Littorio in Rome have been documented in Carol Rusche, 'Progetto di concorso di primo grado per il Palazzo del Littorio a Roma. Progetti A e B', in *Giuseppe Terragni: Opera omnia*, ed. Giorgio Ciucci (Milan, 1996); Maria Grazia Messina, 'L'orma fermata nella pietra: Il concorso per il palazzo del Littorio del 1934', in Sergio Bertelli, *Il teatro del potere: Scenari e rappresentazione del politico fra Otto e Novecento* (Rome, 2000), pp. 117–47.

20   See also a book on the construction industry and its ties with politics and organized crime, *La colata*, which includes a discussion of a judicial investigation into corruption and the construction industry in which one of the characters was Casamonti. Although at the time of this writing the magistrates have not filed official charges against him, his fawning adulation of powerful, criminally connected individuals in wiretapped conversations made the rounds of architectural circles. Ferruccio Sansa, ed., *La colata* (Milan, 2010), pp. 67–71.

21   Vittorio Sgarbi, *Un paese sfigurato: Viaggio attraverso gli scampi d'Italia* (Milan, 2003). Other more serious books that assess the same phenomenon of environmental degradation in Italy include Francesco Urbani, *L'Italia maltrattata* (Rome and Bari, 2003). Vittorio Sgarbi's background includes a troubled career in the Ministry of Culture characterized by absenteeism and false documents (he was charged with and found guilty of fraud, falsification of documents and failure to fulfil the obligations of his job, and subsequently sentenced to six months in prison in 1996); a post in the Ministry of Culture in 2000 as undersecretary for arts and culture; and an elected position as mayor of a town in Sicily.

22   'Una bomba all'Ara pacis', *La Repubblica* (2 June 2004), p. vii.

23   For a summary of some of the polemics with Sgarbi, see Ministero per i Beni e le Attività Culturali, *Contro l'oblio del restauro critico. Rapporto sull'opera di Franco Minissi nell'ambito del restauro archeologico in Sicilia* (Palermo, 2007), esp. pp. 23–7.

24   Sgarbi appears to believe that since he despises the Minissi museum, so should others. Sgarbi therefore argued that a young faculty member at the University of Enna who came out in favour of the museum should not be confirmed in his university post. This from a man who was forced to acknowledge plagiarism publicly in 2008 because the highly paid introductions to a catalogue for a Botticelli exhibition, written by an underling in Sgarbi's name, was copied virtually word for word from an essay of several decades ago by another author. In response to this public airing of a breathtakingly fundamental dishonesty, Sgarbi shirked responsibility for the plagiarism and placed the blame squarely on the shoulders of the underling, also noting that the only problem was that the underling had not been clever enough to disguise the plagiarism. Such an attitude is suggestive of the depth of Sgarbi's knowledge and of his indifference to even minimal ethical standards. Francesco Urbani, 'Sgarbi e quella prefazione copiata', *La Repubblica* (2 December 2008), p. 1. In May 2009 Sgarbi tried to peddle his collection of artefacts to the city of Ferrara, along with the demand that they be displayed in the city's castle and that Gae Aulenti's exhibition design of 2004 be dismantled to make way for his collection. The city politely declined the gift, for reasons not made clear to the public, but given Sgarbi's track record, one can only hope that the city willing to take on the collection also requires complete documentation of the origins of each and every artefact.

25   Ernesto Nathan Rogers, 'Editorial', *Casabella-Continuità*, 199 (December 1953/January 1954), p. 1.

26   The angry outburst from Smithson, Rogers's comments and others are documented in Oscar Newman, ed., *CIAM '59* (Stuttgart, 1961), pp. 92–7.

27   Reyner Banham, 'The Italian Retreat from Modern Architecture', *Architectural Review*, 125 (April 1959), pp. 231–2, 235. Many of the critics of so-called nostalgic architectural

styles celebrated the hopelessly barren and desolate streets and spaces of Oscar Niemeyer's Brasilia.

28 Amit Wolf, 'Superurbeffimero n. 7: Umberto Eco's Semiologia and the Architectural Rituals of the U.F.O.', *California Italian Studies*, II/2 (2011), available at http://escholarship.org.

29 Members of UFO (1967–78) included Carlo Bachi, Lapo Binazi, Patrizia Cammeo, Riccardo Foresi, Titti Maschietti and Sandro Gioli.

30 Adolfo Natalini, *Figure di Pietra: Figures of Stone* (Milan, 1984). Vittorio Savi assesses some of Natalini's designs: 'Story of a Design: Adolfo Natalini and One of His Works', *Lotus*, XL/4 (1983), pp. 19–21. For an earlier article on the Superstudio phenomenon, see Superstudio, Cristiano Toraldo di Francia, Alessandro Magris, Roberto Magris, Piero Frassinelli and Adolfo Natalini, 'Superstudio on Mindscapes', *Design Quarterly*, 89 (1973), pp. 17–31.

31 'Superstudio', *Perspecta*, XIII (1971), pp. 303–15.

32 Emilio Ambasz, ed., *Italy: The New Domestic Landscape. Achievements and Problems of Italian Design*, exh. cat. (New York, 1972).

33 Superstudio, 'Twelve Cautionary Tales for Christmas', *Architectural Design*, 42 (December 1971), pp. 737–42.

34 Tafuri's critiques of contemporary architecture and of capitalist cultural production are many, but two good places to begin are his *The Sphere and the Labyrinth: Avant-Gardes and Architecture from Piranesi to the 1970s*, trans. Pellegrino d'Acierno and Robert Connolly (Cambridge, MA, 1987) and *Theories and History of Architecture*, trans. Giorgio Verrecchia (New York, 1980); for his discussion specifically of Italian radical architecture, see his 'Design and Technological Utopia', in *Italy: The New Domestic Landscape*, ed. Ambasz, pp. 388–404.

35 *La presenza del passato: Prima mostra internazionale di architettura* (Venice, 1980); see also Francesca B. Filippi, 'La Biennale del 1980 e il dibattito sul postmoderno', in *1970-2000: Episodi e temi di storia*, ed. Francesca B. Filippi, Luca Gibello and Manfredo Di Robilant (Turin, 2006), pp. 87–95.

36 Filippi, 'La Biennale del 1980', p. 93.

37 In the wide-ranging investigation into corruption and bribes among politicians, Craxi was found to have been one of the key figures in the system; following his conviction, he went into exile in Tunisia.

38 When I visited my family's ancestral village in the mid-1960s, my relatives proudly showed me the first indoor toilet in the village, and none of my cousins had running water in their houses.

39 An investigation into the reasons for the collapse concluded that the reinforcing rods for the cupola were too thin – thinner than Quaroni had intended.

40 Manfredo Tafuri reserved some of his most pungent criticism for what he termed 'operative criticism': architectural criticism conducted by architects with their own interests as practitioners governing their analyses.

chapter seven: **Landscape and Environment**

1 Rosa Serrano, 'Due milioni di casa fantasma. Foto dal cielo contro gli abusi: Quattro mesi per mettersi in regola', *La Repubblica* (6 March 2008), p. 30. The survey documented 4,238 of the country's 8,103 towns, identifying 1,247,584 illegal buildings.

2 Gabriele Isman, 'Sabaudia, sigilli a 285 villini, Vendite d'oro senza permessi', *La Repubblica* (14 March 2006).

3 Organized crime is a powerful force in Campania, and unfortunately, not only there; see Francesco Barbagallo, *Il potere della Camorra (1973-1998)* (Turin, 1990); see especially the most recent, powerful study that also explores the impact of organized crime on the built environment, Roberto Saviano, *Gomorra* (Milan, 2006).

4   Personal visit, 13 April 2009.

5   Andrea Garibaldi, Antonio Massari, Marco Preve, Giuseppe Salvaggiulo and Ferruccio Sansa, *La colata* (Rome, 2010); the team's research also illustrates the fundamental role of the Vatican in ruthless property development over the twentieth century.

6   Marco Palombi summarizes the events nicely in 'Il PDL si distrae e le demolizioni si bloccano', *Il Fatto Quotidiano* (8 June 2010), p. 9.

7   Pliny predicted centuries earlier that the *latifundia* system would be destructive for Italy in the long run; the essay from his *Natural History* is reprinted in Naphtali Lewis and Meyer Reinhold, *Roman Civilization: Selected Readings* (New York, 1990), pp. 83–90; see also Christopher Duggan, *A Concise History of Italy* (Cambridge, 1994), pp. 31–60.

8   Francesco Erbani, *L'Italia maltrattata* (Rome and Bari, 2003), pp. 36–42.

9   'Crolla terrazzo sulla scogliera, due feriti sono gravissimi', *La Repubblica* (18 August 2007), p. 1; Fulvio Bufi, 'Frana a Ischia, famiglia distrutta: "Il Boato, poi un fiume di fango"', *Corriere della Sera* (1 May 2006), p. 10.

10 Bufi, p. 10.

11 Michelangelo Sabatino, *Pride in Modesty* (Toronto, 2010). Sabatino's study traces the evolution of this notion's appeal, without addressing the class-based distinctions regarding what counted as 'vernacular'.

12 Interview with a mason who worked on the building sites during the 1950s, August 1990.

13 Pier Paolo Pasolini, *Una vita violenta* (Milan, 1959), p. 8.

14 Ibid., pp. 20–21.

15 Maristella Casciato, 'L'abitazione e gli spazi domestici', in *La famiglia italiana dall'Ottocento a oggi*, ed. P. Melograni (Rome and Bari, 1988).

16 Erbani, *L'Italia maltrattata*, pp. 8–9.

17 The earthquake struck L'Aquila on 5 April 2009. Prime Minister Silvio Berlusconi appeared promptly on the scene, promising rapid reconstruction, tax abatements and even shelter in some of his many houses, reaping a wave of free publicity from his fawning media empire. All empty promises. On 7 July 2010 more than 5,000 residents of L'Aquila demonstrated in Rome despite a massive police presence. They decried the empty promises and the fact that reconstruction had not even begun – as indeed it has not, even in 2012.

18 John Foot documented the reality of the *coree* in contrast to contemporary and subsequent popular characterizations in several publications: in particular, see *Milan since the Miracle: Culture and Identity* (Oxford and New York, 2001), in Italian, *Milano dopo il miracolo: Biografia di una città* (Milan, 2003); see also his study of the town of Pero, *Pero: Città di immigrazione, 1950–1970* (Pero, 2002); and 'Revisiting the Coree: Self Construction, Memory and Immigration on the Milanese Periphery, 1950–2000', in *17 Lezioni: Dottorato in Storia dell'architettura e dell'urbanistica a Torino, 2002*, ed. M. Bonino, Cristiana Chiorino, Federico Deambrosis, Laura Milan, Annalisa Pesando and Mario Senatore (Milan, 2004), pp. 111–25.

19 Foot, 'Revisiting the Coree', pp. 112–17.

20 Although there is considerable research on the results of deforestation and the vulnerability of denuded slopes to landslides, see the recent study by Simona Virgiani and Fabio Terribile, 'Soils of the Detachment Crowns of Ischia Landslides', *Italian Journal of Engineering Geology and Environment*, 2 (2007), pp. 51–63.

21 'Ici e concessioni edilizie, oro per i Comuni', *La Voce di Rovigo* (9 March 2008), p. 32. Stefano, an anonymous informant, reported to me that all of the construction workers at Milano 2 were paid *in nero*, that is, under the table, by Berlusconi's company. Interview, 6 May 2010.

22 According to the same survey conducted by CGIA/Mestre, Ravenna and other northern cities such as Cesena, Como, Piacenza, Padua and Rome received the highest percentage (25–35 per cent) of the city budget from permits and residential property taxes, while southern cities such as Trapani (Sicily) and Benevento (Campania) collected between

3.7 and 6.9 per cent of their budgets from the same sources. The figures do not suggest that fewer structures were erected in the south, only that fewer legal ones were.

23 Dozens of books describe Berlusconi's highly questionable meteoric rise to power, alluding to his alleged Mafia associations, charges of bribing judges, money laundering and other illegal practices; Marco Travaglio has been one of his most persistent critics, documenting in minute detail how Berlusconi's lawyers have managed to get him off most charges by delaying the trials until the statutes of limitations expire. See, for example, Travaglio's book written with Peter Gomez, *Lo Chiamavano Impunità: La vera storia del caso sme e tutto quello che Berlusconi nasconde all'Italia e all'Europa* (Rome, 2003); in English, the recent book by Alexander Stille, *The Sack of Rome: How a Beautiful European Country with a Fabled History and a Storied Culture was Taken Over by a Man Named Silvio Berlusconi* (New York, 2006) also explores his illegal enterprises in detail. As shocking as their books are, neither author has been successfully sued over the content of the books – clearly because their accounts are based on facts available in public documents.

24 Giovanni Ruggeri detailed Berlusconi's construction activities in *Berlusconi: Gli affari del presidente* (Milan, 1994). For his activities as a politician and entrepreneur, see also Ferdinando Targetti, *Le complicanze economiche del governo Berlusconi* (Rome, 2004).

25 The figures from Legambiente are reported in Stille, *The Sack of Rome*, p. 269.

26 Ruggeri, *Berlusconi*, pp. 30–35. In 2005, Previti was convicted of bribing judges on behalf of Berlusconi. At the time he conspired with Berlusconi to acquire the villa, lands and family collection of art, in an outrageous conflict of interest he represented both the under-age heiress and Berlusconi – and just whose interests he was protecting soon became obvious.

27 Gian Antonio Stella, 'Villa Certosa, una storia di decreti e segreti', *Il Corriere della Sera* (2 June 2004).

28 The Rome-based group Alterazioni Video documented these constructions in a multi-media exhibition in Rome at the vm21 Arte Contemporanea gallery at the end of 2007; see the review by Luca d'Eusebio, 'Incompiuto siciliano', *Il Giornale dell'Architettura*, 57 (December 2007), p. 32. Alterazioni Video documented some 400 incomplete public works in Italy, some of which have been under construction, with supposedly active building yards, for periods of 30 to 50 years – more than many major historic buildings in the country!

29 The international press published many articles about the waste problems in Campania throughout 2008; among many others, see David Willey, 'Naples battles with rubbish mountain', bbc News Online (28 February 2008); Michael Day, 'Naples rubbish threatens environment disaster', *The Telegraph* (1 August 2008); Tracy Wilkerson, 'A Crime most foul in Italy', *The Los Angeles Times* (30 August 2008). Piles of refuse again fouled the streets of Naples in late 2010, and residents of towns at the base of Mount Vesuvius engaged in public demonstrations against government-operated waste facilities which, not surprisingly, they believe are poisoning them and their children.

30 Gianni Lannes, 'Discarica-killer bonificata a metà', *La Stampa* (9 October 2008), p. 23.

31 Such is the case in the Veneto, for example, where the mayors of the towns of the Alto Polesine serve on the administrative council of Ato Rifiuti and Ato Acqua, consortiums that determine water and waste disposal policies for the province. In August 2009 the mayor of Trecenta, Antonio Laruccia (exponent of the contemporary fascist party, Alleanza Nazionale, prior to its incorporation into Berlusconi's Partito della Libertà), was elected president of Ato Rifiuti, and with the rest of the administrative council of mayors he also served on the other administrative councils, which in turn control, for example, 51 per cent of Polaris srl, a company that treats 'special' waste disposal; the consortium of which Laruccia is president also controls Ecogest, another waste disposal company that operates incinerators in the area. Because service on such councils is lucrative (and public employment as mayor less so) and potentially even greater than the official salaries (waste disposal being one of the most corrupt entities, and not only in Italy, where the presence of organized crime is overwhelming), politicians

fight to serve on such councils – serve being a euphemism for aiding industries in their campaigns to control waste disposal. For the politics behind the distribution of lucrative posts, see Alberto Garbellini, 'Salta l'asse Marangon-Coppola', *La Voce di Rovigo* (31 July 2009), p. 5. Marangon refers to the politician Renzo Marangon, a former owner of *La Voce*; see ref. 36 below, but who was roundly defeated in the 2010 elections. Isa Coppola, treasurer on the regional council until 2010, was re-elected to the council again in 2010, with a different post; she is reportedly the new owner of *La Voce*.

32 Some of the buildings erected along the central spine in Turin were designed with environmental considerations in mind, but most were not. As in the pub at Gibellina, either expensive and ecologically unsound air conditioning will have to be installed to counter the heat gain caused by the extensive glazing on many of the buildings, or the rooms will go unused during the hot and humid summers – and only with difficulty in the frigid winters. For a good summary of the transformation of Turin over the past quarter-century, see Michele Bonino, Giulietta Fassino, Davide Ferrando and Carlo Spinelli, *Torino, 1984-2008: Atlante dell'architettura* (Turin, 2008).

33 Teksid closed its cast iron production at Carmagnola in 2005. Maresita Brandino, 'I sindacati lanciano l'allarme. Il futuro della Teksid a rischio', *Gazzetta d'Alba* (15 May 2007).

34 Many articles have noted the alarming environmental degradation of this region over the past two years; some documentation appears on Beppe Grillo's website, others in the pages of local newspapers such as *Il Gazzettino* and *La Voce di Rovigo*; most of my statistics come from the environmental group InterCom*Ambiente*, material the organization's president, Dr Michelangelo Caberletti, generously provided to me. See also articles in the small local publication *Il Corriere di Bagnolo Po* (2007–2011), some of which can also be found on Grillo's website; Agency for Toxic Substances and Disease Registry (ATSDR), 'Cancer and the Environment', National Cancer Institute (USA), 2003, p. 1.

35 Peter Van Dresser, *Case solari locali* (Padua, 1979); Gabriella Funaro and Emilio D'Errico covered Italy's slim history of solar design in *L'edilizia bioclimatica in Italia. 151 edifici solari passivi* (Rome, 1992).

36 Make no mistake about it; they all have branches throughout the country.

37 *Auditorium Guide*, ed. Corrado Morgia (Rome: Fondazione Musica per Roma, 2005).

38 Ibid., p. 7.

39 Stendhal, *Promenades dans Rome*, vol. I (Paris, 1929), pp. 14–15.

40 Stendhal took his walk on 18 August 1827, *Passaggiate Romane* (Milan, 2004), p. 28.

41 Alois Riegl, 'The Modern Cult of Monuments: Its Character and its Origins', trans. Kurt Forster and Diane Ghirardo, *Oppositions*, 25 (1982), pp. 21–51; see also Robert Ginsberg, *The Aesthetics of Ruins* (Amsterdam, NY, 2004); Michael Roth, Claire Lyons, and Charles Merewether, eds, *Irresistible Decay: Ruins Reclaimed* (Los Angeles, 1997).

42 Mercurio Ferrara, *Descrizione di un viaggio a Pesto dell'abate Mercurio Ferrara* (Naples, 1837), pp. 25–6.

43 Giambattista Vico, *Scienza nuova (1744), Opere di G. B. Vico*, ed. Andrea Battistini (Milan, 1990).

44 Among others, see John Agnew, *Place and Politics in Modern Italy* (Chicago, 2002); Michael Cardwell, *The European Model of Agriculture* (Oxford, 2004).

45 See, for example, Roberta Sonnino, 'For a "piece of bread"? Interpreting Sustainable Development through Agritourism in Southern Tuscany', *Sociologia Ruralis*, XLIV (2004), pp. 285–300.

46 Italo Moretti, ed., *Il paesaggio del Chianti: Problemi e prospettive* (Florence, 1988).

47 As a result of diminishing resources from the state, the Veneto region, for example, has budgeted €400,000 for all cultural activities in 2011. But parliament cheerfully voted a raise on its already bloated salaries, as it has done in previous years, and members of parliament continue to enjoy free phones, cars, plane and train trips, massages, tennis lessons, dental care (unavailable to any other Italian) and many other perks, at the expense of taxpayers.

1 Giorgio Ciucci, 'Pagano und Terragni: Faschistische Architektur als Ideal unds als Staatsstil', in *Faschistische Architekturen: Planen und Bauen in Europa, 1930 bis 1945*, ed. Hartmut Frank (Hamburg, 1985), pp. 123–38.

2 Meredith Clausen, *Pietro Belluschi: Modern American Architect* (Cambridge, MA, 1995).

3 Rino Levi, 'Arquitetura e Estetica das Cidades', *Giornale estado de Sao Paolo*, 15 October 1925.

4 Diane Ghirardo, 'L'alma pellegrina', in *Aldo Rossi: Drawings*, ed. Germano Celant (Milan, 2008), pp. 18–21. The literature on Rossi is extensive; a survey of his buildings can be found in Alberto Ferlenga, *Aldo Rossi: Opera complete, 1959–1987* (Milan, 1987); for Rossi's own writings, in addition to *The Architecture of the City*, see his *Scientific Autobiography*, trans. Lawrence Venuti (Cambridge, MA, 1981), a book published in English nearly fifteen years prior to its appearance in Italian.

5 Renzo Piano and Richard Rogers, *Du Plateau Beaubourg au Centre Georges Pompidou* (Paris, 1987); Nathan Silver, *The Making of Beaubourg: A Building Biography of the Centre Pompidou* (Cambridge, MA, 1994).

6 Carol Vogel, 'The Aulenti Uproar', *The New York Times* (22 November 1987).

7 In one of the best brief accounts of the twentieth-century history of Palazzo Grassi, historian Marcia Vetroq noted how three successive corporate magnates adapted the palace to become a showplace for art as well as a 'vehicle for cultural philanthropy, tony marketing and acceptable vanity': Franco Marinotti, head of the synthetic fabrics manufacturer SNIA Viscosa, in the 1950s, followed by Gianni Agnelli in 1983 and, upon his death, the billionaire purveyor of luxury goods, François Pinault, in 2005. 'A Museum of his Own: The blue-chip art collection of French businessman François Pinault recently debuted at the revamped Palazzo Grassi', *Art in America* (October 2006), pp. 34–7.

8 Guido Montanari, 'Slow Architecture vs Global Architecture: Paesaggi della Modernità', *Atti e rassegna tecnica della società degli ingegneri e degli architetti in Torino*, CXLIII (December 2010), pp. 30–36.

9 Piano so commented during a symposium entitled 'Design and Construction of Tall Buildings', held at the Castello del Valentino, Polytechnic of Turin, on 12 February 2012. Piano's remarks came in response to a challenge from Prof. Guido Montanari. Fuksas was director of the Venice Biennale in 2000, with the theme of 'Less Aesthetics, More Ethics', and specifically challenged the huge scale and consumption of resources in mega-developments in the developing world and elsewhere, and in general, the emphasis on huge dimensions in new projects.

10 Vittorio Gregotti, *Inside Architecture*, trans. Peter Wong and Francesca Zaccheo (Cambridge, MA, 1996); most of his other publications have not been translated into English.

11 Francesco Bottazzo, 'Corte dei Conti, Calatrava sotto inchiesta', *Corriere del Veneto* (12 March 2012). Given Calatrava's status as an 'archi-star', the story appeared in newspapers throughout the country.

12 After the disaster of the Stata Center at MIT, with its endless leaks and the severely water-damaged outdoor amphitheatre, the excessive costs to maintain the pristine purity of the Walt Disney Concert Hall in Los Angeles and the problems associated with glare and elevated temperatures in its surroundings, any civic authority would do well to think twice before budgeting funds for a Gehry design. In Modena, a city where maintenance of the San Cataldo Cemetery has been absent, the prospects that the city would disburse what would clearly be the substantial ongoing maintenance costs required for a Gehry project are less than dim. John Silber, *The Architecture of the Absurd: How 'Genius' Disfigured a Practical Art* (New York, 2007) is particularly piquant on the many failings of Gehry's buildings, conceptual and otherwise; at $442 per square foot, MIT got a building with a series of extensive problems.

13 It was at this same exposition that Le Corbusier displayed his Plan Voisin for gutting

central Paris and replacing its historic centre with towers in a vast park; it was also here that he brashly described the house 'as a machine for living in'.

14 'Si dimettono i vertici del Maxxi: Arriva il commissario Recchia', *Il Sole 24ore* (9 May 2012).

15 Carlo Micono, 'Il percorso dell'architettura sostenibile', in *1970–2000: Episodi e temi di storia dell'architettura*, ed. Francesca B. Filippi, Luca Gibello and Manfredo di Robilant (Turin, 2006), pp. 199–207.

16 The Italian Ministry of Foreign Affairs in collaboration with the Ministry of Cultural Heritage and Activities mounted an exhibition in London in the summer of 2008 showcasing a selection of recent designs by Italian architects where at least some of the focus was on concerns about sustainability, L. Molinari and A. D'Onofrio, *Sustainable Italy: Contemporary Ecologies Energies for Italian Architecture* (Rome, 2008). The MARC project appeared on p. 68 of that publication.

Select Bibliography

50. La nuova architettura italiana: Due generazioni a confronto (Milan, 2002)

Adalberto Libera: Opera completa (Milan, 1989)

Accasto, G., V. Fraticelli and R. Nicolini, *L'architettura di Roma capitale, 1870–1970* (Rome, 1971)

Albini, Franco, *Franco Albini, 1930–1970* (New York, 1981)

Amadori, Gianluca, *Per quattro soldi: Il giallo della Fenice dal rogo alla ricostruzione* (Rome, 2003)

Ambasz, Emilio, ed., *Italy: The New Domestic Landscape: Achievements and Problems of Italian Design*, exh. cat., Museum of Modern Art (New York, 1972)

L'ambiente illegal: Viaggio di Legambiente nel Mal Paese dei signori, delle tangenti, degli appalti, dell'abusivismo (Rome, n.d.)

Amorosi, G., *A Milano: Fra passato e avvenire, 1927–1967, i problemi dell'urbanistica, gli studi e le soluzioni, le opere* (Milan, 1981)

Angeletti, P., L. Cianciarelli, M. Ricci and G. Vallifuoco, *Case romane: La periferia e le case popolari* (Rome, 1984)

Anzaldi, Michele, Erasmo D'Angelis, Enrico Fontana and Sebastiano Venneri, eds, *Architetti in Sicilia* (Cefalù, 1987)

—, —, —, *L'ambiente illegale. Viaggio di Legambiente nel Mal Paese dei signori, delle tangenti, degli appalti, dell'abusivismo* (Rome

Architetture italiane degli anni '70: Galleria nazionale d'arte moderna, Roma, Valle Giulia, 23 aprile–31 maggio 1981 (Rome, 1981)

Arnell, Peter, and Ted Bickford, eds, *Aldo Rossi: Buildings and Projects* (New York, 1985)

Aymonino, Carlo, *Campus scolastico a Pesaro* (Rome, 1980)

—, et al., *Progetto realizzato* (Venice, 1980)

Baborski, Matteo Siro, *Architecture*, trans. Jay Hyams (Chichester, 2003)

Baffa, M., C. Morandi, S. Protasoni and A. Rossari, *Il Movimento di studi per l'architettura* (Rome and Bari, 1995)

Baldrighi, Luciana, *Luca Beltrami architetto: Milano tra Ottocento e Novecento* (Milan, 1997)

Barbagallo, Francesco, *Il potere della Camorra (1973–1998)* (Turin, 1990)

Battisti, Emilio, and Kenneth Frampton, *Mario Botta: Architetture e progetti negli anni '70* (Milan, 1979)

Belluzzi, Amedeo, and Claudia Conforti, *Architettura italiana, 1944–1984* (Rome and Bari, 1985)

Benevolo, Leonardo, *History of Modern Architecture*, trans. H. J. Landry (Cambridge, MA, 1977)

—, *Storia dell'architettura moderna* (Bari, 1960)

Berdeni, Paolo, *Il giubileo senza città: L'urbanistica romana negli anni del liberismo* (Rome, 2000)

Bizzotto, Renata, Luisa Chiumenti and Alessandro Muntoni, eds, *50 anni di professione* (Rome, 1983)

Boito, Camillo, *Un'architettura per l'Italia Unita* (Padua, 2000)

Bonifazio, Patrizia, Sergio Pace, Michela Rosso and Paolo Scrivano, eds, *Tra guerra e pace: Società, cultura e architettura nel secondo dopoguerra* (Milan, 1998)

Bonino, Michele, Giulietta Fassino, Davide Ferrando and Carlo Spinelli, *Torino, 1984–2008: Atlante dell'architettura* (Turin, 2008)

Braghieri, Gianni, *Aldo Rossi*, trans. Graham Thompson (Barcelona, 1991)

Brandolini, Sebastiano, *Milano: Nuova architettura* (Geneva and Milan, 2005)

Breschi, Alberto, *Nuove figurazioni urbane: Disegni, progetti di architettura per Firenze contemporanea* (Florence, 1987)

Buscioni, M. C., *Michelucci: Il linguaggio dell'architettura* (Rome, 1979)

Campi, Mario, *Young Italian Architects* (Basel, 1998)

Capanna, Alessandra, *Roma 1932: Mostra della rivoluzione fascista* (Rome, 2004)

Casciato, Maristella, 'Neorealism in Italian Architecture', in *Anxious Modernisms: Experimentation in Postwar Architectural Culture*, ed. S. Goldhagen and R. Legault (Cambridge, MA, and Montreal), pp. 25–53

—, and Giorgio Muratore, eds, *Annali dell'architettura italiana contemporanea* (Rome, 1985)

Cefaly, Pietro, *Littoria, 1932–1942: Gli architetti e la città* (Latina, 2001)

Celant, Germano, et al., eds, *Aldo Rossi: Drawings* (Milan, 2008)

Cinque progetti per la Cala (Cefalù, 1984)

Ciorra, Pippo, and Marco D'Annuntiis, eds, *New Italian Architecture: Italian Landscapes between Architecture and Photography* (Milan, 2000)

Cipriani, Giovanni Battista, *Architecture of Rome: A Nineteenth-century Itinerary* (New York, 1986)

Ciucci, Giorgio, *L'architettura italiana oggi: Racconto di una generazione* (Rome and Bari, 1989)

—, *Gli architetti e il fascismo: Architettura e città, 1922–1944* (Turin, 1989)

—, and Francesco Dal Co, *Architettura italiana del '900* (Milan, 1993)

Clausen, Meredith, *Pietro Belluschi: Modern American Architect* (Cambridge, MA, 1993)

Clementi A., and F. Perego, *La metropoli 'spontanea': Il caso di Roma, 1925–1981* (Bari, 1983)

Comoli, Vera, and Carlo Olmo, eds, *Guide di architettura: Torino* (Turin, 1999 and 2003)

Comune di Sabaudia, *Angiolo Mazzoni, 1894–1979: Architetto futurista in Agro Pontino* (Latina, 2000)

Conforti, Claudia, *Architettura italiana, 1944–1984* (Rome and Bari, 1985)

—, *Carlo Aymonino: L'architettura non è un mito* (Rome, 1980)

Conforto, Cina, Gabriele De Giorgi, Alessandra Muntoni and Marcello Pazzaglini, *Il dibattito architettonico in Italia, 1945–1975* (Rome, 1977)

Consonni, Giancarlo, *Piero Bottoni: Opera completa* (Milan, 1990)

Crippa, Maria Antonietta, *Carlo Scarpa: Il pensiero, il disegno, i progetti* (Milan, 1984)

—, *Carlo Scarpa: Theory, Design, Projects* (Cambridge, MA, 1986)

Crispolti, Enrico, *Utopia e crisi dell'antinature: Momenti delle intenzioni architettoniche in Italia: Immaginazione megastrutturale dal futurismo a oggi* (Venice, 1979)

Culotta, Pasquale, and Giuseppe Leone, *Le occasioni del progetto* (Cefalù, 1985)

Dal Co, Francesco, 'Architettura italiana, 1960–1980', in Banca Nazionale del Lavoro, *Italia Moderna*, vol. IV: *La difficile democrazia* (Milan, 1985)

—, *Carlo Scarpa: Opera complete* (Milan, 1984)

—, *Villa Ottolenghi: Carlo Scarpa* (New York, 1997)

—, and Sergio Polano, *The 20th Century Architecture and Urbanism: Milano* (Tokyo, 1991)

—, and Manfredo Tafuri, *Architettura contemporanea* (Milan, 1976)

Danesi, Silvia, and Luciano Patetta, eds, *Il razionalismo e l'architettura in Italia durante il fascismo* (Venice, 1976)

De Giorgi, Manolo, ed., *Marco Zanuso: Architetto* (Milan, 1999)

De Luca, Vezio, *Peccato Capitale* (Rome, 1993)

De Martino, Stefano, and Alex Wall, *Cities of Childhood: Italian Colonies of the 1930s* (London, 1988)

De Rossi, Antonio, and Giovanni Durbanio, *Torino, 1980–2011: La trasformazione e le sue immagini* (Turin, 2006)

De Seta, Cesare, *L'architettura del Novecento* (Turin, 1981)

—, *La cultura architettonica in Italia fra le due guerre*, 3rd edn (Bari, 1972)

Della Seta, Piero, and Edoardo Salzano, *L'Italia a sacco: Come negli incredibili anni '80 nacque e si diffuse tangentopoli* (Rome, 1993)

Di Biagi, Paola, ed., *La grande ricostruzione: Il piano Ina-Casa e l'Italia degli anni '50* (Rome, 2001)

Di Stefano, R., *Edilizia napoletana, 1959–1969* (Naples, 1969)

Diamond, Rosamund, and Wilfried Wang, eds, *On Continuity* (Cambridge, MA, 1995)

Dini, Massino, ed., *Renzo Piano: Progetti e architetture, 1964–1983* (Milan, 1983)

Donin, Gianpiero, *Renzo Piano: Pezzo per pezzo: Catalogo della mostra* (Rome, 1982)

Doordan, Dennis P., *Building Modern Italy: Italian Architecture, 1914–1936* (New York, 1988)

Dulio, Roberto, *Introduzione a Bruno Zevi* (Rome and Bari, 2008)

Durbiano, Giovanni, *I Nuovi Maestri: Architetti tra politica e cultura nel dopoguerra* (Venice, 2000)

—, and Matteo Robiglio, *Paesaggio e architettura nell'Italia contemporanea* (Rome, 2003)

Ente Nazionale Industrie Turistiche, *Ten Years of Italian Progress* (Milan, 1933)

Erbani, Francesco, *L'Italia maltrattata* (Rome and Bari, 2003)

Etlin, Richard, *Modernism in Italian Architecture, 1890–1940* (Cambridge, MA, 1991)

Fanelli, G., *Firenze: Architettura e città* (Florence, 1973)

Fava, Ferdinando, *Lo Zen di Palermo* (Rome and Milan, 2008)

Filippi, Francesca B., Luca Gibello and Manfredo di Robilant, eds, *1970–2000: Episodi e temi di storia dell'architettura* (Turin, 2006)

Fiori, Leonardo, and Massimo Prizzon, eds, *Albini-Helg, la Rinascente: Disegni e progetto de la Rinascente di Roma* (Milan, 1982)

Fontana, Vincenzo, *Profilo di architettura italiana del Novecento* (Venice, 1999)

Foot, John, *Milan since the Miracle: Culture and Identity* (Oxford, 2001)

—, *Pero: Città di immigrazione, 1950–1970* (Pero, 2002)

Fraticelli, Vanna, *Roma, 1914–1929: La città e gli architetti tra la guerra e il fascism* (Rome, 1982)

Fried, R. C., *Planning the Eternal City: Roman Politics and Planning since World War II* (New Haven, CT, 1973)

Galardi, A., *Architettura italiana contemporanea, 1955–1965* (Milan, 1967)

—, *New Italian Architecture*, trans. E. Rockwell (New York, 1967)

Garofalo, Francesco, and Luca Veresani, *Adalberto Libera* (New York, 1992)

Ghirardo, Diane Yvonne, 'Architects, Exhibitions and the Politics of Culture in Fascist Italy', *Journal of Architectural Education*, XLV/2 (February 1992), pp. 67–75

—, 'Architecture and Theater: The Street in Fascist Italy', in *'Event' Arts and Art Events*, ed. S. Foster (Ann Arbor, MI, 1987), pp. 175–99

—, *Building New Communities: New Deal America and Fascist Italy* (Princeton, NJ, 1989)

—, 'Città Fascista: Surveillance and Spectacle', in *Journal of Contemporary History* (Winter 1996), pp. 347–72

—, 'Italian Architects and Fascist Politics: An Evaluation of the Rationalist's Role in Regime Building', *Journal of the Society of Architectural Historians*, XXXIX/2 (May 1980), pp. 109–27

—, 'Politics of a Masterpiece: The *Vicenda* of the Decoration of the Façade of the Casa del Fascio, Como, 1936–39', *Art Bulletin*, LXII/3 (September 1980), pp. 466–78

—, 'Surveillance and Spectacle in Fascist Ferrara', in *The Education of the Architect: Historiography, Urbanism, and the Growth of Architectural Knowledge*, ed. M. Pollak (Cambridge, MA, 1997), pp. 325–62

—, 'Terragni e gli storici: Vicende nella tipologia e nella politica della Casa del Fascio di Como', in *Giuseppe Terragni: Opera completa*, ed. G. Ciucci (Milan, 1996), pp. 257–66

Giovannoni, Gustavo, *Vecchie città ed edilizia nuova* (Turin, 1931)

Grandi, Maurizio, and Attilio Pracchi, *Milano: Guida all'architettura moderna* (Bologna, 1980)

Grassi, Giorgio, *Architettura, lingua morta* (Milan, 1988)

G.R.A.U., isti mirant stella: Architetture 1964–1980 (Rome, 1981)

Gregotti, Vittorio, *Inside Architecture* (Cambridge, MA, 1996)

—, *New Directions in Italian Architecture*, trans. Giuseppina Salvadori (New York, 1968)

Gresleri, Giuliano, ed., *Bologna: Guida di architettura* (Turin, 2004)

Grisanti, Ezio, and Attilio Pracchi, *Alfio Susini: L'attività urbanistica nella 'stagione dei concorsi', 1928–1940* (Milan, 1982)

Grossi, Marina Sommella, ed., *Alberto Sartoris: L'immagine razionalista, 1917–1943* (Milan, 1998)

Guacci, Adriana, *Il tempio di monte Grisa a Trieste: Analisi del linguaggio architettonico di un edificio per il culto* (Trieste, 1991)

Guccione, Margherita, Maria Lagunes and Rosalia Vittorini, eds, *Guida ai quartieri romani INA Casa* (Rome, 2002)

Guttry, Irene de, *Guide to Modern Rome from 1870 until Today* (Rome, 1978, repr. 2001)

Hoh-Slodczyk, Christine, *Carlo Scarpa und das Museum* (Berlin, 1987)

Howard, Deborah, *The Architectural History of Venice*, revd edn (New Haven, CT, and London, 2002)

Insolera, Italo, *Roma moderna: Un aecolo di storia urbanistica* (Turin, 1962)

International Architecture Exhibition, *Sensing the Future: The Architecture as Seismograph*, 6th Venice Biennale of Architecture (Venice, 1996)

Ippolito, Achille M., and Mauro Pagnotta, *Roma costruita: Le vicende, le problematiche e le realizzazioni dell'architettura a Roma dal 1946 al 1981* (Rome, 1982)

Irace, Fulvio, ed., *L'architetto del lago: Giancarlo Maroni e il Garda* (Milan, 1993)

Jodice, Romano, *L'architettura del ferro: L'Italia (1796–1914)* (Rome, 1985)

Kirk, Terry Rossi, *The Architecture of Modern Italy*, vol. I: *The Challenge of Tradition, 1750–1900* (New York, 2005)

—, *The Architecture of Modern Italy*, vol. II: *Visions of Utopia, 1900 to the Present* (New York, 2005)

Lanzani, Arturo, *I paesaggi italiani* (Rome, 2003)

Lanzarini, Orietta, *Carlo Scarpa: L'architetto e le arti. Gli anni della Biennale di Venezia, 1948–1972* (Venice, 2003)

Lasansky, D. Medina, *The Renaissance Perfected: Architecture, Spectacle, and Tourism in Fascist Italy* (University Park, PA, 2004)

—, and Brian McLaren, eds, *Architecture and Tourism: Perception, Performance and Place* (Oxford, 2004)

Leone, Giuseppe, *Progetti campione nel centro storico di Palermo* (Palermo, 1985)

Lissoni, Alessandro, *Ville casette* (Milan, 1949)

Loi, Maria Cristina, ed., *Ignazio Gardella architetture* (Milan, 1998)

Lupano, Mario, *Marcello Piacentini* (Rome and Bari, 1991)

McLaren, Brian, *Architecture and Tourism in Italian Colonial Libya: An Ambivalent Modernism* (Seattle, 2005)

Magnaghi, Agostino, Mariolina Monge and Luciano Re, *Guida all'architettura moderna di Torino* (Turin, 1982)

Maltese, Corrado, *Storia dell'arte in Italia (1875–1943)* (Turin, 1960)

Mancini, Daniel, *Giuseppe Terragni: Two Projects* (New Haven, CT, 1991)

Marcello Piacentini e Roma, Bollettino della Biblioteca della Facoltà di Architettura dell'Universita degli studi di Roma "La Sapienza", 53 (1995)

Marcianò, Ada Francesca, *Carlo Scarpa* (Bologna, 1984)

Marcolli, Attilio, *Attilio Marcolli: Per un'architettura anatopica* (Florence, 1987)

Mariano, Fabio, ed., *Terragni: Poesia della razionalità* (Rome, 1983)

Martignoni, Massimo, ed., *Illusioni di pietra* (Trento, 2001)

Martinoli, Simona, and Eliana Perotti, *Architettura coloniale italiana nel Dodecaneso, 1912-1943* (Turin, 1999)

Meeks, Carroll, *Italian Architecture, 1750-1914* (New Haven, CT, and London, 1966)

Meyer, Ester da Costa, *The Work of Antonio Sant'Elia* (New Haven, CT, and London, 1995)

Minardi, Bruno, *Bruno Minardi* (London, 1997)

Mioni, Alberto, ed., *Urbanistica fascista: Ricerche e saggi sulla città e il territorio e sulle politiche urbane in Italia fra le due guerre* (Milan, 1980)

Miotto, Luciana, *Renzo Piano* (Paris, 1987)

Mollino, Carlo, *Carlo Mollino, 1905-1973* (Milan, 1989)

Morozzo della Rocca, and Maria Donatella, *P. M. Letarouilly, Les édifices de Rome moderne: Storia e critica di un'opera propedeutica alla composizione* (Rome, 1981)

Il municipio di Aliminusa (Cefalù, 1983)

Muratori, Giorgio, ed., *Cantieri romani del Novecento: Maestranze, materiali, imprese, architetti, nei primi anni del cemento armato* (Rome, 1995)

—, Alessandra Capuano, Francesco Garofalo and E. Pellegrini, *Italia: Gli ultrimi trent'anni* (Bologna, 1988)

Murphy, Richard, *Carlo Scarpa and the Castelvecchio* (London, 1990)

Muzio, Giovanni, *Muzio* (Milan, 1994)

Nakamura, Toshio, *Renzo Piano: Building Workshop, 1964-1988* (Tokyo, 1989)

Natalini, Adolfo, *Figure di Pietra: Figures of Stone* (Milan, 1984)

Nicoloso, Paolo, *Gli architetti di Mussolini: Scuole e sindacato, architetti e massoni, professori e politici negli anni del regime* (Milan, 1999)

Noever, Peter, ed., *The Other City: The Architect's Method as Shown by the Brion Cemetery in San Vito d'Altivole* (Berlin, 1989)

Nonis, Fabio, and Sergio Boidi, *Ignazio Gardella: Exhibition and Catalogue* (Cambridge, MA, 1986)

Oddo, Maurizio, *Architettura contemporanea in Sicilia* (Trapani, 2007)

—, *Gibellina: La nuova attraverso la città di transizione* (Turin, 2003)

Olivetti, Adriano, *Città dell'uomo* (Milan, 1960)

Olsberg, Nicholas, et al., *Carlo Scarpa, Architect: Intervening with History* (Montreal, 1999)

Pace, Sergio, Cristiana Chiorino and Michela Rosso, *Italia '61: Identità e miti nelle celebrazioni per il centenario dell'Unità d'Italia* (Turin, 2005)

Pagano, Giuseppe, *Architettura e città durante il fascismo* (Rome and Bari, 1976)

Palla, M., *Firenze nel regime fascista (1929-1934)* (Florence, 1978)

Patetta, Luciano, *L'architettura in Italia, 1919-1943* (Milan, 1972)

Pellegrini, Pietro Carlo, ed., *Lo spazio pubblico in Italia (1990-1999)* (Florence, 1999)

Peressut, L., and I. Valente, *Milano: Architetture per la città, 1980-1990* (Milan, 1986)

Pettena, Gaia, *Architettura e propaganda fascista nei filmati dell'Istituto Luce* (Rome, 2004)

Pettena, Gianni, ed., *Superstudio, 1966-1982: Storie, figure, architettura* (Florence, 1982)

—, and Milco Carboni, eds, *Ettore Sottsass Senior: Architetto* (Milan, 1991)

Piano, Renzo, *Renzo Piano: Buildings and Projects, 1971-1989* (New York, 1989)

—, *Renzo Piano: Progetti e architetture, 1987-1994* (Basel, 1995)

Piantoni, Gianna, *Roma 1911* (Rome, 1980)

Pica, Agnoldomenico, *Architettura italiana ultima* (Milan, 1959)

—, *Recent Italian Architecture* (Milan, 1959)

Pirazzoli, Giacomo, ed., *Paolo Zermani: Architetture* (Milan, 1995)

Poretti, Sergio, *Modernismi italiani: Architettura e costruzione nel Novecento* (Rome, 2008)

Porta, Marco, *L'architettura di Ignazio Gardella* (Milan, 1985)

Portoghesi, Paolo, *Dopo l'architettura moderna* (New York, 1982)

I progetti per la ricostruzione del teatro La Fenice 1997 (Venice, 2000)

Purini, Franco, *Luogo e progetto* (Rome, 1981)

Rispoli, Ernesto Ramon, 'Italia-America anni '70: Intorno all'IAUS di New York (1967-85)', unpublished PhD thesis (Politecnico di Torino, 2010)

Rossi, Aldo, *The Architecture of the City*, trans. Diane Ghirardo and Joan Ockman

(Cambridge, MA, 1982)

—, *L'architettura della città* (Padua, 1966)

—, ed., *La Biennale di Venezia: The Third Exhibition of Architecture* (Venice, 1985)

Russo, Antonella, *Il fascismo in mostra* (Rome, 1999)

Sabatini, Michelangelo, *Pride in Modesty: Modernist Architecture and the Vernacular Tradition in Italy* (Toronto, 2010)

Samonà, Alberto, *Ignazio Gardella e il professionismo italiano* (Rome, 1981)

San Pietro, Silvio, *Discodesign in Italia* (Milan, 1996)

—, ed., *New Villas 2: In Italy and Canton Ticino* (Milan, 2000)

—, *Nuovi negozi in Italia* (Milan, 1990)

Sartoris, Alberto, *Alberto Sartoris, 1901–1998: La concepción poética de la arquitectura* (Valencia, 2000)

Savi, Vittorio, ed., *Casa Aurora: Un'opera di Aldo Rossi* (Turin, 1987)

Saviano, Roberto, *Gomorra: Viaggio nell'impero economico e nel sogno di dominio della camorra* (Milan, 2006), trans. Virginia Jewiss

Scardino, Lucio, *Itinerari di Ferrara Moderna* (Florence, 1995)

Schumacher, Thomas L., *Il Danteum di Terragni, 1938* (Rome, 1980)

—, *The Danteum: Architecture, Poetics, and Politics under Italian Fascism*, 2nd edn (New York, 1993)

Sgarbi, Vittorio, *Un paese sfigurato: Viaggio attraverso gli scempi d'Italia* (Geneva and Milan, 2003)

Smith, George Everard, *Italy Builds: Its Modern Architecture and Native Inheritance* (New York, 1955)

Soroka, Ellen, 'Restauro in Venezia', *Journal of Architectural Education*, XLVII/4 (May 1994), pp. 224–42

Stille, Alexander, *The Sack of Rome: How a Beautiful European Country with a Fabled History and a Storied Culture was Taken Over by a Man Named Silvio Berlusconi* (New York, 2006)

Superstudio: In-arch, Istituto nazionale di architettura: Roma, Palazzo Taverna, 20–23 marzo 1978 (Florence, 1978)

Suzuki, Katuyuki, *Guido Canella* (Bologna, 1983)

Tafuri, Manfredo, *The Sphere and the Labyrinth: Avant-Gardes and Architecture from Piranesi to the 1970s*, trans. Pellegrino d'Acierno and Robert Connolly (Cambridge, MA, 1987)

—, *Storia dell'architettura italiana, 1944–1985* (Turin, 1986)

—, *Theories and History of Architecture*, trans. Giorgio Verrecchia (New York, 1980)

Terranova, Antonino, *Mostri metropolitani* (Rome, 2001)

Tintori, S., *Piano e pianificatori dall'età napoleonica al fascismo* (Milan, 1985)

Torino fra le due guerre (Turin, 1978)

Vandelli, V., *Il liberty nell'Emilia* (Modena, 1988)

Vasumi Roveri, Elisabetta, *Aldo Rossi, 'L'architettura della città', 1966: Genesi e costruzione del testo*, PhD thesis (Politecnico di Torino, 2008)

Volpiano, Mauro, *Torino, 1890: La prima esposizione italiana di architettura* (Torino, 1999)

Zevi, Bruno, ed., *Omaggio a Terragni* (Milan, 1968)

—, *Storia dell'architettura moderna* (Turin, 1950)

Zucchi, Benedict, *Giancarlo De Carlo* (Oxford, 1992)

Acknowledgements

As my editor, Vivian Constantinopoulos, will corroborate, nearly a decade went by before I completed this book. Partly the slow pace was due to my desire to visit as many of the projects I planned to discuss as possible, and in this I was quite successful, having visited over 95 per cent of the buildings discussed in the book. In the course of doing so, a number of projects I initially planned to include gave way to others, so I encourage readers to turn to any of a number of fine general surveys, such as that by Terry Kirk, for such a study. I must also attribute the delay to the slow development of my ideas as I mulled over what I saw, read about and discussed with innumerable interlocutors over the years. The scope and range of the questions I asked expanded vertiginously: how did the developments in architecture intersect with political events and changes, with other cultural expressions, with international trends? How could one reconcile the country's enormous environmental disasters with the drive to build in the same wasteful patterns, in the same risky areas, over and over again? How could I delineate the connections between a thuggish and predatory political class – the caste, as they are quite publicly known (organized crime) heavily invested in cement and waste disposal of all types – and the desire of many Italians to curate and care for a grievously wounded national landscape? There are no easy answers, but I have tried to adumbrate the contours of these issues and fill in some spaces where appropriate and, I need hardly add, I have made my own views quite clear.

It is almost impossible to count the many people who have contributed, in ways great and small, to this book. Some accompanied me on trips to visit particular sites, some argued with me endlessly over particular interpretations or about specific buildings, others read various chapters or versions of the manuscript, and some generously provided better photographs than I was able to produce on my own. Some showered me with reading materials in the hope of modifying my views, and others simply helped finance the enterprise, more than once, such as Dean Qing-yun Ma at the University of Southern California. Not only did he give me time to work, he created an atmosphere where such research is encouraged. Along with funding, these two factors help make the work a joy. My biggest debt is to Vivian Constatinopoulos, my patient and exacting editor, who put up with a lot of nonsense over the decade but who never stopped believing in the project, and Martha Jay, also of Reaktion, who helped usher the book through the last phases. Among those I must acknowledge for their contributions, whether simply providing photographs or debate and moral support, are Morris and Lisa Adjmi, Luigi Ballerini, Giacomo Beccaria, Cecilia Bellelli, Michele Bonino, Marino Bortolotti, Michelangelo Caberletti, Gaia Caramellina, Maristella Casciato, Ciro Cellurale, Pippo Ciorra, Maria Cristina Coreggiolo, Serenella Crivellari, Manfredo Di Robilant, Andrea Faoro, Vittorio Fava, Alain Fievre, Francesca Filippi, Joseph Flynn, Mia Fuller, Sonia Gessner, Gay Ghirardo Engles, Carmine Granito, Vittorio Gregotti, Luca Greselin, Victor Jones, Sandra Macat, Mark Mack, Brian McLaren, Gino Malacarne, Claudio Manari, Guido Montanari, Andrea Nascimbene, Maurizio Oddo, Sergio Pace, Rebecca Pasternak, Fausto and Vera Rossi, Michela Rosso, Isabel Rutherfoord, Valentino Sani, Natasha Schottland, Marcella and Dante Spinotti, Benedetta Tagliabue, Marida Talamona, Ferruccio Trabalzi, Michela Tramarin and Chiara Visentin. Needless to say, they are not responsible for the views expressed in this book.

Photo Acknowledgements

The author and publishers wish to express their thanks to the below sources of illustrative material and/or permission to reproduce it:

Arassociati: pp. 169, 202, 203, 204 and 205 (photo Michele Crosera), 293 bottom, 294 (photos Mario Carrieri); Cecilia Baratta Bellelli: p. 109; Giacomo Beccaria: pp. 44, 172, 173; BVV Architects: p. 293 (top); Michelangelo Caberletti: pp. 16, 46, 250; Maria Christina Coreggiolo: pp. 27, 189; David Dunham: p. 77 (top); FARE Studio: p. 302; Vittorio Fava: p. 267; Joseph Flynn: pp. 73, 140, 165, 219; Massimiliano Fuksas: pp. 265 (photo © Aki Furudate), 266 top (photo © Aki Furudate), 266 bottom (photo © Massimo Brugè), 279 top (photo © Maurizio Marcato), 279 bottom (photo © Moreno Maggi); Diane Ghirardo: pp. 15, 24, 25, 26 (both), 28, 29, 31, 32, 33, 35, 36, 38, 40, 42, 48, 49, 51, 60, 63, 81, 84, 85, 87 (top), 91, 94 (top), 97, 108, 118–19, 122, 123, 130, 133, 142, 143, 145, 146, 147, 159, 160, 161, 166, 167, 184, 193, 194, 206, 210, 214, 215, 218, 220, 221 (top and bottom), 222, 227, 229, 233, 234, 235 (left and right), 237, 240, 241, 242, 243, 247, 249, 252, 254, 256, 258, 259, 262, 263 (bottom), 270, 271, 272, 274, 275, 277, 281, 282, 284, 285, 287, 288, 290; courtesy Diane Ghirardo: pp. 12, 14, 21, 30, 64, 67, 68, 69, 74, 79 (top), 83, 86, 87, 94 (bottom), 95, 96, 102, 103, 104, 105, 111, 114, 115, 121, 189 (top); Beppe Giardino: p. 296; giotti/BigStockPhoto: p. 273 (bottom); Giorgio Grassi: p. 191 (photos P. Balaguer); Gregotti Associati: pp. 162, 163, 176, 177; Aimaro Isola: pp. 157, 168; Gino Malacarne: p. 292; Elena Manferdini: p. 295; MARC and Beppe Giardino: p. 297; matteocozzi/BigStockPhoto: p. 273 (top); Guido Montanari: pp. 149, 150, 154; Maurizio Oddo and Alessandro Baracco: pp. 300, 301; Eredi Aldo Rossi, courtesy Fondazione Aldo Rossi: p. 263 (top); Michela Rosso: pp. 179, 180, 181, 182; Kevin Stringfield: p. 77 (bottom); Studio di Architettura, New York: p. 269; Marida Talamona: p. 106; Federico Tomasini: p. 260; Ferruccio Trabalzi: pp. 61, 100; Wolfsonian Foundation, Genoa: pp. 127, 128; ZPZ Associati: pp. 298, 299.

Index